Web 2.0 Heroes

Interviews with 20
Web 2.0 Influencers

Web 2.0 Heroes

Interviews with 20
Web 2.0 Influencers

Bradley L. Jones

Wiley Publishing, Inc.

Web 2.0 Heroes: Interviews with 20 Web 2.0 Influencers

Published by
Wiley Publishing, Inc.
10475 Crosspoint Boulevard
Indianapolis, IN 46256
www.wiley.com

For general information on our other products and services or to obtain technical support, please contact our Customer Care Department within the U.S. at (800) 762-2974, outside the U.S. at (317) 572-3993 or fax (317) 572-4002.

Library of Congress Cataloging-in-Publication Data is available from the publisher.

For me, Web 2.0 is about community and more. My community starts with my family and it is to them that I dedicate this book. To my daughters, Lilian (Lili) and Aubrey, and to my wife, Melissa.

About the Author

Bradley L. Jones works for Jupitermedia Corporation, where he oversees a number of high-profile web sites such as Developer.com, DevX, CodeGuru, VBForums, Gamelan.com, and more. He is an international bestselling author and has spoken internationally as well. His writing credits entail more than a dozen books, including *Alan Simpson's Windows Vista Bible Desktop Edition* and *Windows XP in 10 Simple Steps or Less*. He has received a number of recognitions, including Microsoft's MVP award for the past four years.

Credits

Acquisitions Editor
Katie Mohr

Development Editor
Maureen Spears

Interview Transcriber
Kathy Jones

Production Editor
Elizabeth Ginns Britten

Copy Editor
Christopher Jones

Editorial Manager
Mary Beth Wakefield

Production Manager
Tim Tate

Vice President and Executive Group Publisher
Richard Swadley

Vice President and Executive Publisher
Joseph B. Wikert

Project Coordinator, Cover
Lynsey Osborne

Book Designer and Compositor
Maureen Forys,
Happenstance Type-O-Rama

Proofreader
Candace English

Indexer
Jack Lewis

Cover Image
Michael Trent

Contents

Acknowledgments

It is important to acknowledge the people listed at the top of each of the chapters in this book. They were gracious enough to provide their time and energy to not only do an interview, but to help make sure that I didn't take them out of context. Their time was greatly appreciated. I know that I gained a number of valuable insights from them, and I hope that you do as well.

I'd also like to acknowledge all of the public relations, marketing, and other folks who helped me to schedule interviews with the heroes within this book. There are too many of them to list; however, most of them are just a step or two away from the leaders in this book. Without the help of many of them, I doubt schedules would have been coordinated to make this book happen.

At Wiley Publishing, there is also a large number of people that deserve to be acknowledged. You can find most of their names listed on one of the first pages of this book. I'd especially like to thank Katie Mohr for her patience with me. The scheduling with the heroes took far longer than I had hoped, and Katie was understanding and even supportive even though I was no hero at holding a schedule. The same is true of Maureen Spears, who was the primary editor helping to craft this book into its final, more-cohesive form. Their patience allowed me to target the big sites and companies. Their patience allowed this to be a better book.

I would also like to do a special thanks to Kathy Jones. Kathy helped to transcribe many of the interviews. In doing that transcribing, she also provided some great feedback. It was good to see someone who has a very low interest in the computer world finding some of the comments and insights in this book interesting to the point where she did comment. Her help in the grunt work of transcribing this book made it a much better process for me.

When Katie at Wiley said this book would be "easy," I thought it would be. It seemed easy enough. In retrospect, I don't think any book will ever be easy to create. This one wasn't because we chose not to cut corners. That meant I took a lot more time away from my family than I had hoped. So most importantly, I have to acknowledge my family. I thank my wife, Melissa, and our two girls, Lili and Aubrey, for their understanding and patience while I did this book. The value of our time together is great, so I thank them for the cost they paid in letting me write.

Introduction

Web 2.0 is a term used quite frequently today. The fact that you've picked up this book indicates that you have probably heard it used. In fact, at the time this introduction was written, a search on Google for "Web 2.0" would return 14.7 million results. On Live Search the number of results was 56 million. If you don't put quotes around the phrase, then you'll get even more results—73.8 million results on Google and 243 million results on Live Search.

With so many search results on the phrase, it should be no surprise that if you ask 10 people what Web 2.0 is, you are likely to get 11 different answers. The inspiration for this book centers, however, on these responses. When you add numbers after a name, it often implies a version. Is Web 2.0 a second version of the Web? Was there a Web 1.0? Is Web 3.0 the next version of the Web?

With so many people having ideas about what Web 2.0 is or isn't, how is a person to actually get a solid understanding of what is an important topic to understand for web developers and web site owners? Is the term just hype? Does it have real meaning? There are those in the industry who have tried to define what Web 2.0 and Web 3.0 are. Others in the industry say the term is not definable.

Is it important to know the meaning of Web 2.0? In some cases it seems like it is. After all, venture capitalists looking at Web-based companies seem to be more interested in companies doing Web 2.0 versus those that are not. Additionally, some people have a perception that if you are not doing Web 2.0, then you might be using old technology and are potentially dooming yourself to fail. It seems that the leading-edge sites, or those that are getting the highest traffic, also tend to be tied to the concept of Web 2.0. Search for top Web 2.0 sites and you'll see that the lists often match the top sites on the Web.

While there are many areas where people disagree about the term Web 2.0, there is also a lot of agreement by most of the industry leaders I talked to. One area of agreement is that the Web has evolved and is evolving. Technology has made the Web more dynamic and more responsive. However, it is the social interaction occurring on the Web that is changing it even more. The impact of blogs, wikis, and social networks, along with the freer flow of information through instant messaging, email, RSS feeds, and other such means are all causing an evolution or change. But are these changes Web 2.0?

To help define Web 2.0, the thing to do is to ask those people heavily involved in the Web. Leaders within high-profile sites and companies can simply be asked what Web 2.0 is or isn't. These leaders should be from some of the most popular sites and companies that are on the leading edge or associated with key innovations on the Web. After all, if their sites and companies are building Web 2.0, then they should know.

Would asking CEOs, CTOs, web strategists, and other high-level people at such highly visible organizations result in more answers than questions? The best way to find out was to start asking. Instead of asking 10 people and getting 11 answers, I chose to ask double that number. More important, I stuck with people who are known as leaders in regard to their sites or with technologies for building sites. Most of these site and company names should be familiar: sites like eBay, LinkedIn, and del.icio.us as well as companies like Adobe, IBM, Microsoft, and Sun. These sites and companies are well known and successful. It could even be said that their success makes them heroes in the industry.

In reading this book, you will discover exactly what these heroes' thoughts are on Web 2.0. What you will find is that there are themes that come up in a lot of the interviews about Web 2.0. You'll also find that not everyone is in agreement. Is Web 2.0 simply a designation to a time in the evolution of the Internet, is it social networking, is it the application of various technologies, or is it simply marketing hype?

And since we have these heroes' attention, why not ask a few extra questions? Is Web 3.0, the Semantic Web, the next big thing, or is it an academic topic? What about Software as a Service (SaaS)? Is it fact or fiction? And an even more interesting question: if today it is Web 2.0 that is the big thing, then what is the next big thing or revolution on the Web?

The people interviewed in this book are on the leading edge of the Web. All have different backgrounds and thus all bring different perspectives. Their companies or sites stand out. That makes them and their sites heroes to anyone looking to tap into the Web or even into Web 2.0.

What do they have to say? Read on!

Max Mancini:
eBay

"You blur the lines between a desktop experience and a Web experience, and that's really where everything is headed."

—Max Mancini

If you ask anyone about online auctions, chances are the first place they would name is eBay. Ironically, eBay is more than just an auction. In fact, eBay's business is transactions. It just happens that their most known transactions are those of people selling items to buyers on an auction site that carries their name.

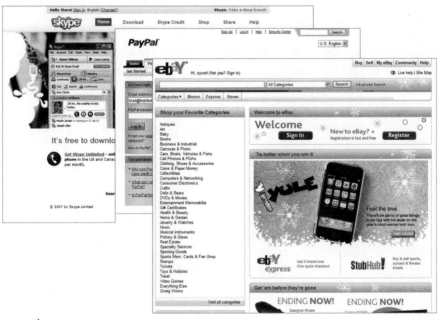

www.ebay.com

eBay's business is centered on charging a fee for bringing a seller and a buyer together. This transaction fee is how eBay makes money regardless of whether a marble, a car, or a piece of land in Texas is sold. It really doesn't matter what is sold as long as a transaction occurs.

eBay also provides a number of other services for doing commerce, including PayPal, which, like eBay, makes money when transactions happen, but instead of buyers and sellers exchanging products, PayPal makes it easy for two people (or other entities) to exchange money. Using this simple transaction model, eBay and PayPal both became leaders in the spaces they target.

If You Can Create a Compelling Experience for the Consumers...

Max Mancini is the senior directory of disruptive innovation at eBay. Prior to this role, he led over 70 developers at eBay, focusing on eBay Stores, registration, sign-in, merchandising, and more. He has also worked with eBay's classified business, Kijiji (www.kijiji.com).

Can you tell a bit about who you are and who you work for?

I'm Max Mancini, I work for eBay, and I run eBay's Platform and Disruptive Innovation team.

"Platform and Disruptive Innovation team" is an interesting title. Can you expand on that?

> *"[Our] role is to inspire innovation through experimentation."*

Sure. There are two parts of my team. On the platform side, our job is to enable innovation. We want to ensure that eBay is an E-Commerce operating system, or platform, that can be accessed by third-party developers to create applications and other innovations that accelerate commerce around eBay. Anywhere.

To give some context, our developers program, which is the responsibility of my platform team, is seven years old. As part of the program, and central to our platform strategy, we offer a series of web services that let any third party create applications that tie into eBay's "ecosystem."

Our ecosystem is composed of developers as well as applications and customer needs. Critically, our ecosystem has a clear value proposition for third-party developers. And today, more than 25 percent of the listings on eBay come through third-party tools.

Disruptive Innovation's role is to inspire innovation through experimentation. We study trends and provide infrastructure and resources that encourage developers, internally—and also externally—to think and create within the boundaries of their known silos. The trends we concentrate on shift over time.

Presently, the two big trends we see are, first, that buyer expectations have grown in terms of what they demand from online commerce. Today, people expect rich, interactive experiences: things like Flash and AJAX and JavaScript enabled across the Web. The second trend

> *"You can't necessarily rely on individual sites being where the Internet economy is going."*

we are closely monitoring is social commerce, which relates to the comfort people have sharing contact information and defining their relationships online, across their social graph in every place it exists, i.e., Plaxo, LinkedIn, Facebook, or MySpace. How much we share directly impacts the overall trust models that exist. That's something on which eBay has been building, so we think it's important to experiment with social environment participation and learn how that affects what other people are doing in commerce and how that affects the business. Across eBay, PayPal, and Skype, eBay accounts comprise a lot of our social graph with a high emphasis on the trusted relationships where commerce flourishes.

Are you finding that people are willing to share more information now?

Absolutely. That's the trend we're seeing. We've launched a Facebook application as well as neighborhoods within eBay. Obviously there's a different twist to what you expect to do when you're on eBay versus when you're on Facebook.

On Facebook, you're in a social environment, and what interests you is discovery with an entertainment factor—what are your friends doing? What are *their* friends doing that *I* might have some interest in? It's not as action-oriented as you would expect on a site like eBay, of course. In eBay's case, you're there to have some amount of entertainment but also to look for and discover new things.

This leads into the primary question: How would you and eBay define Web 2.0?

I consider the first mashup—the Craigslist/Google Maps mashup—as an embodiment of my view of Web 2.0. Somebody once described it as the "atomization of the Web." It's taking all of the components and making them available so that people can combine them in ways that you would never have considered, or that are very personal for an individual experience.

So, the components that I see really defining Web 2.0 are platform or web services, innovation that's built on top of that platform or web services, and distribution of that information. You see some of the embodiments of that sort of thing today—for example the proliferation of widgets across MySpace, Facebook, Google, and Yahoo!. Now you can combine information from multiple sources easily and distribute that information around.

Distribution means that you can't necessarily rely on individual sites being where the Internet economy is going. Rather, you must ask what compelling value are you delivering, and how do you monetize that value?

Getting back to eBay, it's easy for us because the service that we provide is all centered on transaction engines, and payments, through PayPal. As a result, there are inherent monetization models both for eBay as well as for developers and people who are using things that are distributed.

> *"What needs to evolve is the monetization models...Otherwise a lot of companies will go out of business."*

Another defining moment for the trend in Web 2.0 was the development of ad-supported models that made it possible to monetize things that would have otherwise been unmonetizable. So integrating ads to contextually relevant information—whether it's somebody's blog, or somebody's personal home page, whatever it happens to be—meant you could make money off of these things in ways that never existed before or couldn't scale before.

Of all the things you mentioned, are any more important than others?

Right now there's an explosion of web services that have opened things up. That's an important enabler. However, that's not going to be the definition of success in the long run; it's going to be expected out of everyone.

What needs to evolve is the monetization models. The commerce-based transaction model and the pure ad model as they exist today need to evolve significantly. I don't know what that's going to look like, but it will have to evolve; otherwise a lot of companies will go out of business.

Having some companies going out of business seems to be a part of how things do evolve.

That's true. I like to look back to 2000/2001, because the deal flow and VCs [venture capitalists] and everything else sure look similar to today—in fact, you're starting to see some similar companies pop back up on the radar screen. The difference is that these companies have a way to last longer and bootstrap more because of advertising models, frankly, and affiliate programs. They have a longer rope, if you will, but that still doesn't create the real economic value that needs to be put in place in some of these businesses.

You mentioned "2000/2001," and the bubble that "burst." Do you see a bubble now as well and is there a risk it will burst?

There's a bubble now. I don't know if it has the same risk of bursting because the previous bubble was created entirely as a result of the IPO market and that mechanism. The current bubble seems more tied to the M&A market, but it's not as aggressive as what the IPO market was. And, there's a bit more revenue backing to some of these startups.

So, there is a different kind of bubble although I don't know how early we are in it; it's certainly very aggressive right now. I don't think it has the same risk of bursting as quickly as the previous one did.

> *"The bigger the target, the more attention you get from the bad guys."*

You mention monetization and the sharing of information. This leads to the question of security. Do you see security continuing to be an issue?

Security hasn't been addressed yet in a lot of these models. I'm in a unique position of being able to sit back and see some of these things. We saw the value in creating this kind of model due to the selling side of our business, and we're expanding on the buying side much more aggressively now.

So, getting back to the definition of Web 2.0, it's creating a lot more openness so you can integrate things that you would have had to build from scratch before; how you manage rights and security within that model has yet to be determined.

In the early days, even Facebook was hammered on how much they shared information. They probably have the biggest head start in terms of creating a model where you can define trust a little bit more specifically.

> *"As messed up as our cell phone service is in the United States, I can't imagine us in a situation where we always have connectivity."*

I'm not sure that's addressing all of the security issues. Social networking isn't really addressing any of it right now, but people are going to address this; security always shows up. It's a function of how much monetization occurs in the model and how early, and we're not quite at the big levels of monetization yet where security becomes as big of a concern as it should.

eBay has done security and what we internally call "trust and safety" pretty significantly. Obviously being a huge marketplace means that people will try to figure out how to take advantage of others. The security model gets built in and the bigger the target, the more attention you get from the bad guys. With the exception of something like click fraud in CPC kinds of models, none of the Web 2.0 stuff is at that scale yet.

All of that will happen, but you address it when it happens. Much of that will evolve with Web 2.*whatever*.

On Web 2.0, everyone has his or her own definition. Is there anything about Web 2.0 you believe people are misunderstanding?

That's a good question. Everybody seems to have a derivative or a variant on the same theme—at least among the people I talk to.

Let me ask a different question then. AJAX, Adobe's AIR, Microsoft's Silverlight—a lot of these technologies coming out— how do these fit into a Web 2.0 world?

People have defined Web 2.0 as AJAX, so that's missing the boat. AJAX is a component; it's an enabler to things that are evolving with Web 2.0, and it's a contributing technology, but in and of itself it doesn't define Web 2.0.

I can speak more specifically about Adobe AIR because we've built a product on that. There's a lot of momentum around creating interactive experiences leveraging Web 2.0 technologies and web services, so what Adobe is saying is, "Why can't we do even better by taking those same technologies and bringing them to the desktop *and* allowing you to leverage the web services in the same way and as simply as you were able to through the Web?"

Adobe is jumping on something that could be quite significant in terms of how we experience the web, which is, the web really isn't about a web browser—we experience it that way today, but it doesn't have to be.

If you think about it (and I don't think this example is the best), Yahoo!'s desktop widgets don't take advantage of the same dynamic that normal web widgets do, which is viral distribution. That's another important dimension of what's happening on the Web.

> *"I believe in enabling your business to operate no matter what the next big thing is, and letting other people catch up."*

So, the concept of Adobe AIR, and in theory, Silverlight (although I'm not familiar with it) is smart, in that you blur the lines between a desktop experience and a web experience, and that's where everything is headed.

A colleague on my team likes to say that Web 3.0 really happens when people stop talking about the Web, the desktop, and Web 2.0—it's just the way we interact with our computer. It's transparent whether it's local or on the Net. AIR is just a first step in that direction.

That brings up the issue of online versus offline and the topic of connectivity. Do you foresee a day when connectivity availability is not an issue?

I've thought a lot about that since we've invested in our eBay desktop product on the AIR platform. One of the benefits is that you can do offline activities.

As messed up as our cell phone service is in the United States, I can't imagine us in a situation where we always have connectivity—I'd love for us to get there. I don't know when it's going to happen; if you're willing to pay enough, you can get it, right? I just don't see the average person being connected continuously, with the exception of through their mobile device.

In developing countries, mobile is *the* way most people connect to the Internet. Although there's a lot of innovation and excitement around Web 2.0, certainly in Silicon Valley, the mobile investments are starting to pick up again. The first wave of investments may have been too early; I don't know what it was. I don't know if this next wave is going to stick, but if I were looking at where the real opportunity to reach the majority of the world is, it's not going to be in the PC in the home.

That leads into the question, what do you see as the next big thing coming?

That's a good question.

There's plenty of opportunity in mobile; people are just going to have to be there, to engage with people when they're connected. It's hard to tell.

I believe in enabling your business to operate no matter what the next big thing is, and letting other people catch up.

Let me describe what I'm talking about.

I would rather spend money building our platform structure and web services, so that when the next big thing happens, our platform is that next big environment. For eBay, obviously we have our three major businesses, PayPal, Skype, and eBay marketplaces, and those are independently very huge markets for us. I'm not specifically looking beyond our marketplaces' business and how buyer experience and social commerce might affect those.

Shifting back to an earlier comment, you mentioned Web 3.0. Some define Web 3.0 as the Semantic Web. Do you have any opinions or thoughts on the Semantic Web?

Well, I don't think it's the Semantic Web.

The next generation of search and find for discovery across the Web will be much more like what my interpretation of Semantic Web is, which isn't necessarily what everyone else shares. It's a trend I did mention on Web 2.0; one reason Web 2.0 happened was that it became so easy and cheap to publish, right? As an individual I can create a hugely popular blog with almost no marketing experience or background team. Self-publishing has enabled many things to happen; frankly, it's supporting a lot of the economy, from a page-view perspective, in that you can distribute widgets in content, things like that.

So I think that the same thing will happen with the Semantic Web, or next-generation finding experience on the Web which is, "How are people identifying content in a way that can be aggregated and useful to browse through, or search through, or discover." The concept of meta tags and tagging clearly had some early momentum and we acquired a company, StumbleUpon [see Chapter 15 for more on StumbleUpon] which takes into consideration this concept of not only identifying the social bookmark aspect of it, but tagging things.

I over-simplify the concept of Semantic Web because I don't foresee people assigning detailed attribute definitions to everything that's in their content out there. I think there's a huge opportunity. I used to run a company called Consumer Review, and our objective was to get product reviews from passionate

> *"Stop worrying about having to manage your infrastructure; start worrying about your products and your innovation."*

enthusiasts on particular product categories. Consumer- or community-generated content is huge. It creates huge value, and it's even easier to do now. The Semantic Web can evolve out of stuff like that over time.

I just don't know how the value chain works. Where's the incentive structure?

Another company that eBay has acquired, Epinions, was a consumer-generated review site. They set up a virtual economy for motivating people to do things, but ultimately, the majority of the contributors are a small percentage of the population.

So, in order for the Semantic Web to really come about, there needs to be a shift in people's ability and willingness to help tag and categorize information across the Web. Some of the bigger companies are going to have to participate a bit more in standardizing around this.

Do you believe that shift will come? Do you think people will be willing to tag information?

I actually do, but I don't know what the trigger is going to be. Let me tell you why I think that: I hate to use Facebook as an example, but they changed a lot of things with some basic activities.

By opening up their platform, they got every major Internet company to ask, "How do we open up our platform more?" Google responded with OpenSocial, which while it's a marginally off-of-a-paper-napkin kind of launch, might just take off! They started off with the right things, and they know they need to get into the game more aggressively off their platform than they have in the past and get other people to do the same thing. OpenSocial encourages other companies, who have typically held their information very tightly, like a LinkedIn [discussed in Chapter 9] and a Plaxo, to open their platforms more.

SalesForce has understood this concept for a long time. We've understood it. Yahoo has understood it to a certain extent. And, Amazon actually jumped on this bandwagon a few years back and has made great progress.

Let's jump to another term that is being used today—Software as a Service (SaaS), or Software plus Services (S+S). What is your thought on these?

Great ideas. Once again, the real test for adoption on those won't be small companies; it'll be the big companies. The small companies will adopt it, because economically it makes a lot of sense.

> *"Big companies love control; they need predictability. Wall Street does not like unpredictability."*

The general philosophy is, "Stop worrying about having to manage your infrastructure; start worrying about your products and your innovation." And that's a great message. So, if you can focus your business and your employees to do things that truly matter to the bottom line and not worry about infrastructure to support your software and manage it as a service, it makes a lot of sense.

Big companies are going to be reluctant, because they don't want to have core-business infrastructure in a place that they don't control. Big companies love control; they need predictability. Wall Street does not like unpredictability, and if you release that control too much, you run the risk of catastrophe. That's why it will take a long time to get there.

Shifting back to Web 2.0, what has eBay done in the Web 2.0 space that you would consider really cool?

First, we built a widget in May of this year called eBayToGo. You can take a look at it at `http://togo.ebay.com`. As simple as widgets are, the reason that this one is meaningful is that it creates a compelling interactive eBay Anywhere experience delivering unique and customized content from our site and publishing it on a third-party site or blog. From our perspective, it also helps show that distributing eBay off of eBay.com is very important to our business.

The other cool thing is desktop.ebay.com, which my team is developing. This application is written on Adobe's AIR platform, which creates an experience that you just can't get on the Web today in this environment on your desktop.

For us, once again, it's distribution. I look at delivering the eBay experience off of eBay.com in four places. The first is delivering it across the Web through distribution of widgets and core functionality. I'm talking buying experience now, not selling, so this is enabling widgets, not just

> *"If you can create a compelling experience for the consumers, then that's really important."*

promoting items that are on eBay for sale, but also allowing people to purchase directly from the widget. That's something that we're working on internally, and we talk about. Hopefully in Q1 of next year we'll start to see this stuff proliferate across the Web. That's cool because you can put something up on your blog and not have people leave the blog but stay in that experience and have very relevant, very tailored kinds of products, depending on what you're talking about. So, that's distribution across the Web.

The second place is distribution on the desktop. There are a lot of desktop PCs that are shipped, and it's always great to have a desktop link on shipping PCs. While having a Web link is okay, if you can create a compelling experience for the consumers, then that's really important. Our eBay desktop product is one of those examples.

The third is distribution into the digital living room, which is one of those fits and starts. It's tried, but hasn't gone anywhere. Third parties have created things for eBay through our platform, like this company called BuyOff, in Austin, Texas, when they launched with Time/Warner cable in Austin. They're also launching across a lot of Time/Warner areas with eBay in the cable set-top box. Pretty interesting. We've got a third party who developed a Windows Media Center application. We're really looking at that, but it's more of an early "Hey, let's see what's going on." But it's pretty important to learn and know how these things develop.

And then the last one, of course, is mobile, from a distribution perspective.

> *"One of the other beauties of the Web 2.0 evolution is that it's a lot cheaper to develop things."*

From my point of view, in five years, eBay is going to be much more about eBay across the Web than it's going to be about eBay.com. Every big company needs to think that way. Although the trend is there, big companies, I don't think, are necessarily…it's a tough one. It's a lot easier to control and predict behavior when it all happens on your web site.

Do you see Web 2.0 features justifying their cost? Do some of the things you've done at eBay justify the cost of development?

It depends on how you compare cost. I would say that one of the other beauties of the Web 2.0 evolution is that it's a lot cheaper to develop things like this, because it's easy to write or integrate with a REST API or to leverage a web service. Now you're seeing some tool companies come out with creative tools that automatically read in the WSDLs that define different web services that are out there and allow you to drag and drop to create things; things like Yahoo! Pipes.

All of these tools are designed to make it easy to leverage web services to create widgets and distribute applications. The cost of development is going down for those things, but the early days of development are pricey, although not as pricey as writing a desktop app—I can tell you that! It's all relative. For me, it's cheap compared to core development/core infrastructure costs.

That's another reason that there are so many companies out there right now—because they can actually launch their company without having to invest a lot of development dollars. The differentiation is not going to be investment dollars on the technology side; the technology is getting easier and easier to use. It's going to be entirely based on user experience and what information are you combining in the right way.

Is there anything about Web 2.0 or eBay that you'd like to add?

Just that the sheer volume of content and interesting stuff—which is proliferating at an accelerated pace, coupled with the ability to find it, has enabled this economy, if you will, the ability to create widgets and distribute them.

Without the early days of personal home pages evolving into blogs, evolving into creating mashups easily, or whatever—self-publishing in any way—obviously video through YouTube—all those things are really foundational elements. It is important to note that.

Sound Bites

eBay is one of the best-known successful web sites. When you add PayPal and Skype to the mix, you have a company with great web experience. Max Mancini, who runs the Platform and Disruptive Innovation team for eBay, is in a great position to provide insights on Web 2.0 and more. Some of his perspectives follow:

- Internet users expect rich, interactive experiences. On sites, differentiation will be based entirely on user experience and how information is combined. A defining moment for Web 2.0 is people opening their platforms to allow others to use the information in ways that the platform provider never thought of. Web 2.0 is really defined as enabling people to create new things.
- "Atomization of the Web" is taking all of the components and making them available for combination in unconsidered ways, or in ways that are very individual.
- You can't necessarily rely on individual sites as being where the Internet economy is going. Rather, you should determine what compelling value you are delivering and how you can monetize that value.
- Another defining moment for the trend in Web 2.0 is being able to monetize things that would have otherwise been unmonetizable. The

monetization models really have to evolve. The commerce-based transaction model and the pure ad model as they exist today need to evolve significantly.

- Web 2.0 is creating more openness in integrating things that you would have had to build from scratch before. Nobody has even started looking at how you manage rights and security within that. We're not quite at the big levels of monetization yet where security is as big of a concern as it should be.

- Blurring the lines between a desktop experience and a web experience is where everything is headed. There is a lot of momentum for creating interactive experiences leveraging Web 2.0 technologies and web services. We're taking these technologies, bringing them to the desktop, *and* allowing people to leverage the web services in the same way and as simply as they could through the Web. After all, the Web really isn't about a web browser—we experience it that way today, but it doesn't have to be.

- Big companies love control; they need predictability. Wall Street does not like unpredictability, and if you release that control too much, you run the risk of catastrophe. Enable your business to operate no matter what the next big thing is, and let other people catch up.

Alan Meckler:
Internet.com

2

"Going back into the 1990s, I believe that there really were Web 2.0 properties; it's just that nobody knew to call them that. In fact, they were mocked."

—Alan Meckler

There is the Web and there is the Internet. There is only one Internet.com and Alan Meckler and Jupitermedia oversee it. Internet.com is a site name that is very easy to remember for obvious reasons; however, it is just one of the many web sites and company products that make up Jupitermedia.

www.internet.com

Internet.com is more than just a site. It is also a channel into some of the other parts of Jupitermedia. As such, to fully understand what Internet.com is, you need to know what Jupitermedia is.

Jupitermedia bills itself as a leading provider of images and information for creative, business, and information-technology professionals. It is divided into two primary divisions. Jupiterimages provides photos and other graphic images electronically. JupiterOnlineMedia provides information to IT professionals, developers, and creative professions through five different channels as well as through event (JupiterEvents) and job (JustTechJobs) areas. Internet.com is one of the channels within JupiterOnlineMedia. When you dig into these various divisions, you'll find that there are over 150 web sites, including 30 discussion forums, and more than 180 newsletters. Included within this impressive group are highly visible properties such as FlashKit, WebReference, Developer.com, Codeguru, WebDeveloper, InternetNews, LinuxToday, Webopedia, and MegaPixel.

We Tend to Think that We've Seen it All, When in Fact We Haven't Seen Anything Yet

Internet.com is a portal to an impressive list of sites. Even more impressive is Alan,the CEO in charge. He is one of the early pioneers in tapping into the Internet, particularly from a media perspective. As such, he has some interesting insights and perspectives, as the following interview shows.

Can you tell a little about yourself and about Internet.com?

I've been in the publishing business since 1969. I also have a PhD in American History, so I have an interesting perspective on media and history. My PhD was actually on the history of micropublishing, which was considered high-tech back when I first started publishing in 1969–'70.

Along the way, I've been involved in every phase of publishing, from printing letters, journals, magazines, monographs, reference books, novels, fiction, non-fiction, and all forms of business-to-business publishing and technology publishing. I was fortunate in that my career took me on a path from the micropublishing, which is really about the delivery of information, and opened my eyes to the fact that this would evolve. I was therefore ready to grasp new ideas. So when the microfiche micropublishing aspects of the world changed, and this so-called technology or medium became somewhat obsolete, I grasped the video disc and optical disc, which came about around 1979 to '80, and then when CD-ROM came along in the early 1980s, even though it wasn't commercially viable for another eight or nine years, I started to report on CD-ROM way before anyone was actually using it other than research libraries.

When the personal computer came along, it was a natural evolution for me to understand that the PC was obviously going to be a very important next-generation way to deliver information. Fortunately, because I primarily worked with academics, research libraries and research organizations in my specialty publishing, I was exposed to the Internet in 1990. At that time, the Internet was really only used by certain government agencies and academic institutions. Certainly, very few people knew about it, even in the technology space.

I saw it immediately as the next frontier for the delivery of information. But it's important to note that in 1990, and until late 1993, the idea of the World Wide Web—or as I understood it to be, the multimedia aspects of the Internet—was unknown to anyone in the world. The Internet in 1990 was strictly a contextual way of delivering information.

In 1990 I started what I believe was the first commercial venture in the world to deal with the Internet, when I started a newsletter called "Research and Education Networking," which covered what the Internet would be able to do primarily for academics and research libraries. By 1992, before the World Wide Web had been announced—or started to appear in any form or in the press—I had one of these amazing experiences due to a speech that I was listening to by Mitch Kapor. Many people don't know who he is anymore, but he was the creator of Lotus. Mitch was giving a talk at a trade show I was running, and he was speculating about the Internet. It was while he was speaking that it dawned on me that the Internet was going to be much broader and wider than anything that I had ever thought about. I had only thought of it in terms of how it could be used in an academic setting.

> *"The Internet was going to have a greater impact, perhaps, than the computer and it was going to be all-encompassing."*

I then realized that the Internet was going to have a greater impact, perhaps, than the computer and it was going to be all-encompassing.

I decided at that point in my business career that, as a small company, that I should essentially roll the dice, take anything that I had, sell any products that I had that I could use to raise money, to concentrate 100 percent on the development of the Internet, in terms of reporting on it. I was not really successful in being able to raise money, I went to venture capital firms, banks; very few, if any, believed in the Internet or understood what I was talking about, as you can well understand in 1992.

> "What was really needed was a web site that would be very, very specific or vertical that would cover a topic really well."

By 1993, in order to do what I wanted to do, I finally had to get a mortgage on my home in order to raise the money to take the newsletter, which was now starting to grow, turn it into a magazine, and change the name to *Internet World*. At the same time, I started a trade show by the same name. That first trade show took place in New York City in December of 1993. The day that the trade show opened was the first day that I had ever heard about the World Wide Web. There was an article in the New York Times by John Markoff about the World Wide Web. As it was explained, I couldn't quite grasp what it was all about, but I did understand that the Internet now had a multimedia aspect to it. That first trade show attracted about 1,400 to 1,500 people, but it only had about eight exhibits that were Internet-related because in those days there were virtually no commercial applications.

From that point on, my work has always been in the Internet space, for the most part, with a number of web sites and other related products, including trade shows. I was sort of always trying to take the role of the middleman. In other words, if you went back to mining days, there were the prospectors who went out and dug for the gold and took some greater risks, and then there was the fellow who had the general store, who supplied perhaps the information as to where the miners ought to go, and also sold the supplies. The supplier is sort of the role that I've taken over the years. That's essentially my background in the Internet.

Can you talk a little about where Internet.com and Jupitermedia are today?

The evolution of my company in the 1990s, once the Internet started to take off, basically moved, sort of by accident, into becoming a dominant trade show producer of the Internet World trade show I mentioned. The show started at eight exhibits with around 1,500 people in attendance in 1992, and by the time I sold the business in 1998 it was a show running three times a year in the United States and in 20 different countries around the world. The big U.S. shows were attracting four to five hundred exhibitors, with 60,000 to 75,000 attendees, depending on where the shows were located.

What happened to me then was that I was approached by several companies in 1998 about buying the business, and we sold the company in 1998. We had been building the company along the way, from 1993 on, and had one of the first web sites in the world, launched in early 1994, and at the time it was known as "Meckler Web" as a codeword, but it got picked up by the press and it was written up in *Fortune* and *Forbes* magazines.

It was a very interesting model; it was basically built on the concept that we would be a master web site for all types of organizations because it was so difficult and arcane to build a web site. Servers were so expensive—as I remember, in those days, they were about $50,000. We would become a sort of general portal for any type of organization and we would create a lot of verticals. We soon realized, after doing this for a few months, that this was too broad. I went back to my roots, feeling that what was really needed was a web site that would be very, very specific or vertical that would cover *a* topic really well, much like a good magazine or a good newsletter. At that point, we scrapped the original "Meckler Web" and became iWorld and launched a web site that covered the growing Internet industry, the business-to-business aspects of the Internet, as well as general IT and enterprise issues.

That evolved, but in terms of the company, the trade show and the print magazine were what really were bringing in the money. With the web site in those days, of course, there was very little advertising that one could glean, and it was a loser.

> *"I made the first web site acquisition in the world, and it was a web site called thelist.com."*

However, I felt, as early as 1996, that certainly in technology reporting and information, that the day of the print magazine was fast approaching its end and that ultimately all technology information (business-to-business information), would be online. If someone continued to invest in magazines, they would be doomed. The type of information that technology professionals wanted was yesterday, and you could get that out very cheaply and inexpensively and rapidly around the world, on the Internet, but you couldn't do that in print.

So, I started to buy web sites. In fact, in 1994 I'm sure I made the first web site acquisition in the world, and it was a web site called thelist.com. I then bought several other web sites in 1994, '95, and '96. Interestingly, we were condemned by Wall Street and financial institutions that followed us. We were now a public company, and they didn't see any future in the commercial side of web sites in terms of making money. We were an extremely profitable company, and the only part of our company that was losing money was the building out of our web site, iWorld.

> "I am one who thinks that many Web 2.0 properties are jokes. Very few will ever be profitable"

In 1997, we got an opportunity to buy the domain name Internet.com from a company that was going bankrupt. We bought that for $250,000 in the spring of that year, and changed our name to Internet.com. In 1998, when our company was acquired, interestingly, we had five suitors—some fairly famous companies like the Gartner Group, United Business Media in England, Penton Media, Advanstar, and others who wanted to buy us. In the discussions, none of them wanted the web site assets. They wanted the trade shows and they wanted the print magazine that we had, which was now being published weekly as a newspaper-size tabloid but in magazine format. It was a fascinating experience, because while I was willing to sell the whole company and walk away, these companies—some of them sophisticated professionals—were telling me that they didn't want the web site assets because they felt that you could not make money on them, and would I consider running them for these companies as a subsidiary. Ultimately, when we made our deal and sold to Penton Media in November of 1998, Penton decided to keep an interest in the web sites, and they sold back to me an 80.1% interest in the web sites. I had a partner. I thought this was a tremendous opportunity because I had already felt two years earlier that print was doomed, at least in technology publishing, and that the Web was the way to go.

We built up Internet.com into what today is one of the larger networks of web sites covering the enterprise IT and the Internet. We have over 150 web sites and companion email newsletters; we have 15 million unique visitors a month, which clearly makes us one of the bigger web sites in the world. We have five million subscribers to email newsletters, and we continue to evolve with those web sites. Some web sites have topics that aren't as relevant, and we have to discontinue those. We continue to be selective in acquiring new web sites, and we also create sites organically. That is, we think of ideas and start web sites or blogs to cover technology on the Internet.

With that history, it is interesting to ask you how you define Web 2.0.

Web 2.0 as I see it is just a continuing evolution of the ability to inexpensively get information, data, and now entertainment out to the consumer and to the business world. I actually don't think it's as radical as some do.

Going back into the 1990s, I believe that there were Web 2.0 properties; it's just that nobody knew to call them that. In fact, they were mocked. When the Internet had its bubble crash in late 2000, those properties became known as the laughingstock of what brought the

> *"More than 99 percent of all Web 2.0 properties will never make a dime."*

Internet down, or at least the people who had invested in it. I refer to sites like The Globe (www.theglobe.com), The Tripod (www.tripod.com), and many others that were essentially community sites—user-generated content sites with major traffic, page use, and unique visitors that really had no way of making money.

What we see today is really just different forms of technology taking advantage of software and speed to turn what was the laughingstock product in the late 1990s and 2000 into something that is now very much in demand. But, the similarities go on, because I am one who thinks that many Web 2.0 properties are jokes. Very few will ever be profitable.

While you certainly have your very successful organizations that have sold for amazing amounts of money like MySpace, YouTube, and others, relatively speaking, they still don't do very well at making money. There are, however, thousands of others out there that are getting venture capital funding that will never make money. While there will never be the crash in values that we saw in 2000 to 2001 from the 1990s, I do believe that a lot of venture capital firms and organizations that have made investments in so-called Web 2.0 properties will end up taking it on the chin because I would say that more than 99 percent of all Web 2.0 properties will never make a dime.

Why do you believe venture capitalists (VCs) are investing the money if there isn't a business model?

It's very similar, again to the late 1990s to 2000, where we're seeing the rise of eyeballs as being valuable, even if there's no money. It is the idea that if you have the traffic, the revenues will come in one form or another. It will be translated into economic reward.

I still don't believe that that is the case.

> *"There might be less than half of one percent [of Web 2.0 sites] that are going to make it."*

I think that a Web 2.0 property, with that revenue—when it's tied into a sideline or another companion business that does have an E-Commerce offering—can be extremely valuable. But, I think most Web 2.0 properties standing by themselves with the idea that they will be the next MySpace, YouTube, or Facebook is a pipe dream. Therefore it's the VCs and investors chasing these ideas that they can create great traffic and then sell it for hundreds of millions of dollars, and I just don't think that's going to happen. I'm even dubious, personally, about how valuable Facebook really is. It certainly has massed a lot of people, but I'm still not convinced that, by itself, it is going to be that successful dollar-wise.

Is just having community in and of itself not an asset?

It's an asset depending on how you're using it. Our company, for example—and obviously we're not in the same league and valuation as YouTube and some of the others that we've mentioned—has a number of E-Commerce offerings and properties where we sell advertising. We also have user-generated content in the form of discussion forums and the like with a fairly good-size membership.

In our case we feel that these forums are extremely valuable because they are part of web sites or services where we advertise our own E-Commerce offerings to like-minded people. So, in that sense, community is very valuable because we hopefully can interest them in buying images from us, or attending one of our webinars or webcasts where we get advertising dollars, or going to our online job-sites, which are related to some of the topics being discussed. When they fit hand-in-glove like that, I believe community Web 2.0 aspects can be very valuable. When they rise and have a very big community by themselves, but there are not economic or E-Commerce offerings that do fit hand-in-glove, I question the value.

Is advertising by itself enough of a driver?

I don't think so. Obviously, Google with AdSense and keywords, it works for Google. With the Facebooks, the LinkedIns, and the others, the idea would be that you can deliver focused advertising to the vertical interests of the people. It's quite possible that will work. I don't necessarily believe that people who use Facebook and LinkedIn and whatever will be happy with the advertising that they see on Google where it's expected. I think that might be the flaw.

But, of course, I'm talking about two of the more popular Web 2.0 properties. When you think of the vast number of others that are out there, which is really what my theory is, yes, there might be less than half of one percent that are going to make it—or even less than that—

> "Web 2.0 is great, but I feel that it's just an extension of what was already there in '98/'99."

and they'll make it really big. But the vast majority, ninety nine and a half percent or more, is not going to make it. Even if they're able to build up a reasonable amount of traffic, I still don't believe that they're going to be able to attract advertising. I also think that the advertising will be more like keywords, and I don't think that they'll get the same economic return that Google gets. I don't think that they will get the traffic in proportion to what Google gets, so that the values that are being placed on these with the assumption that you're going to get keyword advertising and the like—I just don't believe that the numbers will pan out to be satisfactory in terms of the investment value that is being placed on them.

Is there anything about Web 2.0 that you believe people might be misunderstanding or hyping in the wrong way?

The hyping, of course, is the ability to make money, because we have certain stellar performers that have gotten extraordinary returns. Again, there were a lot of Web 2.0 properties in the late '90s that didn't make it, and I imagine that if they were to come along today, (i.e., The Globe—I don't even know if it still exists), they would probably be considered more valuable than they were considered back then. I do think Web 2.0 is great, but I feel that it's just an extension of what was already there in '98/'99, and that the really exciting thing that is coming along might be Web 3.0, which would be the ability to leapfrog searches we know today and to be able to string together a whole bunch of thoughts and ideas and get very concise response.

That leads into the question of what you think of Web 3.0, or of what is known as the Semantic Web?

I think there are tremendous possibilities. The better term for Semantic Web might even be Linked Data, which I think is a little more understandable. I think Semantic Web may be too esoteric for people to understand. Linked Data Web is easier to understand.

I think that the opportunities in that field are extraordinary in that Google might not be the final answer. In other words, although Google has a lot of engineers and tech professionals obviously thinking about these issues, Google is vulnerable.

It would be a great mistake to think that what we see today is what we'll see in five years. It is just as YouTube came along, totally unexpectedly out of nowhere. And to a degree, who would have even thought in 2002 that Yahoo! would have to take a backseat to anybody? We really would be foolish to think that Google has it absolutely locked. I would expect that with all the brilliant people in the world who are now exposed to technology, somebody is going to come up with a better mousetrap and do to Google what Google did to Yahoo!. And it will be this Linked Data concept that we've been talking about.

Then you don't believe that the topic is too academic or too manually intensive. You believe the linking of data could be truly automated?

Yes. I think that's the trouble with the term "Semantic Web;" it's too esoteric. Anyone who has used the Internet enough for searching can immediately understand when you use the term Linked Data. The great dream—I believe, within 10 years—[will be that] you'll talk to your computer or your browser or whatever service you're dealing with, and it will find the information for you, and that that is what's coming. That will be the next great thing—and it will all be through linked data and to a degree, a bit of artificial intelligence.

So is voice recognition then the next big revolution you see, or is it something else?

I think that's what I see—that, and entertainment increasing. The mobile phone will lead us in being able to attain more instantaneous and spectacular businesses. For example, I believe I read the other day that there are over three billion mobile phone handsets in the world. At the rate of change, what's happening is that those people are changing over, not several times a year but certainly much faster than people changed computers in the '90s when that was the standard.

Now, it's not speed on the mobile phone, but rather the services that a person will be able to get, and it is also the E-Commerce that will be able to be conducted over the mobile device. Voice recognition will be the key there. A lot of people are making a mistake by thinking that communicating with services is going to be a browser for the cell phone as we understand a browser

> *"The Internet over the next 20 to 30 years…is still going to be incredibly revolutionary, in terms of what's going to happen."*

for the computer. But because we talk into a phone to use it, I think that the next great thing will be the ability to use the device by talking to it and it giving you answers back, whether the answers be directions or whatever.

You mention services. Software as a Service (SaaS) and Software plus Services (S+S)—what do you think of these?

I'm not sure that I have enough knowledge or instinct about it, but I presume you're talking about the idea of getting your services off the Web versus actually physically having the software, so to speak, on the computer?

A similar question, although not the same would be will the desktop application go away?

I don't think they go away, but I do think the days of buying the next version of the software are over. That's definitely gone. Obviously storage, software, and those types of services will be obtained from the Web. I don't think one is necessarily going to need a huge reservoir of software and other types of things because you're going to be able to get that through the ether. This is much like the smart phones—they're just going to keep getting smarter and you'll be able to do more and more things with them: information is going to be stored on the telephone.

The Internet over the next 20 to 30 years, through the phone and whatever form the computer takes, is still going to be incredibly revolutionary, in terms of what's going to happen, but I really foresee a virtual melding of the smart phone and the computer with more and more voice recognition and intelligence in terms of being able to link things and buy.

One of the things that I believe is going to happen—I've read about it, but I haven't seen it—is being able to drive down the road, see a billboard that has a bar code on it, aim your cell phone at it, and get more information from the vendor or even to buy something right on the fly that way.

By just aiming your phone at the sign, it will pick up the bar code. The bar code will talk to the phone, the message will then go back to the vendor because of the software on your phone and the transaction could essentially then be made or the information could be delivered. That's where the really big money is going to come from.

That presumes that connectivity will be at a level where we will always be connected. Do you believe we will get to that point?

Absolutely. To me, the greatest mystery is why we're not always connected on an airplane. There were some attempts over the last two or three years with Boeing's Connexion service, but there are new ones coming from a company called Aircell and others so that you'll always be connected on an airplane. It's the combination of satellites, ground stations, and such.

I live in New York City, and I always know with the number of Starbucks around, and other stores that have Wi-Fi, I can duck into a store and in less than 30 seconds, I'm on the Internet. I would say that in three to four years that in most cities you won't need to be ducking into a store. The Net will be omnipresent.

Do you have anything you'd like to add about what we've discussed?

The big point is that we tend to think that we've seen it all, when in fact we haven't seen anything yet.

It seems that those of us in the United States are not using our cell phones and mobile devices like people in many other countries.

It's been like that for years. The other thing that's exciting is the coming of the openness of it—you don't have to be locked into one network.

When you think of the evolution, five to six years ago, even your cell phone number was locked into a network, and they at least opened that up. That was considered quite wild at that time. Those kinds of things that had previously taken three to four years will now start jumping down to months in terms of the portability.

Sound Bites

Alan Meckler has been involved with the use of the Web since the days it was opened to the public. With his experiences and with the number and scope of sites he is involved with, it is no surprise that he has a number of interesting insights, such as the following:

- Web 2.0 is just a continuing evolution of the ability to inexpensively get information, data, and now entertainment out to the consumer and to the business world.
- As a result of technology, software, and speed, what was the laughingstock product in the late 1990s and 2000 has turned into something that is now very much in demand.

- A lot of venture capital firms and organizations that have made venture capital investments in so-called Web 2.0 properties will end up taking it on the chin pretty hard because most Web 2.0 properties will never make a dime.
- A Web 2.0 property can be extremely valuable if it is tied into a sideline or another companion business that does have an E-Commerce offering. Most Web 2.0 properties standing by themselves with the idea that they will be the next MySpace, YouTube, or Facebook are pipedreams.
- It would be a great mistake to think that what we see today is what we'll see in five years.
- Within 10 years, you'll talk to your computer or your browser or whatever service you're dealing with, and it will find the information for you. That's what's coming.
- The mobile phone will make it possible to attain more instantaneous and spectacular businesses.

Eric Engleman: Bloglines

3

> *"Web 2.0 brought the learning curve down to a really low level so you didn't need to be a computer engineer to be able to run your own blog site."*
>
> —Eric Engleman, general manager, Bloglines

If you ask a number of people to name the most popular sites related to blogs, you'll quickly see that Bloglines is near the top of their lists. It seems only natural that if you ask about Web 2.0 sites, you will again see Bloglines appear often in people's lists.

Bloglines started as a tool created by Mark Fletcher in 2003. It quickly grew from there. Today the site bills itself as a free online service for newsfeeds, blogs, and rich content. It helps you to search, subscribe, and share these services without requiring you to understand the underlying technology.

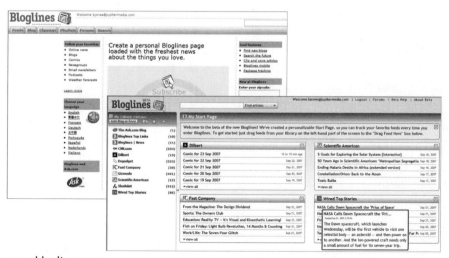

www.bloglines.com

Bloglines is a brand of Ask.com. Eric Engleman is the general manager who leads the Bloglines team today.

I Don't Think There Is Anything Right or Wrong about Web 2.0

As general manager, Eric brings his experience at Bloglines along with his past experiences at other leading web sites, including Earthlink and Excite. Eric offers some interesting perspectives on what he sees as Web 2.0 and more.

Can you say a little bit about who you are and what you do?

I'm Eric Engleman, I'm the GM of Bloglines, so basically I run the Bloglines team here at Ask. Prior to being here, I worked in major companies like Yahoo!, Earthlink, and Excite/Excite@Home. Even earlier I had an old-media background and made a transition to online at CNN. And as far as the old-media world [goes], I worked at big places such as CNN and smaller places like *LaundryNews*—the newspaper for the industrial launderer.

I have a wide range of experiences, with a lot of focus on start pages beginning in 1996.

At Excite I launched Excite Live, which became myExcite and won an award in 1998 as best start page. I've also worked on start pages at EarthLink and Yahoo!, so I'm familiar with the RSS feed reader space and have been tracking it for a while.

Can you provide some background on Bloglines?

Bloglines was one of the early innovators for Web 2.0. It launched in 2003. It was really a self-funded operation by the founder, Mark Fletcher. Mark built the tool for himself, basically. He saw that there were a lot of blogs that were coming online, and people were writing a lot of really interesting things. He didn't want to spend all his time going to these different sites individually, so he built this application to grab the content via RSS and display it in one application.

Subsequently, it was a real grass-roots operation. Mark would chat with people, build a feature, and then push it out that night. Maybe it worked. Maybe it didn't. He would then fix it until it worked.

It grew by word of mouth within the blogging community that was around at that time.

Let's ask the big question: To you, and to Bloglines, what is Web 2.0?

There are so many answers to that question. It is such a big thing.

When I look at Web 2.0, I look at two documents to center the conversation. Those are the *The Cluetrain Manifesto* and the O'Reilly Web 2.0 doc. I think it is interesting because *The Cluetrain Manifesto* was one of the earliest conversations leading to Web 2.0. It's kind of this crazy manifesto (manifestos are usually in this hyperbolic language). It's really out there. I think it was published in 1999, or 2000. That's pretty early for it to be Web 2.0, but it's talking about online conversations and how companies need to take part in this new conversation.

THE CLUETRAIN MANIFESTO

The Cluetrain Manifesto was published in hardback in 1999 and released in paperback in 2001 for $14.00. It is authored by Christopher Locke, Rick Levine, Doc Searls, and David Weinberger. The English version is published by Perseus Books Group.

For the O'Reilly document, which was published in 2005, I would call out a few things. If you grew up on the Web, then you'll find a lot of the things they called out are just second nature. Like the Web is the end of the software cycle; if you've been working in the Web for a few years, then you had already gotten into this concept of the Web as a service, and you were already doing releases all the time.

For me now, it's "the app as a platform," whereas he [O'Reilly] talks about "the Web as a platform." But really, now it is about trying to

> *"It is really about end users."*

make the app as a platform. The app is an ecosystem of users and consumers of the application and the data that is created by the user. That data can be user-generated or application-generated.

It is really about the user. It is about creating a user-controlled experience and leveraging the end user to create added value. In the O'Reilly Web 2.0

document, they talk about rich user experience and things like that. The whole AJAX thing is cool, but it is really about end users and how they can organize data and how that collective organization of data adds increased value. Kind of like tagging or monitoring to see what is popular. Another example is Facebook with the activity stream. That is where we're focused now. It is about the app as a platform and it is all about breaking down these silos of applications and content so they can be distributed very easily. Widgets can be distributed very easily. Applications can be joined together and mashed up very easily. So the things I think are interesting are the app as a platform.

Really being data-driven, being able to gather information about the users, and offer up that information in valuable ways, and then creating a user-controlled experience—those are a few big things.

How does Bloglines fit into that?

Bloglines may not be the app as a platform yet, but it is definitely "web as the platform." Bloglines is all about consuming data, all about consuming RSS feeds.

App as a platform—we have a few developers that have created applications on top of Bloglines. One of the great things about Bloglines is that people have created different JavaScripts to enhance their Bloglines. They have created skins so that Bloglines will look like a Mac OS view, for example. Others have built whole applications on top of our APIs. Snarfer uses our APIs for a desktop version. That is kind of interesting. That is definitely app as a platform.

Then data-driven—we have a lot of public data, so the user can consume their data, or they can set their privacy setting and make their blog world public. We aggregate the top 250.

Third parties look at what is popular within Bloglines to inform their blog readings. So a number of people have started using or coming up with "what's hot" in a specific category. I don't know if you've seen the Advertising Age 150 and other very specialized services. In the future, we will be doing more with recommendations to allow the community to highlight what they like in any given topic. That way we can make this feed universe more accessible to the average person. They spend a lot of time trying to set up and figure out how to make a feed reader work.

And lastly, a user-controlled experience. A feed reader is all about user control. It is all about the user defining what feeds, what content they want to subscribe to, and then pulling that all into a single interface. We have launched an AJAX version and that addresses the whole rich user experience, the desktop experience on a web site.

Is the new Bloglines look [one] where the user can move things around on the Web page and such?

It is very funny because you would think, "it is only drag and drop," but in fact it really changes your computing experience. Now that I have drag and drop capabilities with my library in the left-hand pane, I constantly reorganize my lists because I constantly see new relationships between the feeds that I didn't see before. That is one of the great things about Web 2.0 in that it is lowering all of these hurdles so that users can discover new relationships, discover new ideas. Just accomplish things in a lot easier fashion. It allows a lot of different types of people to do these tasks, even outside of Silicon Valley.

> *"People need to be constantly talking to their customer base, constantly innovating and coming up with great ideas."*

Can you expand on what you mean by "a lot of different types"?

Web 2.0 brought the learning curve down to a really low level so you didn't need to be a computer engineer to be able to run your own blog site. You don't need to be a computer engineer or advanced scientist to get your message out to the Web. Anybody can customize your web experience nowadays as simply as drag and drop.

Does this mean that tomorrow someone could create "Bloglines the Sequel" and put you out of business?

Oh, yeah! That is also one of the great things about Web 2.0. The barriers to entry are really low. So, lots of ideas get out there, and lots of ideas are getting attention. I started in '96. Building a web site then was complicated. It wasn't easy stuff.

Nowadays, there is all of this technology that is available for people to leverage, and therefore they focus on solving really interesting, big problems or interesting small problems. It means that people need to be constantly talking to their customer base, constantly innovating and coming up with great ideas. If you really enjoy this space, then that is fun.

You have touched on this, but let me ask: How does Bloglines, or any Web company, continue to survive in the next year and the year after?

Yeah, I think it is a matter of really talking to the customer base. The other thing in the tech world we need to understand is that a lot of these things are still really complicated for the average person. We had Nick Douglas, who was doing some stuff for Justin.TV, in the other day, and he had his camera on top of his head and whatnot. In the demo/interview he is broadcasting live across the Web. I don't think the average person can do that. Not yet.

You mentioned AJAX. There are all these technologies. There are some people who would say that AJAX and similar technologies such as Silverlight, JavaFX or Adobe AIR, are Web 2.0. Are these Web 2.0?

> *"Web 2.0 is a kind of resurgence of the Web after the dotcom bust."*

If that is Web 2.0, then that is pretty limiting and boring. I wouldn't define Web 2.0 as being just the display and creating a desktop experience on the Web. I think that the reason that Web 2.0 is so...it is kind of like any generation; it is very hard to understand when there is a beginning or end of something.

Web 2.0 is a kind of resurgence of the Web after the dotcom bust. I don't think that AJAX is entirely Web 2.0. What all of these things have in common is that they really lower the hurdle for the user. AJAX is just one of those. It lowers the usability hurdle for the average person. User-driven application—it lowers the usability hurdle of those applications being able to get your content syndicated or distributed across a wide variety of different applications. Again, it lowers that user hurdle, or developer hurdle, for making those things happen.

What do you see as some of the most misunderstood areas or aspects of Web 2.0?

Wow. Well, since you asked the first question about AJAX, then maybe some people do define the presentation layer as Web 2.0. I think there is more to it than that.

What I also think is "change." Web 2.0 today is very different from Web 2.0 in 2005. Flickr started in 2004 or something. Web 2.0, like all terms, is constantly evolving. Right now, I think that most people are focused on Web 2.0 as a social graph. I think that is a really hot topic...

> *"The users are now in control, whereas in the past they were not in control."*

You pause. I expect a "but..." at the end of that statement.

When you look at O'Reilly's stuff, I don't think they talk about user control. They talk about the collective harnessing of group intelligence and what-not, but not necessarily user-controlled applications. It is more about the user producing data, which can be leveraged by the people.

I think there is a slight difference. Greater user control is really one of the key things for Web 2.0. The users are now in control, whereas in the past they were not in control. It was really what big companies wanted to broadcast or distribute, whether it is a broadcast via a media model or via an old software model. Now, you can modify and take apart your application. Kind of like the modders who souped up their Toyotas, jack them up, or do whatever. A lot of people are doing that. That is one of the really cool things in how the users take control of their user experience.

You've said that Web 2.0 has evolved to where it is today; where do you see Web 2.0 evolving to in 2009, 2010?

You mean Web 3.0 and all that?

That seems to be a different question. What would you define to be Web 3.0, the Semantic Web?

So in the current path, we'd see more data being created and distributed, and therefore data being created by non-humans and other actors, blog-jets, and things like that. That is pretty interesting. Here's an example: I have a buddy who goes surfing. He monitors the buoys off the Pacific coast. And he understands the information that the buoy generates, so he can figure out where the best surfing spots are going to be. There is all this data that is being generated and can be consumed by people. I think there will be a lot of data that will be generated. We have yet to really understand all of the data that is going to be generated. Facebook is an example of that. There is lot and lots of data. Twitter is another example of that. "I'm hungry for grapes right now." What the heck!

So there is that piece and then the Semantic Web. It is interesting. It is saying, "How can you take all that data out there, and how can you add intelligence to it?" Any time you get into intelligence, it usually takes a lot longer to solve those problems. Artificial intelligence has made a lot of strides, but it has yet to radically change the average person's life.

Do you think the Semantic Web, giving intelligence to data, will actually happen?

It will be augmented in the short term. We have a lot of data. We are looking at how we will mine that data so it will be valuable to people, whether we do that ourselves or with a third party. Everyone is trying to solve that problem, whether it is a recommendation engine, a collaborative filter, or whatnot. Within structured content it is pretty easy, but at Bloglines we have a lot of unstructured contact, and that is where it gets difficult.

What I think will really happen...

In the near term, people have a lot of data. You'll be able to mine the data. You'll be able to offer up maybe not recommendations, but more like augmented options. You'll then be able to watch the users to see what they do, so your recommendations will become better and better over time. A few people are trying to solve this with lots of data and lots of unstructured content.

On Bloglines, if I were to look to find data on "Orange" the company, versus "Orange" the bike or "Orange" the fruit, do you see that ability happening?

I think that Ask3D is interesting in that...maybe this is a plug for the corporate parent....

What I thought was interesting about Ask3D, besides bringing a broad range of rich content to the user via a three-panel interface, is the way it works with disambiguation, or with the user. Ask3D offers up related search terms that the user can use to really easily disambiguate these different terms. Do you mean Orange the bike, or orange whatever, or do you want more oranges?

Ask3D.com recommendations

Generally people think that there should be no user involvement, but that is really, really tough.

Will the Semantic Web happen, or is it more academic?

I think that it needs to have some sort of user interaction. If you look at Ask3D, just as a good example, nobody really talks about what this left-hand part of the page is doing. People usually talk about how Ask3D is prettifying or "sexifying" the page. They rarely talk about how it is helping the user to disambiguate these terms.

Then the other is if you look at music recommendations, oftentimes you need some user interaction to say that "I want this kind of music." Then you are able to create a good stream for a certain period of time, but you'd likely be able to create a great stream if you could stay within a very narrow set of musicians, but they don't have the rights to play that music over and over.

There are Internet radio stations that let you indicate what was good or bad, that will then refine its suggestions based on that feedback.

The book *What the Dormouse Said: How the Sixties Counterculture Shaped the Personal Computer Industry* talks about artificial computing and augmented computing.

Here is what is going on in Silicon Valley, and why it became "the place." Then there is a really interesting note on the battle between artificial intelligence and augmented computing. Artificial intelligence is more common now. The computer is a tool for the human, and working with a computer as an extension of a human is a more tangible function or dream for the near future. For a good example of this, you can look at places like a music site or Ask3D. I think that the key there is that you need to have applications that produce flow. Kind of like a game, so that it has really low hurdles, the right level of challenge, the right level of response. That is really hard to do.

With unstructured data, I think that is very difficult to do, and with fast-moving data sets, it [all] is very difficult to do. With Pandora, they will choose a data-storage structure because of the music genome project. You'll see some of these recommendations and wonder why they made it. But they offer some information on why they recommended a song, band, or album.

> *"One of the things I think is really great about Web 2.0 is that it is a lot of constant delight and surprise."*

I think that oftentimes with AI, you can't always explain why you made a choice. Amazon is a good example: "Why did you make this recommendation on a fishing book...?" It was because I bought a fishing book for my dad, and I probably won't buy another fishing book for another year.

What would you consider some of the "coolest" things you've seen with Web 2.0 inside of Bloglines or elsewhere?

That is an interesting thing. I'm thinking that normally there would be really, really big things, but one of the things I think is really great about Web 2.0 is that it is a lot of constant delight and surprise. Whether you use them as great utility functions is not necessarily the case. The first is that, because the barrier to entry is so low, companies are constantly doing new and interesting things.

It is kind of like the beginning of the Web, where you'd have this cool site of the day. At Digg you could see different ways for Digg data to be displayed. Some work very well, some don't, but all are really cool. The same thing is true at Flickr. With Flickr mashups, you can do fun things and display data in a fun way. That is really a great thing about Web 2.0—because the barrier is so low, just about anyone can do something. If they have a dream, they can just get out there and do it. So you are constantly energized.

The other is that these applications have become, with AJAX, a lot easier to use. An example is the next generation of Bloglines that is currently in beta. You forget how simple drag and drop is and things like that within some of these interfaces. Why can't I just drag it here and drop it across the page?

Another thing I'm finding interesting is the variety of bookmarklets. This innovation is just happening everywhere. Bookmarklets are pretty easy to do, so there are a lot of people who created all these bookmarklets. It is a tech crowd, but whether it is coComment (`www.cocomment.com`), or Blummy (`www.blummy.com`)—which is a kind of bookmarklet for bookmarklets—it is a constant surprise out there.

One other thing I love is how all this information is public. We have information on Bloglines where people can see your blog rolls. On Flickr, you can go to a folder and view who attended the same event as you.

All of this stuff is more and more public and available for you to view, where in Web 1.0 you had to get past the subscription wall or a registration wall. You then had to get into an application. It wasn't easy to find. There might not have been an easy search. Or, the data wasn't tagged, or there was no metadata associated with the item. Now with Web 2.0, all this information is public. It is most likely tagged in some way. It is much more accessible.

Doesn't public data raise issues? Google ran into this issue regarding their policies on public data. Isn't there intellectual property and copyright issues?

Yes and no. I think that in the case of Google applications, they should have been a little clearer with their policies. I think there are a few cases you bring up.

One is that the information is public, and the application is public. Therefore using a public application, what does that mean about the data? Is it public? Is it private? Does it have some restrictions? I think in the case of Google, they didn't clearly communicate what it means to use the Google applications. Do you actually own your data or not?

The other issue is, what does it mean to be public? As in, "If the data is available, and you made it public, then can I use that data and make money off of it?"

I think that all of these issues, such as copyright, are changing. People are still trying to figure out what the new version of copyright is.

How does Bloglines make money?

Our revenue stream is evolving and somewhat straightforward. Feed readers and start pages really work in that they create retention of the user. These products are an entry point into a user's daily content experience. One clear way of monetizing is offering relevant monetizable products within the application—that would be search—so offering up Ask search, which is monetized.

> *"I think that, although it is contradictory, 95 percent of the Web is not monetizable."*

It is evolving because the RSS world and RSS advertising are still evolving. A lot of people are doing tests with RSS advertising, or advertising within the feed, or supplementing the feed. One could imagine that in the future these feeds will have ads, so the opportunity for the feed reader or another aggregator is to offer value-added advertising for the publishers.

Do you see business models changing with Web 2.0, or do you see your business model changing?

I think that Web 2.0 has definitely pushed the advertising model first and foremost. Google AdSense made it very easy for Web 2.0 companies to derive a revenue stream. You put some keyword advertising up there and—bingo—you have a revenue stream. In the past, where people might have pursued a subscription model or some other type of model, they now have an advertising model available for them. So I think the subscription model has gone to the wayside.

In our case, has Web 2.0 changed our model? Since Bloglines is really a part of Web 2.0, you can't really say that Web 2.0 changed it.

Do you see the business model of banner ads changing? There doesn't seem to be banner ads on Bloglines.

We don't include any advertisements on Bloglines, including banner ads.

I think that, although it is contradictory, 95 percent of the Web is not monetizable. How do you monetize the rest of the Web? I think that the Semantic Web will allow for some of this non-monetizable space to be monetized. You'll have an understanding of what is going on out there, so therefore you'll be able to figure out if the pages are monetizable, whereas right now you have no idea of what these pages are, so you can't even make a recommendation or know whether that recommendation would be monetizable.

So there is kind of this dark Web out there.

I'm not sure if that is a great thing.

That's one. And two, banner ads as we know them will change and will definitely change with video. Banner ads are all about brand building and driving brand awareness. Video advertising is definitely effective in doing that. Now that video on the Web is so mainstream, everyone is using [it]. So I think that banners as pixels, as a GIF image, that is not going to be the great thing. But, a video ad as a brand-building ad; that I think will be much bigger.

> *"SaaS is 24/7. It is nonstop. It is constant contact with the customer."*

What do you consider to be video? Are you including Flash videos and such?

Rich media. Is it CPM or CPA advertising? I don't think that CPM is going away. I think it will have resurgence in video and other rich media context. I also think that about one percent of advertising is going to video, and that seems really small to me.

It is small; overall online adverting is only two or three percent, and video is only one percent of that.

Any thoughts on Software as a Service or Software plus Services?

The original part of Web 2.0 talked about Software as a Service, as an ongoing, living thing as apposed to software as a package, as a box, that gets shipped around. So SaaS is 24/7. It is nonstop. It is constant contact with the customer. If you didn't work in desktop software, then, of course, it is Software as a Service. I'm assuming that in some of your other interviews some of the people haven't worked in packaged software, so of course, it is 24/7—it needs to be nonstop; I always need to be talking to my customers—it is always out there.

> *"A lot of people were saying [Web 1.0] was a fad and was going to go away like the CB radio."*

The notion of service changes. You really are offering great service for free.

If you lose your photos on a photo-sharing site, then you get upset. You don't expect them to lose your photos even though you are not paying any money. The bar for customer service has gotten higher, because people now expect that service to be 24/7, very reliable, and they expect it to be free.

It's kind of mind-boggling.

Earlier you mentioned the initial Web bubble, and that things have evolved since then. Do you think that Web 2.0 is another bubble?

First, it is interesting to talk about Web 1.0 and what people were seeing in that time, because a lot of people were saying it was a fad and was going to go away like the CB radio. But then a lot of people realized it was not like the CB radio, but more like the printing press. There was fundamental change, and it was just going to take some time.

In any market there is a period of initial exuberance, then a low, then exciting exuberance, then irrational exuberance. And that really did happen.

So is Web 2.0 going to be like that? Generally not. In markets as they evolve, the follow-on market goes through a period of competition and consolidation.

If you look at the railroad market, they went through that initial excitement exuberance, irrational exuberance, and then crashed. Then they matured and just became a regular industry. I think Web 2.0 is pretty much like that.

Why is Web 2.0 different? The technology cost is far less, and people are a little more prudent. They are not inviting the Rolling Stones to perform at their company picnic. There are also more clear revenue models, so people can measure and figure out if a particular product is making money.

With Web 1.0, when Yahoo! and Excite went public, there was no clear revenue mode.

That is another big difference between Web 1.0 and 2.0. With Web 2.0, if you look at the actual numbers, Flickr was bought for something like $20 [million] or $30 million. That is not a big acquisition for something that everyone talks about and that had a lot of users. In Web 1.0, they would have gone public for like $1 billion. There is real risky stuff still happening, but it is way out there. It is like the artificial intelligence stuff where there is a lot of work still going on. Who knows how those models might evolve?

What do you see as the next change or big revolution that will happen on the Web?

It is funny, because my first reaction was to say the Semantic Web. I've been reading about this for so long. Tim Berners-Lee's stuff has been out there for several years, but it is one of those things that is very elusive. I do think that a lot of the basic problems are being solved and that the promise of making sense of all this information is possibly quite near.

If you look at some of these sites like Techmeme, you'll see they are able to sort out all the news and postings that are happening on the Web. I think that this is a distinct possibility based on the work that is happening with the microformats. People taking off little chunks and then documenting what those formats might be, whether it is an event format or a calendar card format. That is really evolving at a grass-roots level around specific use-case levels that people do right now. There is this hope that this kind of intelligence will start evolving within the Internet.

I think that a lot of people are trying to solve that, and I think that people at Bloglines are helping to solve that. We are already tracking a large set of data. We are gathering between 6 million and 10 million posts a day. We also have a fairly good-sized user base, so we can start monitoring what they do and then hopefully make intelligent recommendations of what they want to read. I think that a lot of other people are in that position now.

Any parting words or thoughts?

One thing I'd like to recommend is that you check out or reread *The Cluetrain Manifesto* that I mentioned earlier. It is really kind of mind-boggling, because it was published so early and out of context. They were really thinking of something when they wrote that.

Sound Bites

Bloglines and Eric Engleman provide a number of insights on Web 2.0. Eric talks about the generation of lots of data, the differences between Web 1.0 and 2.0, Artificial Intelligence, and much more. His comments include the following notable observations:

- Web 2.0 today is very different than Web 2.0 in 2005. Today's Web 2.0 offers plenty of delight and surprise. It lowers all of these hurdles so that users can discover new relationships and ideas. Web 2.0 brought the learning curve down to a really low level, so you didn't need to be a computer engineer to run your own blog site.
- Web 2.0 has definitely pushed the advertising model first and foremost. Although it is contradictory, 95 percent of the Web is not monetizable.
- Why is Web 2.0 different? The technology costs become far less. People are a little more prudent.
- In the past, users did not have control. Today, having a user-controlled experience and leveraging the end user creates added value. The bar for customer service has gotten higher, because people now expect that service to be 24/7, very reliable, and they expect it to be free.
- The whole AJAX thing is cool, but it is really about end users and how they can organize data. That organization of data collectively adds increased value.
- People need to constantly talk to their customer base, to constantly innovate and come up with great ideas.
- In the tech world, a lot of these things are still really complicated for the average person.

Gina Bianchini: Ning

4

> *"I think the freedom that is enabled by the Internet and what people are doing with it today is just really profound."*
>
> —*Gina Bianchini*

To many, social networking is at the core of what defines Web 2.0. One of the most dynamic, user-driven social networking sites on the Web is Ning.com, which was started by Marc Andreessen and Gina Bianchini back in 2004. Marc you might remember from the days when he was working with Netscape.

www.ning.com

What sets Ning apart from other social networking sites is that it is actually a platform for *creating* social networks and not necessarily a social network itself. In other words, people can go to Ning and set up a social network on any topic for any people with any features they want. Ning provides the platform for creating the social network and leaves it to individuals to decide the topic of their social network. The end result is well over (at last count) 145,000 social networks and growing on the Ning platform.

Creating a social network on Ning takes only a matter of minutes. You can then decide if your social network is going to be public or private. Additionally, you can choose features such as videos, blogs, photos, forums, and more.

Of course with more than 145,000 existing networks, you don't have to create your own. Rather, you can join one that already exists. Examples of the categories of existing communities include religion, moms, health, television shows, books, movies, sports, and about anything the mind can imagine.

I Don't Think It Matters...

For many, Gina is a hero in the Web 2.0 space, and her work on Ning has helped propel her to that status. It is interesting to hear perspectives on the topic of Web 2.0, social networking, and more from a hero in the space. It is worth pointing out that not every person is sold on the term Web 2.0.

Can you tell a little bit about yourself?

Sure! I grew up in Cupertino, which is about 20 minutes south of Palo Alto, so I was born and bred in the Silicon Valley. I started Ning about three years ago now, with my friend Marc.

> *"I think it [Web 2.0] just means a lot of different things to a lot of different people."*

We started with a really simple premise, which was based around, "What if everybody had the opportunity to create social networks for anything? That's been the driving premise for the last three years. We really look to try to enable freedom at every level.

What motivates me personally is the fact that we've seen the networks used for so many amazing and diverse purposes. We've seen everything from teachers using these networks for connecting with other teachers, to independent journalists connecting with each other as they're covering different crises around the globe, to people affected by diabetes. That definitely gets me up every morning and excited to move forward with what we're doing at Ning.

What do you consider Web 2.0 to be?

I don't think about it [Web 2.0] that much.

I mean, sincerely, the thing that motivates us here at Ning, and me personally, is giving people the freedom to create. Thinking about the term Web 2.0—and spending a lot of time on defining what it is—doesn't matter. I think it is more of a buzz word. Ultimately, what really motivates people to be involved in social networking and social media is giving people freedom, giving people choice, giving people the ability to meet and connect with people they would never otherwise meet. I find that so incredibly motivating that I don't spend a lot of time thinking about what Web 2.0 means.

Isn't Web 2.0 the current "buzz jargon" for what you just described?

Maybe; I think it just means a lot of different things to a lot of different people. People a lot smarter than me have spent a lot of time trying to define it. The whole point in having a definition of something is to have something that people agree on, and people don't agree on what Web 2.0 means. I think it's just another thing for people to talk and have a dialogue about, which is fine. But, at the end of the day, I think the freedom that is enabled by the Internet and what people are doing with it today is just really profound, and should be the focus. But that just might be me.

While you've discounted Web 2.0 as a buzz term that you'd prefer not to define, let's go ahead and still ask a few questions around the topic. For example, what do you consider to be the most misunderstood issue surrounding Web 2.0?

The problem is thinking that there should be a definition. I don't think there should be or that there needs to be.

If people can focus in on enabling new and interesting ways of connecting people, then you don't really need to have a shared understanding of the specific term.

People like to put terms on things that are out there. The Web is dynamic and changing. Trying to peg a time in the changing evolution of the Web with a term almost seems binding in a way that doesn't work.

And I don't think it matters.

Part of the reason for this book is because there are many ways of defining a term. In this case the term is Web 2.0. In most cases people are willing to define what they believe Web 2.0 to be. Most center on the communities being more in charge.

Actually I had a really interesting conversation earlier today with a music label. The technology guy said the funniest thing I've heard all day. He was talking about services like imeem or Facebook or MySpace, and he said, "Well, the community really seems to love it but... but we think there should be..."

And I thought, "Maybe you should be paying a little bit more attention to what this "community" is actually doing as opposed to what your CMS [content management system] system is integrating into." Perhaps that was mean, but it's true!

> *"I think about the time we're living in and it is really, really cool."*

As somebody who has always been passionate about grassroots organizing and empowering individuals, what I love about right now is that it's putting out of work the whole set of big, gigantic systems integrators. You know "47,000 stakeholders" having to agree in order to implement something. Now it's just about someone with a good idea creating something out of nothing. That's really cool.

There's a media company that announced in May 2006 that they would have up and running a "MySpace" for women in middle-age. It's now January 2008 and they still haven't launched anything. The technology is moving so fast that those layers of coordination and centralization just don't apply anymore. They're irrelevant, and if you spend too much time on those things, you'll become irrelevant, too.

So this company could set this community up on Ning in a matter of a few minutes?

That's my point. In the time the company has had many meetings, interviewed stakeholders, hired enterprise software companies to build them out this "special thing," they could have been up and running with a social network on Ning.

In that same time, more than 145,000 social networks have been created on Ning. It's pretty profound in terms of just how fast these things are moving. This kind of innovation and power of individuals is phenomenal. I think about the time we're living in and it is really, really cool.

What is the cost to set up a community on the Internet now?

It's free and takes less than five minutes on Ning.

Having said that, how does Ning make money?

It's straightforward. On the free service, we reserve the right to run advertising. If you want to buy that right from us, you can do so, as well as purchase from us a number of other premium services.

Are ad blockers an issue with this?

No because, for the most part, we're actually talking about AdSense text ads. We're not talking about flashing banners that are going to get blocked by ad blockers. More importantly, especially as an analyst, I would think that the incredibly large numbers associated with online advertising would be a clear indication that there is a market here for free Web services that are advertising-supported. I don't think that's controversial. Maybe in 1997 it was controversial, but not in 2007.

I see ads being accepted, but I see communities pushing back and saying that sites should be free and that they shouldn't be subjected to ads.

But then people would go out of business and they wouldn't have any services. In our case, you *can* buy the right to not have ads. You have a choice. I don't think it's that big of a deal.

The other thing that's going on here—that you hear as a criticism, or as a naysayer warning of doom—is that social networks don't have very targeted advertising; the CPMs are very low…. That has a lot more to do with the fact that you can't do good targeting when the generic one-size-fits-all social networks just based on profiles. In our case, social networks on Ning are targeted and specific. So, for the most part, it's actually pretty easy to drive targeted advertising here.

Where do you see the community taking the Internet next?

I don't think there's one community. There are 1.3 billion people online. More and more, the Internet is going to closely reflect how people organize in the real world. The Internet certainly enhances and extends the real world, but fundamentally you're just going to continue to see an exaggerated set of human nature. I think that's a good thing.

There are technologies like Google Gears and Adobe AIR that are looking to take Web applications offline. Do you believe there will be a move to take the Web back offline?

For Google to have desktop apps, I think that's great. Cool. Do I think that that's going to replace Google search? No.

Do I think that it would be in Adobe's best interest to have offline desktop applications? Sure. I just don't think that it will replace online efforts. I think that the genie is out of the bottle on the internet.

S+S (Software plus Services) seems to be getting more important, especially in the enterprise space. Do you have any thoughts on these pieces of jargon?

I'm getting further and further away from the enterprise world. I am seeing that there are companies that are creating social networks on Ning for internal purposes or for intranet.

The whole concept of "behind the firewall" is slowly but surely being challenged, at least on the edge of the network for things like, "Hey, we want to put this thing together and if we can do this with software in our consumer lives, or in our individual lives, why can't we do it for this company too?"

Sticking with jargon, what is your thought on Web 3.0 and the Semantic Web?

It's an interesting, theoretical discussion amongst a small group of people who really care about it. I don't think it is a mainstream behavior.

I believe that Ning fits squarely into what many people describe as Web 2.0. It has been awarded as such. Are there any social community–driven sites or other sites that you would consider great Web 2.0 type sites (from a social, community aspect)?

I really like these guys out of Chicago called skinnyCorp. They've done a great job job of saying, "Hey, this is the kind of company that we want to build and we want to create all these interesting sites like Threadless, and ExtraTasty.

It's just a fascinating way of organizing company ideals. If I was 22 years old, I would basically be sleeping outside their offices in Chicago until they hired me.

What do you see as the next big change or revolution on the Web?

I think it's going to be people organically organizing in new and interesting ways, and communicating in ways that we can't even fathom today. That, to me, is incredibly exciting.

But you look at me, or people like me, in the world of social networking, and there are only less than 20% of the total 1.3 billion–person online population who have actually been on a social network, which makes this an incredible opportunity.

> *"The best, most innovative ideas, we haven't even come close to seeing yet."*

Facebook is, at least from a Silicon Valley perspective, taking over the world. However, they have only 41 million total registered users out of 1.3 billion people online, which is comparably small and represents huge potential going forward.

We're not even close to full market penetration yet.

In what other market would you say that the game is over when only 43 or even 100 million out of 1.3 billion people are using something? Not very many.

One of the things that's really, really important to us here at Ning is localization and the opportunity for people to create social networks in whatever language they choose. We have a drop-down list of about six languages, including British English. You sit there and look at things like this and think, "The opportunity is so big!" The best, most innovative ideas, we haven't even come close to seeing yet. When you're in the heat of the moment, you think, "Oh, online video is over," or, "Oh, social networking is done and it's not even begun in many places around the world."

I remember that social networking was considered a finished fad here in Silicon Valley when Friendster was pronounced dead. Then MySpace happened.

I just think the thing that's so cool is that we're living in a day and age where the Web continues to mature rapidly. Even though we're 12 to 14 years in, and that the potential for what's going to happen is even more profound than what has happened so far. And what's going to happen is even more profound than what has happened so far. While I might have some ideas and could place some bets on what happens next, I certainly don't know what the next big thing is going to be. I do know that it's going to be fun to watch what happens next.

Would you place any bets?

The biggest bet I would place is on a broadening base and definition of social networking.

> *"It's so global, and it's so cool."*

We're going to see a massive increase in the number of social networks for every conceivable niche, need, interest, location—in every conceivable language, for every conceivable purpose, in ways that extend and expand communication that we can't even think of today. And that kind of future certainly, from my perspective, gives me goose bumps.

How important do you believe localization is going to be?

Critical. Absolutely critical.

We have registered users today in 176 countries, and we're pretty small relative to where we want to be in the next 12 months. Half of our traffic is outside the U.S. already.

The idea that we still live in the U.S.-centric world is just insane to me. It's so global and it's so cool.

Do you have anything you would like to add? Any additional comments you'd like to make on Ning?

Not at this point, but thanks for asking!

Sound Bites

Not everyone agrees that the term Web 2.0 is a good thing or that it should be defined. Regardless, Gina provides a number of great insights into social networking and the world of the Web. Following are some of her key comments.

- What is happening right now really puts that whole set of big, gigantic systems integration out of work.
- The technology is moving so fast that the layers of coordination and centralization just don't apply anymore. They're irrelevant, and if you spend too much time on those things, you'll become irrelevant, too.
- The incredibly large numbers associated with online advertising Would be a clear indication that there is a market here for free-based web-services that are advertising-supported.
- Increasingly, the Internet is going to closely reflect how people organize in the real world and, with it, you're going to see an exaggerated set of human nature online.
- The whole concept of "behind the firewall" is slowly but surely being challenged.
- [Web 3.0 or the Semantic Web is] an interesting, theoretical discussion amongst a small group of people who really care about it. I don't think it is a mainstream behavior.
- There are only less that 15 percent of the total 1.3 billion person online population who have actually been on a social network.... In what other market would you say that the game is over when only 43 or even 100 million out of 1.3 billion people are using something?
- You're going to see an increase in the number of social networks for every conceivable niche, need, interest, location—in every language, for every conceivable purpose, in ways that extend and expand communication that cannot be imagined today.

Dorion Carroll:
Technorati

5

"For Technorati, a lot of Web 2.0 is about authenticity, accountability, interaction, and this idea of the people-powered or the social web."

—*Dorion Carroll*

According to the Technorati site, there are more than 175,000 new blogs every day. They would know because they are in the business of tracking them. If Web 2.0 is about people or blogs, then they are deep into it. Technorati currently tracks more than 100 million blogs and more than a quarter of a billion pieces of tagged social content.

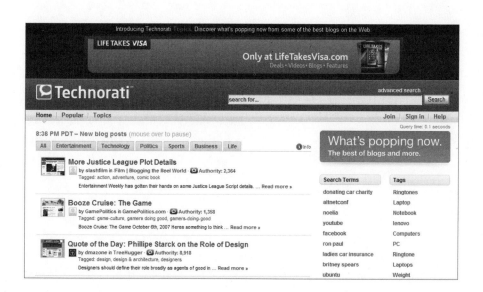

Dorion Carroll is Technorati's vice president of engineering. Prior to working at Technorati, Dorion worked with companies such as Postini, Excite@Home, Electronic Arts, and Oracle. His experiences are in search, email processing, E-commerce, CRM, ad targeting, and numerous web and enterprise technologies, thus making him an expert in his field and a great person to discuss the topics of Technorati and Web 2.0.

See if it Sticks. If it Doesn't, Fail Fast; Move on to the Next Idea.

Dorion's time and position at Technorati, along with his prior experiences at companies such as Oracle, make him a perfect candidate to glean information regarding the world of blogging and, more importantly, Web 2.0.

How about telling a little bit about yourself.

Technorati is just past its fourth anniversary as a company. I'm just passing my third year with the company. So [for] three of the last four years of the company, I've been here. My background is dealing with large-scale Internet applications, databases. I'm a data junkie. I worked at Postini for three years running their anti-spam engineering as they kind of grew from 5 million messages to approximately 500 million a day. Lots of text processing, large-scale systems, and distributed systems.

> *"What are people saying about me?' ...It turned out that [David Sifry] wasn't the only person asking that question."*

I was at Excite before that, running internal ad-serving, reporting, partner reporting, sponsorship serving, building out the Excite shopping channel; large Internet, lots of growth, lots of fun things, lots of interesting challenges, mixtures of search and database work. And building products that actually help the company make money.

I like to think some of my unique talents are being able to understand complex problems [on a] large scale, and actually matching those to business needs—not just the technological side, but also trying to understand the business application of things. And before that I was at Electronic Arts (EA) for four years, building P&L systems, data warehouses, point of sales and analysis systems for EA as they grew into kind of a giant of the gaming industry.

I was at Oracle for three years before that building out CRM apps before CRM was called CRM; it was just sales-info systems and lead-tracking systems. And I'd been in financial services building lead tracking and contact management before that.

So, I have been at this for almost 20 years, doing various things that were originally database-driven, then I moved to Internet applications, then started sprinkling in search, ultimately doing things that deal with millions and millions of people. I love doing things that impact millions of people.

What is Technorati?

The company was founded by Dave [Sifry] and a couple of people that he brought in. That first year was a lot about inventing something that didn't exist at all, recognizing this phenomenon of blogging. For Dave, as a blogger and as somebody that was kind of self-publishing, it was about realizing a way to find the good stuff and to find the people that are actually referencing him. Again one of these things with blog-publishing platforms and with moving into that Web 2.0 concept was the ability for people to recognize each other, build community, and create connections where they couldn't really do that before. In the print world, clearly you would have citations in a scientific journal or things of that sort, but moving at a very slow pace.

All of a sudden these things started happening in near-real time, and from a very pure, ego-driven perspective. "What are people saying about me?" That was kind of the

> *"'Blogging,' back in 2004, was not a common word."*

first problem Dave started trying to resolve. It turned out that he wasn't the only person asking that question. A bunch of other folks started recognizing that Technorati was a place to go to find out, "What are people saying about me?" and developing some kind of interesting things beyond just classic search, such as, "Is anybody looking for my name, or did anybody mention my name?" and actually developing things like, "Who's linking to my blog?" "Who's actually writing another blog?" or "Who's writing some other web page and linking?" These were lightweight social gestures, something that says, "I have a connection to this person, and as I'm writing, I'm choosing to make a citation to them, either to confirm what they say, to augment it, or to dispute it."

"Blogging," back in 2004, was not a common word—it started to take off, and from that the next things we developed were ways to find out where people were focusing attention as expressed by these lightweight gestures. There was the ability to simply reference something on a free or relatively easy-to-install-and-operate self-publishing platform, a blog platform, WordPress, TypePad, Blogger, or any number of the other ones that came out. People could start creating connections.

Technorati was able to find these connections again in near-real time. Real time is important because some of the basic underpinnings of blogging are different from the rest of the Web, fundamentally. When you hit that pub-lish button on a blog post, there's a thing called a ping, which is really just a notification that gets sent out to the Internet, and there are a bunch of ping-collecting services out there. Technorati is one, [as there's] Ping-O-Matic, and others. A ping just says, "Something on this blog changed; there was an update." It doesn't tell you what the update was, only that it changed.

Some of the unique technologies that Dave and a couple of the other guys developed could respond to those notifications in a matter of seconds, grab the content, figure out whether this was brand-new content or different content, put it into an update, put it into a database or an index, and then make it available to people for search and discovery and aggregation in two minutes or less. So that in near-real time, they were publishing to where somebody else could then discover what you just wrote. So again, it is this whole concept of community and discovery and the ego. You could just sit there, refreshing, going, "Is anybody talking about me now? I just wrote something that I think is brilliant; did anybody read it yet? Did anybody link to it yet?"

That's still core to what we do. We developed these notions early on around accountability with blogging. At least in those early days there was this notion that you weren't anonymous. You had to put yourself out there, you had a profile, you had a name, you had a voice, you weren't a journalist, and you didn't have to hold yourself accountable to the ethics in journal-ism, but it was your voice and other people would link to [it], and say, "I agree," or, "I disagree," or, "You got this wrong," so you also got this sense of a real-time public discourse around concepts, whether it was technology or politics, entertainment or health, or who knows what.

By the time I started, which was in August of 2004, Dave was approached by CNN to see how this blogging phenomenon might actually start to play into the political race, and for 10 days straight the guys basically slept in the offices and built out a brand-new version of Technorati for the Democratic National Convention (DNC). They built a view of political blogs with charts and an emphasis on what was being said about the convention, the participants there, the candidates, etc. Bloggers were starting to blog about the convention. Dave was standing there on TV next to Wolf Blitzer and giving bloggers commentary.

Again, "blogging" wasn't really a common household word at that time, and I think that was the first point where Technorati came onto the mainstream. People at least saw our logo, our brand—Dave was up there. This concept of people just writing about whatever they wanted with no control raised the question, "Is this going to be the Wild West and totally out of control?" But it turned out that some of these guys are actually pretty good political commentators, and they have some interesting things to write. This thing called Technorati Authority, which says how many people, how many other blogs have linked to this blog in the last six months, which says, "Hey these people actually went to the trouble to reference this guy, and we're not counting how many times you referenced it, so if you link every day you only count as one vote," that was the beginning of a way to link blogs, which is key to the way that Dave had envisioned a lot of this. But that notion of Technorati Authority and which were the top political blogs, and how can we came up with 5,000 to 10,0000 core political blogs—that seemed to open a regular discourse referencing each other, referencing external materials.

The interesting things that came out of that were not only did political bloggers exist, but we found that liberal bloggers would link to liberal blogs, right-wing conservatives to conservative bloggers, and the guys in the middle would link to either or neither. So we were able actually to break things down into three different sections. You could get a sense as to what the left was saying about a specific candidate, what the right was saying about that candidate, what the middle was saying about that candidate. Quite often the exact same issue, the exact same article in *The Washington Post*, *The New York Times*, or *The Wall Street Journal* about that candidate would have these wild swings of commentary and the reactions of other bloggers to that commentary. It was really interesting; instead of getting your morning paper with just that one editorial view, all of a sudden you have hundreds if not thousands of different views about these things and the reactions of others about them.

Again, that idea of the authenticity of voice, the nature of accountability that you weren't hiding behind a mask, your blog was there—anybody could read it and say something about it—became really important. When I joined, we then did the same thing with the Republican National Convention (RNC), and that went pretty well; site traffic grew dramatically at that point.

> *"It's no longer the one-way Web."*

The DNC and RNC site development set the tone for what we wanted to do going forward. The first year was kind of that science-fair project; Dave and a couple of people were figuring out what this thing might be, how it could go, getting some financing, incorporating. The second year was, "Okay, now we've got to scale this thing; it's starting to catch on—going from hundreds of thousands of blogs a day to maybe millions." The third year was, "Alright, now we know what the technology does. We've got too much opportunity to pursue, so let's take a couple of things and build some great product on top of it." This fourth year was, "How do we create a sustainable business?"

For me, this is what I really love. How can I then turn this into something that millions of people want to use, are addicted to using, and understand the value of and can appreciate the ability to find out what people are saying about them, what people are saying about things that matter to them, and how they can be connected to or participate in this new thing that's happening out there. It's no longer the one-way Web, where a bunch of corporations or people with deep pockets can actually afford a web site and they put a message up so you can read it. Rather it's a place where, anybody, for free, can put their opinion out there and have the opportunity to be discovered.

This doesn't mean people will voice their opinions, or that anybody will read them, but through some of these social gestures, if you reference somebody and you use a tool like Technorati to find those references to you, I personally feel I want to reference these people back, even if it's just a thank you, or to leave a comment on their blog, so I actually link back at their post. It's just a way to get people connected and there are these myriad of clusters of communities of people discussing all kinds of different things. It can be a lot of fun.

Quite often I'll get into these comments back and forth on people's blogs or link to them, only to realize later that they're in New Zealand. We've launched a couple of products. Being a data junkie, I watch real-time traffic coming in. It's like, who's the first person to have written a new blog post to link to the new product we've just launched?

We launched a product about 18 months ago called Favorites, which lets people keep track of "What's your favorite blog?" Then you can come back to Technorati, and we'll give you a synopsis from this collection of blogs in real-time sort, time-sorted results. The first to link to

> *"One person can now communicate with a mass audience, most of whom they'll never encounter."*

Favorites was some guy in Germany. I speak German poorly and probably write it even worse! I wrote a blog post on my blog and linked back to him, congratulating him on being the first person to have a link to our new Favorites product. The next person was in Brazil. I don't speak Portuguese, couldn't write Portuguese, but it was interesting. The third person was a Wiccan lesbian somewhere on the East Coast. What? All these people are watching Technorati. They saw that we had just launched this thing and felt compelled to blog about it. These weren't a bunch of Silicon Valley, classic engineer geeks sitting one block from me here in San Francisco or farther down the peninsula. These were people all over the globe, and [the reaction] was really quite fascinating. It had to be the fourth or fifth person to link who you'd consider the mainstream—more what you'd expect! I certainly didn't expect a Brazilian or a lesbian Wiccan! It was fun.

I work with a number of high-profile discussion forums. It is interesting the diversity of the people that visit the forums. It is amazing how well the world is represented.

Transitioning, let me ask a simple, core question: What do you consider Web 2.0 to be?

It can be a bunch of different things, and Technorati has been part of the creation of what is Web 2.0. On the one hand it's this idea of public social discourse, that aspect of the social Web that lets people connect, that gives an opportunity to have an open sharing of ideas. People can be published quickly, easily, found, discovered, and read, and other people can react to those things. There's also more of an emphasis on this notion of a people-powered Web, whether it's through lightweight social gestures of linking, reading, voting, or sending and sharing via email—just discovering and connecting with people. Email is basically a back-and-forth between two people; with blogging, the video sites, photo sites, all of these different types of social media, one person can now communicate with a mass audience, most of whom they'll never encounter, but they can actually see their own stuff rising in rankings and getting better and see a wave building around it; there are a lot of folks out there that really like that.

On the other end of the spectrum, there's a lot about 2.0 that is about the Semantic Web—upgraded from that first course of HTML and web-server architectures to an infrastructure that anybody can participate in. The web page itself might now start relaying structural information that is also easily displayed. Some of what Technorati has been known for is an area called microformats, where you can use structured HTML to represent things like a contact record, or an event. In the past, people had to write all kinds of complex XML or complex text analysis just to figure out what's the likelihood that this is actually a person's name and that, gee—these patterns look like they might be their address.

Today, using microformats, you can easily format standard HTML, add a couple of extra class descriptions, to say, "Oh, by the way, this is the first name, last name, address, zip code," or whatever it might be. And when other programs come along, they can see that information as structural and valid without complex calculations going on. But, for a browser looking at it, it's just HTML, and the CSS guys and the web page developers can actually style that information. So you get the best of both worlds, because it's semantically valid, has actual meaning, but can also be easily rendered and displayed.

Tantek Çelik, our former chief technologist, would say, "Your web page is your API." That if you're using HTML, and you have strict and valid HTML, from a technical perspective, your web pages are valid and can be displayed and styled in lots of different ways. But at the same time, they can contain fully recognizable, parse-able, structured information. So there's this one aspect of Web 2.0 that is about the social connections, the openness, the democratization of ideas and the ability of others to react to it, whether it's on Facebook, or MySpace, or through something like a Technorati, and at the same time, there are underlying pieces [that define] how different services create open APIs, whether those are through XML, or RSS, or just using semantic HTML and making things structurally parseable right off the main web sites. At Technorati, we do all of the above. We have RSS feeds, we have XML based APIs, and our web site validates XHTML strictly, well—most of the time.

Semantic Web is often pegged as Web 3.0. The other things you've mentioned are topics that have come up from others as a part of Web 2.0. You mention microformats. Are there standards for microformats?

Part of the idea of microformats.org is an open web site you can go to. The site has definitions. It has discussion forums. It has proposals. Just like any standards body, there is a process with a committee.

One of the microformat philosophies in putting these things together is not to rehash decisions that have already been made. The folks behind microformats look to adopt existing standards like vCard and avoid the battles over naming conventions and

> *"Tags are probably the most widespread microformat out there."*

such. They favor function over form, in this regard. FN is First Name. LN is Last Name. You know—just get over it. So then, basically they're taking an already existing standard, that is widely adopted—but is technically proprietary—and turning it into a completely open and easily adapted HTML-based standard. So that you can take something like a "list item," or a "DIV" in HTML, and give it a class. That class has a name, so that class equals FN. All of a sudden you've just said that this thing that's already a standard—everybody already knows what a V-Card is—can now be represented in HTML.

At Technorati we've done some prototype and some lab work, and put things out there. We have a proxy server that allows somebody to point to a web page and the proxy server. It will actually consume the HTML on the page and turn any hCards that it finds into vCards, and it will open up and automatically download. You can simply click to add to your address book.

There are similar things for the calendaring standards; an hEvent is a standard representation of an event at a time and at a specific location with a description. Actually, an hEvent might contain hCards for the people that are going to be there, so these things can be nested. You can, again, send this microformatted content through the proxy server. It'll find those hEvents and automatically turn them into iCals. If you want to just download and save it to your calendar automatically, you can send it through the proxy. The proxy can go either direction: take a VCF file and it'll turn [the calendar] into a vCard.

There are a number of simple, easy-to-add JavaScript widgets and things that let an end-user who doesn't know anything about DIVs and classes just type things into a form of which the output is a chunk or snippet of HTML that's a valid hCard.

I think with tags—tags are probably the most widespread microformat out there. It just uses a little-known attribute of the HREF in HTML called the rel attribute, or the relationship. It basically says, "Okay, the standard anchor tag, you know, you have the HREF, and you have your link text. You just add inside the first part of the anchor declaration, rel=tag." So I can create something that says, "Here's a link you know, Technorati tags." I've just written something about Web 2.0, so I say:

```
<a href= http://technorati.com/tag/Web2.0 rel="tag" >Web 2.0</a>
```

Then I can put the word that I want to show up as the link tag. I've just created a microformatted tag reference. The rel= says, "The relationship of this link text is a tag relationship," in that you'll find the post that contains this tag in the tag space referenced at that link. Something in the neighborhood of 55 percent of the posts we process every day have tags on them, whether it is from the RSS feeds or actually from people using blogging platforms, which now have simple things to make it really easy to add tags. Huge phenomenon.

In many ways, Technorati is probably known, discovered, and found by new people through the use of tags across the Web. Through Google, for example, if you search for something like *iPhone*, it turns out there are a bunch of bloggers who have blogged about the iPhone. They've tagged their posts *iPhone*, and we aggregate those and put them up on a search result or on a content page on Technorati under technorati.com/tag/iPhone. The Google bot comes by and visits and sees that there are lots of people that are referencing this, and that we have a reasonable amount of page rank. So if you're trying to find out what's going on about iPhone right now, the real-time nature of peoples' reactions, as represented through the aggregation that we do, becomes very compelling search-result material on a Google result page. To say, "If you want to see what people are saying about the iPhone right now, click on this link and go to Technorati," then you'll see a collection of blog posts like, "This is great!" or, "This is the latest hack," or, "It's coming soon," or, "I just got one," or whatever it might be. But the tags in terms of microformats are probably the most widely spread of all of the microformats out there.

You stated that in your second year you worried about scale. One of the concepts stated by Tim O'Reilly in regard to Web 2.0 was, "Worry about scale later. Worry about getting users and customers first." You scaled in your second year, so do you agree with that philosophy?

To me that isn't a yes or no answer, so let me answer it in a qualified way.

I'm a strong believer that in start-ups, you absolutely have to cut lots of corners. Technorati would not be where it is now if we hadn't cut corners. That meant, "Okay, we don't need the purity of essence architecture to solve this particular problem; what can you hack together this weekend? Let's get it out there, see if it sticks. If it doesn't, fail fast; move on to the next idea." In those early years of invention, that's what you need to do. It's basically a human-driven, rapid genetic algorithm for code and product. "What works?" and, "What doesn't?" If it takes off, then you worry about the scaling of it.

When we were tracking 100,000 blogs and maybe 200,000 to 300,000 blog posts a day, you can run that on a box, if you want to be able to then let people query it in real-time. At that scale, with the number of writes that are coming in and the number of reads, because you're still a little web site, you could probably let people run the queries right from the web site. You could hit the same box that the spiders are filling up with data. You don't have a lot of read and write contention and everything's fine. The numbers of transactions per second are such that the underlying systems can deal with it.

By the time we were prepping for the Democratic National Convention, it was too much information to sit on one server, and also allow the runtime components to hit the same computer that was getting all of the writes written to it. So we have this concept of the "truth" or our internal master records of what we spider that gets saved into our master databases. Then we replicate that information to other boxes, in sub-second time so that the queries are hitting one set of infrastructure and the writes are going into the "truth," whose sole job is to store that truth and replicate it to a bunch of servers. To scale things, we need to separate the high-volume writes from the high-volume reads and distribute the reads horizontally based on demand.

> *"We're a 30-person start-up, and Google isn't."*

So, on the one hand I agree with Tim in that you definitely want to figure out what you're doing and get your customers, get your name and your product out there, but at the same time, for a company like Technorati, we're basically trying to pull together all of this information in near-real time and present a compelling search experience for people, with algorithmic and not editorial bias; part of what we do is simply amassing large amounts of data. Our challenge was to make sure that this scaled, because your product wouldn't be the product if you didn't have the data supporting it.

Is scale a competitive advantage for Technorati?

There are a bunch of companies out there that do parts of what we do. It seems at this point that there is only one company that has successfully entered and is running head-to-head with us, as far as blog search, and that is Google. Depending on who you ask, some people will say that Google is better, some will say Technorati, or, "Well, you know, Technorati has their bad days," or maybe, "They've done this or that not quite right." The fact of the matter is: We're a 30-person start-up, and Google isn't.

I feel very proud of the fact that we're able to do something that as far as I can tell, nobody else on the planet except Google can do. That's pretty amazing! It's not me; I didn't do this. There are a bunch of really smart people who work here who have done a lot of this before; it's really a team effort. It's about really smart people getting together and doing really great things. Sometimes pretty amazing things, and with the number of people we have, sometimes we don't get everything right. It is not uncommon knowledge that we have our outages or our slow times, or we missed spidering this or missed spidering that, but the fact of the matter is, when I started 3 years ago, we had three million blogs in the index, and 3 years later, we've got 100 million. So, a lot of the kind of criticism that we do get,

pages and the conversa-
try to put spin on it, if
't get this to work," "It
—on a Sun blog, because
lutely right; we screwed

urned their engagement
ith their customers. So,
; where again, as we're
er the world, organizing
g things, if you want to
ry by more well-known
ail, however, you might
ing together and change

olks out there doing the
dation. We have a lot of
nority on blogs; what do

f years ago, marketers
ere's this thing called cit-
n and these people aren't
l they might think bad
us; how can we keep
om us?" We pioneered
this sort of social media
of *The Washington Post*,
aming blogger reactions
y writes an article about
ion to the story.

dia trying to understand
can be the Wild West.
controls on it), but fun-
this is something new,
just "that media site" or
ith these folks and give
e benefit from it as well.

I think is well-founded. We were down, or we are slow, or we missed that blog post. But the fact of the matter is, we have to figure out how to process updates on about a million blogs a day, which translates into about 2 million to 3 million blog posts a day, which represent about 10 million links every day from one place to another. And keep all of that running in a way that queries are sub-2-second if not sub-second, and that the latency between when someone hits Publish and the data is then available in our index is under 2 minutes, and when we're running in that "magic zone," it's under a minute. That's almost real time.

Email *used* to be, "I'll just send an email, and someone will get it later, and that's fine." I'm sure you've had the situation where you've either hit the Send button or somebody else has hit the Send button, you're on the phone, and they say as soon as they hit send, "Did you get it?" The expectation is, email is instantaneous now. It is like IM except that it has an archive. Blogging and Live-Web and those kinds of things aren't there yet.

> *"[People]…taking photographs, capturing the moment…writing quick instant messages…about their reaction or what they saw—it is kind of mind-boggling."*

We're sitting on top of something that has that potential and I've seen search results show up that are 26 seconds old. It's a completely different kind of experience. It definitely plays to those situations. Going back to Web 2.0…people are reacting; people have a connectedness to things—disasters, major faux pas, or things of news-worthiness that follow that same kind of news cycle. Britney Spears bombed on the VMAs [Video Music Awards]; 30 seconds later, while people watched it, held back any bile they have, and reacted to it in real-time, other people picked that up and reacted to it. You're not going to get that on *Entertainment Tonight* until the next day!

It's not always mind-boggling that somebody said they just went and saw the Rolling Stones and that was 22 seconds ago and it's like, "Who cares?" But things like major events have really showcased Technorati's potential. Things like Hurricane Katrina, the tsunami, Dan Rather's passing; things like these are where there's an outpouring from people on the ground, or

people and their expressions around these types (
people can be very, very different. I think that is [
difference between Web 1.0 and commercializatio
Tim Berners-Lee and the Web were all there in th
connecting and open sharing of ideas, but it wasn

With Web 2.0, there is the ability for anybody to
digital camera and shoot some photos or video ar
millions of people have the opportunity to see it.
bombing—the people there with the cell phones
capturing the moment, and instantly uploading
Flickr or some other photo-sharing site. Or, peo
messages and sending them through a gateway
instant blog post about their reaction or what the
boggling. Technorati brings this instant flow of in

You mentioned this is Technorati's fourth ye
You stated that this year, the focus is on cre
business. How has the business focus change
of Technorati to today?

We're basically a media company powered by rea
suing two ways of extracting revenue from this
and the product potential that we have. The first
a destination web site; a place where people can
looking for, have these moments of surprise and
of ego-satisfaction, or discovery, or very intent-d

Again, one of the basic differences between what
engine like a Google or a Yahoo! is that if you
your first hit's going to be the Sony web site.
Technorati, your first hit is going to be the last pe
product, and the Sony web site is never going to
So, it's much more about what people are say
something that in terms of how people react to pr
ization of things, is something that we can then
"Here's a destination-driven web site. Here's an
Here's how we can organize things topically. Her
very different than other sites." So for us, the firs
pretty classic, advertising-driven web site, reven

product managers actually manage those produc
tions. What they learned very early on was, dor
somebody says "This product sucks," "I could
doesn't do these things." To come back on a blog
Sun has a lot of bloggers—and to say, "You're abs
up, and here's what we're doing to fix it."

I think Sun embraces the blogosphere and has
into an advantage. They've created a dialogue
there is this notion of conversational marketir
aggregating this real-time conversation from all o
it topically or around specific search terms, filter
filter by authorities—I only want to get the st
blogs, or I want everything from the whole long
want to do this—this is something that we can b
the nature of marketing.

We haven't figured it all out yet. There are other
same kind of thing, so I think we've got some va
people coming to us saying, "You guys are the au
we do?"

> "*We can't necessarily control [blogging]… maybe actually talking to people is a good idea.*"

Two-and-a-ha
were like, "Th
izen journalis
journalists ar
things about
them away f
integration of
into the likes
The Wall Street Journal, and *Der Spiegel*. We're str
on those web sites. *The Washington Post*, someboo
Iraq, bloggers react to it, and there it is—the reac

There were a few early pioneers in mainstream m
how to embrace these folks who have opinions.
There can be swear words (there have to be some
damentally, they were open-minded enough to sa
this is something different, and we don't want to b
just "that print material;" we want to be engaged
them a chance to participate and get recognized. V

I think is well-founded. We were down, or we are slow, or we missed that blog post. But the fact of the matter is, we have to figure out how to process updates on about a million blogs a day, which translates into about 2 million to 3 million blog posts a day, which represent about 10 million links every day from one place to another. And keep all of that running in a way that queries are sub-2-second if not sub-second, and that the latency between when someone hits Publish and the data is then available in our index is under 2 minutes, and when we're running in that "magic zone," it's under a minute. That's almost real time.

Email *used* to be, "I'll just send an email, and someone will get it later, and that's fine." I'm sure you've had the situation where you've either hit the Send button or somebody else has hit the Send button, you're on the phone, and they say as soon as they hit send, "Did you get it?" The expectation is, email is instantaneous now. It is like IM except that it has an archive. Blogging and Live-Web and those kinds of things aren't there yet.

> *"[People]…taking photographs, capturing the moment…writing quick instant messages…about their reaction or what they saw—it is kind of mind-boggling."*

We're sitting on top of something that has that potential and I've seen search results show up that are 26 seconds old. It's a completely different kind of experience. It definitely plays to those situations. Going back to Web 2.0…people are reacting; people have a connectedness to things— disasters, major faux pas, or things of news-worthiness that follow that same kind of news cycle. Britney Spears bombed on the VMAs [Video Music Awards]; 30 seconds later, while people watched it, held back any bile they have, and reacted to it in real-time, other people picked that up and reacted to it. You're not going to get that on *Entertainment Tonight* until the next day!

It's not always mind-boggling that somebody said they just went and saw the Rolling Stones and that was 22 seconds ago and it's like, "Who cares?" But things like major events have really showcased Technorati's potential. Things like Hurricane Katrina, the tsunami, Dan Rather's passing; things like these are where there's an outpouring from people on the ground, or people and their expressions around these types of events, or this is where people can be very, very different. I think that is fundamentally the biggest difference between Web 1.0 and commercialization of the Web. The ideas of Tim Berners-Lee and the Web were all there in the spec—it was about the connecting and open sharing of ideas, but it wasn't available to everybody.

With Web 2.0, there is the ability for anybody to pick up a cell phone or a digital camera and shoot some photos or video and upload it instantly, and millions of people have the opportunity to see it. That can be the London bombing—the people there with the cell phones taking the photographs, capturing the moment, and instantly uploading them to the Web to a Flickr or some other photo-sharing site. Or, people writing quick instant messages and sending them through a gateway because they've got an instant blog post about their reaction or what they saw—it is kind of mind-boggling. Technorati brings this instant flow of information to the Web.

You mentioned this is Technorati's fourth year and your third. You stated that this year, the focus is on creating a sustainable business. How has the business focus changed from the beginning of Technorati to today?

We're basically a media company powered by real-time search and are pursuing two ways of extracting revenue from this underlying infrastructure and the product potential that we have. The first is through advertising on a destination web site; a place where people can come, find what they're looking for, have these moments of surprise and delight, or these moments of ego-satisfaction, or discovery, or very intent-driven search.

Again, one of the basic differences between what we do and a classic search engine like a Google or a Yahoo! is that if you type "Sony" into Google, your first hit's going to be the Sony web site. If you type "Sony" into Technorati, your first hit is going to be the last person writing about a Sony product, and the Sony web site is never going to show up in those results. So, it's much more about what people are saying about things. That is something that in terms of how people react to products and topical organization of things, is something that we can then present to advertisers as, "Here's a destination-driven web site. Here's an advertising-driven model. Here's how we can organize things topically. Here's how it's the same as or very different than other sites." So for us, the first piece of what we do is a pretty classic, advertising-driven web site, revenue model.

On the other hand, we've got these more recent endeavors. Although we've been dabbling in this for over the last year-and-a-half now, for us as a four-year-old company, it's not actually brand-new at all, and that is the syndication of our indexed and topically organized data off technorati.com.

We had early successes with things around Al Gore's movie, *An Inconvenient Truth*. What they wanted to do was not just put up a bunch of facts and charts, but to actually engage people in a discourse: pro, against, scientific fact but not proven to be, human-related, or these are the issues that we have to solve, and then varying other topics of conversation that are related in terms of green issues, and energy-saving issues, reviews of products that work and help, and all of these underlying topics of conversation. We powered that by streaming this real-time conversation into that web site.

And we developed similar capabilities for the Dixie Chicks; that sort of mounted their comeback, their *Shut Up & Sing*. We had a campaign with them called "Shut Up and Post," where we had a flash-based ad unit where people could post a comment that would get posted to the site.

> *"It's not about controlling the message. It's not 20th-century, one-to-many mass marketing."*

Again we were streaming in the real-time conversations of a handful of searches so the people who are writing blog posts across the globe as they were doing this comeback could get syndicated into a single site; people who were encountering these ad units could post, land on that site, and see that their voice actually was one of many voices, and they would either love them, thought they got the shaft, or didn't think it was right, or it was un-American, or whatever the issue was.

The key with this whole thing for *An Inconvenient Truth*, for the Dixie Chicks, or for something we did a few months back with Microsoft sponsoring the Live Earth concerts, is that it's not about controlling the message, it's not 20th-century, one-to-many mass marketing, but it's about honestly trying to engage an audience and hear what they have to say. If it's bad, it's bad.

On sun.com and a lot of their product pages—in fact, I think all of their product pages—we syndicate blog posts, the conversation, about whatever it is, you know, the "X2000" server, or this particular storage array. The product managers actually manage those product pages and the conversations. What they learned very early on was, don't try to put spin on it, if somebody says "This product sucks," "I couldn't get this to work," "It doesn't do these things." To come back on a blog—on a Sun blog, because Sun has a lot of bloggers—and to say, "You're absolutely right; we screwed up, and here's what we're doing to fix it."

I think Sun embraces the blogosphere and has turned their engagement into an advantage. They've created a dialogue with their customers. So, there is this notion of conversational marketing where again, as we're aggregating this real-time conversation from all over the world, organizing it topically or around specific search terms, filtering things, if you want to filter by authorities—I only want to get the story by more well-known blogs, or I want everything from the whole long tail, however, you might want to do this—this is something that we can bring together and change the nature of marketing.

We haven't figured it all out yet. There are other folks out there doing the same kind of thing, so I think we've got some validation. We have a lot of people coming to us saying, "You guys are the authority on blogs; what do we do?"

> *"We can't necessarily control [blogging]… maybe actually talking to people is a good idea."*

Two-and-a-half years ago, marketers were like, "There's this thing called citizen journalism and these people aren't journalists and they might think bad things about us; how can we keep them away from us?" We pioneered integration of this sort of social media into the likes of *The Washington Post*, *The Wall Street Journal*, and *Der Spiegel*. We're streaming blogger reactions on those web sites. *The Washington Post*, somebody writes an article about Iraq, bloggers react to it, and there it is—the reaction to the story.

There were a few early pioneers in mainstream media trying to understand how to embrace these folks who have opinions. It can be the Wild West. There can be swear words (there have to be some controls on it), but fundamentally, they were open-minded enough to say this is something new, this is something different, and we don't want to be just "that media site" or just "that print material;" we want to be engaged with these folks and give them a chance to participate and get recognized. We benefit from it as well.

That stuff sort of showcased that blogging was coming into the mainstream and after that people started saying, "Oh, well, we can't necessarily control it, we certainly can't ignore it, well darn it, maybe actually talking to people is a good idea." And I think that's kind of where things are now. It's not about mass marketing; it's about actually understanding the masses. This is a lot of what Technorati can do.

Our discipline now is not to pursue every last technology or opportunity that we have, because, fundamentally, with only 30 people, we just have so much more under the hood than we can possibly get out to market. Let's pick two ways that we can run a business, manage our expenses to those revenue lines, grow those revenue lines, hold ourselves accountable, and deliver something that nobody else has done before.

Do you see resistance to advertising on Technorati due to the fact that blogging can be the "Wild West"?

There are those who aren't ready for it. Absolutely. There's sort of a continuum. There are those who are ready and willing—they see high click-through rates. We have a unique audience, a very influential audience, a highly participatory audience, and they see that as a place to go—that Technorati at least has a brand, an authority, and is a place to start engaging. That they don't have to take all the risk and, yes, their advertising might be right next to something that's questionable or unsavory, but they're willing to do that. Those are the kind of people way at the forefront.

At the other end of the spectrum they are like,

"But, can't I edit it? Can't I control it?"

"No, thank you."

"Okay, fair enough."

The people in the middle who are interested—I mean, we have a sponsor right now, Scion, who is sponsoring the conversation around independent film; for them, it was really important to associate their brand not just with auto people, because these are people associated with independent film, and Scion actually sponsors an indie film festival. Conversations about a lot of indie film festivals are going on all around the country right now. They wanted something that was actually on Technorati.com. They did not want to create a stand-alone web site that was sponsored by Scion and looked like a shill; they said, "Look, you guys are the authority on blogs.

You're the place where people go. We want to associate our brand with this audience that we believe in, but we want that to be authentic—a place where bloggers actually go and believe it. And, we want this to actually be something where you're either building it already, or that you plan on running even when we stop sponsoring it."

Great! So let's build this thing together!

> *"You need to be transparent, you need to be open."*

That's somebody who's actually recognizing the value we bring. Granted, there can be some loud, rough material in there. There are others, who were looking at it from the conversational point of view, who said, "You know what? I actually have my own web site, or I need to build a web site." Like Microsoft Live, when they had a specific event. There we actually do have ways of filtering objectionable content, and allowing greater degrees of control. We have pretty strong recommendations around, if you're editorially selecting things, you need to make that clear. You need to be transparent, you need to be open, you need to say, "These are featured bloggers," or, "These are featured posts." You can't say, "This is the true or honest conversation" because you've taken editorial control.

We strongly recommend that people don't just cherry-pick the "best" posts. It's really good to have some opposing points of view there. We don't necessarily control everything that they do, but we do let them know, when those links come back to a Technorati search result, it's not censored anymore; it's everything. If you cherry-pick a handful of things that don't say anything bad about you or product, when somebody follows that link through and actually your product is a horrible disaster, that's what's going to show up on Technorati. You have to know that—and, so far, we've had a bunch of success with that. So, there are these different levels; not everybody's ready for it.

Let me ask a few general Web 2.0 questions. For Web 2.0, what would you consider the most important feature?

For me personally, it really is about the open sharing of ideas and recognition of other people; it's the social aspect of sharing things in an open medium that anybody with an Internet connection can get access to.

Would you say the same is true for Technorati?

For Technorati, it's actually that plus some of the other technical pieces that I talked about earlier. As sort of the cornerstone of a lot of the Web 2.0 growth, the technical aspects are very important—the idea of open APIs, RSS, sharing information, being able to take your information with you wherever you go. I think from a very high-level point of view, for Technorati, a lot of Web 2.0 is about authenticity, accountability, interaction, and this idea of the people-powered or the social web.

What do you think is being misunderstood about Web 2.0 in the blogsphere or in general?

Web 2.0 can be used in a derogatory fashion, sometimes used synony-mously with "Bubble 2.0;" if Web 1.0 was about the first bubble, then Web 2.0 must be about the second bubble. It's all going to blow up pretty soon. There are a bunch of companies that survived Web 1.0, actually added value, created completely new things that had never been done before, and actually delivered on a promise that people love and use all the time.

I think the same is going to be true of Web 2.0. There are a bunch of frivolous things. From the social perspective, we're human beings. The original ideas about the Web, and some of the original ideas about Web 1.0—uploading photos, and linking ideas, and sharing with each other, and recognizing people as human beings, being social—some of that can be to the better-ment of humankind, some of that can be frivolous, and some of it can be downright mean.

Andrew Kean is writing a book focusing on some of the negative aspects about Web 2.0—and it's probably fair to say that it's out there. But, to blame Web2.0, or to say this is nothing or it's meaningless, it's like television—television kind of went through this as well—and you choose to dial into the channels that you choose to dial into. If you want to watch something inane, or something degrading, you're doing that. If you want to tune into something that's going to expand your mind, or just entertain you, or sur-prise and delight you, you get to do that, too. And I think Web 2.0 presents pretty much the same kind of things but on a much larger scale.

Do you believe there really is a "bubble" and that there is a chance it could burst?

I don't think so. In the words of Alan Greenspan, I don't have an *irrational exuberance*. I think that there's an awful lot that people learned from the first time around and there are a bunch of lessons that either people have forgotten, or are new lessons that have to be learned. I don't see a mass IPO series of events going on out there. There aren't a ton of companies getting bought at ridiculous multiples. I mean, I look at Excite, when it was purchased by @Home in a $7.2 billion acquisition and then two-and-a-half years later they sold off the assets for 10 million bucks.

> *"It's a good time to be in this industry, but it's also a challenging time."*

We're not there at all. I don't see that kind of capital going in there. I don't see the public markets reacting that way. Venture capitalists invest their money and don't expect a huge return on every investment. They would love it if that happened, but that's not what happens. They scatter the money around, they choose and pick, they look for things that are likely to be successors, but the whole idea is to take risk. They're not taking completely crazy risks and just pouring money down the drain.

I don't see New Year's parties or Super Bowl ads for Web 2.0 companies. Those are lessons that have been learned. I know that now. Where I am in the Bay Area, the market's really hot. Engineers can command a premium, there's a lot of movement, and it's a good time to be in this industry, but it's also a challenging time.

In the Web 1.0 world, it seemed that having a business plan was not a requirement. That doesn't seem to be true today.

There are a number of companies that have had to shift gears. I think [of] companies that have done this fairly well, such as LinkedIn, and I'm not sure they had a business model. They're growing and making money and doing things right, but they've had to shift. I think a lot of people reacted negatively to some of the things that they did, but at the end of the day, they're growing. They've got a bigger audience now than they've ever had, and they seem to be doing some things right—but they had to shift their business plan around.

Take something like Flickr—they were gamers! The game never ended. They were trying to build something completely different. And they realized, "Uh-oh: We're spending the last of our Angel money, or our investment money. We actually need to figure out something that's going to make a difference." Then they did, and then they sold it to Yahoo! It ended up being incorporated there.

Again, people learned that lesson. Those people that want to survive have to learn to make things work and learn the lesson. Those people that don't, go under.

What do you think are the "coolest" Web 2.0 things you've seen?

There are kind of two parts to that.

When I was at Oracle, I was building sales information systems, CRM systems. Most everything we did was host-based computing, with VT220 terminals. I know, I'm dating myself. At that point, things were starting to move into client-server computing, and I left Oracle because I really wanted the opportunity to pursue some of those new technologies, some of those new ways of interacting with content or with applications or transactional systems that were presenting themselves. The ability to have multiple windows open and do things; actually do all the parallel processing, not just have one terminal window; block mode, or whatever.

Client-server and a bunch of those companies kind of came and went and I had a great time doing that stuff. Interestingly, Web 1.0 and a lot of basic web sites today are a lot like block-mode terminals of the '60s. The big IBM mainframe, although it's huge, it's distributed, it's connected, and the back-ends are all over the planet. The user experience is that you get one page at a time and all the information is right there. If it's not what you want, you have to go grab another whole page and display the whole thing.

Along comes AJAX, and all of a sudden you have the ability for lots of different parts of a site to be active and be reactive without forcing a complete and total reload of the page, without having to go to every back end system to generate the page. Things can be very quickly updated and very lightweight.

Things seem so simple, like the ability to vote on a web site by just clicking a little star and having that little star fade out and then fade back lit up because your vote was recorded. Just something like that lightweight gesture with a very elegant user experience, where the whole page doesn't reload, makes it easy to interact. You get visual feedback because of the JavaScript components and the AJAX components that make it so easy and delightful to use.

We use those kinds of things; lots of people use those things. And I'm not saying that AJAX is the thing; I'm just saying that that's no longer the block-mode-reload-the-whole-darn-page experience. All of a sudden it's this component-oriented approach. Obviously the porn sites and the advertisers figured this out a long time ago. About a year, year-and-a-half ago, the rest of the Web caught up to a lot of that. Changing the way people interact with computers, interact with each other, and interact with the Web—that is a pretty dramatic shift in the user experience. I think that's pretty cool. And again, the ability to map that to the social gestures that in so many ways, from my point of view, define the social web or define Web 2.0—that's a pretty key one.

The other one is just this massive growth of all of the different social media, whether it's blogging, or YouTube videos, or other kinds of photos, or other types of media, podcasts, and all these kinds of things that people can express the different kinds of ways that they want to share their ideas or just stream their ideas out there. And then ways to pull that information together, organize it around a theme, and present it to others through the open APIs and a sense of openness, but also attribution, accountability, and authenticity. You have the ability then to deliver millions and millions of things a day. We do 3 million blog posts a day—I don't know how many books there are in the Library of Congress. Clearly, blog posts are not of the same caliber as book pages, but pages in a library versus a week's worth of blog posts; the volumes are huge, unfathomable. So having the ability to sort, store, organize, index, aggregate, and associate terms or topics—with this Niagara Falls, not just a fire hose, of information coming through, the technical challenges that go with that, the possibilities of extracting things, and the ability to do those things in real-time—probably just aide and abet our A.D.D. culture. It's great! It's really, really great.

What do you see as the next big revolution on the Web?

It could be one of two things. Either it's not on the Web at all and the Web starts to move into other things, and I don't mean talking refrigerators and stuff like that, but the ability for the manufacturers and governments to finally figure out how the computer and the TV are one and the same. It just seems crazy that you have to go buy a $2,500 laptop and you need to get your $2,500 flat-screen and you can't just use the same darn monitor. From the technology point of view I don't know the details of that; I'm not a hardware guy, and I don't have any interest.

I also see there being the ability for people to just have a single place in a home where they can interact with all this other content with all of these other people. It would be great if we could reintroduce some of the people aspects of this social web to the sharing, so that you could actually have physical gatherings of people at the same time as you have this widely distributed gathering of people. Some way of interactive television with community and social sharing—sort of the next-generation video conferencing. That sort of raises the question of how does the Web enter the home and permeate people's lives as opposed to everybody going to some little table in the corner on a computer and not being able to be physically social in any way.

The other area I see change is within video. I'd expect really great video search where you can search the images inside the stream of a video. Where we are right now is being able to tag data and associate metadata around those things. Companies like Technorati and Google and Yahoo! are great at indexing text and doing analysis and matching, but you're not actually looking at what those images are. Because human beings are incredibly visual, I imagine that those kinds of things will happen, and that those things will create breakthroughs. I hope to live to see it.

Is there anything you'd like to add about Web 2.0, Technorati, or the Web in general?

In terms of Technorati, there are some very talented people that are here now, that have been here in the past, and have just contributed amazing things to this real-time engine and platform that we've developed that I think has the potential to change the way people interact with each other and interact with web content.

Sound Bites

While a number of people contribute to the success of Technorati, Dorion Carroll is in a position to comment about that success and their ventures into Web 2.0. Some of the key ideas from Dorion follow:

- Web 2.0 lets people recognize each other, build communities, and create connections where they couldn't before. It's public social discourse that lets people connect, that gives an opportunity to have an open sharing of ideas. Anybody can pick up a cell phone or a digital camera and shoot some photos or video and upload it instantly, and millions of people have the opportunity to see it.

- People can now communicate with a mass audience, most of whom they'll never encounter, and not know who saw their stuff. Instead of getting your morning paper with just one editorial view, all of a sudden you have hundreds—if not thousands—of views about and reactions from others about these things.

- In start-ups, you absolutely have to cut lots of corners. You don't need the purity of essence architecture to solve a particular problem. What can you hack together this weekend? Get it out there, see if it sticks. If it doesn't, fail fast; move on to the next idea. If it takes off, then you worry about the scaling of it. Those people that want to survive have to learn to make things work and learn the lesson; those that don't go under.

- Actually talking to people is a good idea. You need to be transparent, you need to be open. It's not about controlling the message. It's not 20th-century one-to-many mass marketing. It's about honestly trying to engage an audience and hear what they have to say and if it's bad, it's bad.

- It's not about mass marketing; it's about actually understanding the masses. A huge swell of people can react positively to a major corporation acknowledging their mistake, putting a plan out there and letting folks engage.

- Technorati strongly recommends that people don't just cherry-pick the "best" posts. It's really good to have some opposing points of view.

- For Technorati, a lot of Web 2.0 is about authenticity, accountability, interaction, and this idea of the people-powered or the social web.

Raju Vegesna:
Zoho

6

"Enterprises have some complex work flows, and I don't think online applications...are ready to really fit into the complex workflows in enterprises yet. They'll get there someday, though"

—*Raju Vegesna*

You've likely heard of Google Apps and Microsoft Office Live. While these two giants are working in the online office space, you might believe others don't have a chance. Before you bet on the giants, you might want to note a few smaller companies that are building online office and collaboration-type products. One such site that has shown they can compete is Zoho.com.

ZOHO
Work. Online

Zoho Home | Forums | Blogs | Contact Us   Toll Free : 888 900 9646

Zoho Writer
Online Word Processor   Try Now

Zoho Sheet
Spreadsheets. Online   Try Now

Zoho Show
Online Presentation Tool   Try Now

Zoho Meeting
Web Conferencing   Try Now

Zoho Notebook
Online Note Taker   Try Now

Zoho Planner
Online Organizer   Try Now

Zoho Projects 1 Project Free
Project Management Software   Try Now

Zoho CRM 3 Users Free
On-Demand CRM Solution   Try Now

Zoho Creator
Create Database Applications   Try Now

Zoho Wiki
Group Wikis made easy   Try Now

Zoho Chat
Make Group Decisions Faster   Try Now

Zoho Mail (private beta)
Collaboration Groupware   Try Now

Sign In

Username: [_____]

Password: [_____]

☐ Keep me signed in

[Sign In]

Forgot Password ?

New User? **Sign Up** for Free!

ZOHO Business Request access
Powerful online solutions for your business

Utilities

Site 24x7
Website Monitoring Service   Try Now

Zoho Polls
Online Polls in a snap   Try Now

Zoho Viewer (new)
View and Share Documents Online   Try Now

Zoho Challenge
Easiest Way to Evaluate Candidates   Try Now

SERVICE OF THE WEEK:
Zoho Start
Dashboard for all your Office Files

[EVENTS]   [NEWS]

• iZoho

www.zoho.com

Zoho.com is an office productivity suite from AdventNet. Zoho provides a number of tools including an online word processor (Zoho Writer), an online spreadsheet (Zoho Sheet), an online presentations tool (Zoho Show), an online conferencing tool (Zoho Meeting), an online notebook (Zoho Notes) for taking notes, a scheduling and planning tool (Zoho Planner), a project-management software tool (Zoho Project), and a mail program (Zoho Mail) that allows for a mail account.

There are other tools as well, including CRM (Customer Relationship Management) tools, a database application, wiki tools, and chat. Utilities include a web site monitoring tool, a viewer, online polls, and more.

While companies like Google and Microsoft are moving forward in the online office space, it is easy to see that when it comes to collaboration and online office productivity tools, Zoho has already got a foothold in the areas.

That's What Web 2.0 Is: a Combination of the Wisdom of the Crowd and the Read/Write Web

Zoho has a number of people contributing to the products and making the site run smoothly. Among them is Raju Vegesna, who is a spokesperson for the site.

Can you talk a little bit about yourself and what you do at Zoho?

I'm Raju Vegesna and I've been working with Zoho and the parent company [AdventNet] for the last seven years. I am the evangelist for Zoho currently. I have been with the company for about seven years and prior to that I started my own start-up back in India. Literally this is the second company I have worked with.

What is Zoho?

Zoho is not a company; it's a division. Many people think that Zoho is a separate company. In fact, it's a brand, not a division, within a larger organization called AdventNet, a private company that was founded in 1996 and has been profitable from the first year. [Over] the last 11 years, AdventNet has [had] more than 20,000 customers, not considering Zoho. It has been very profitable without raising any venture money. It is a private company.

It's a different company, I would say. Zoho is one of the brands of AdventNet, and AdventNet has several brands; one of the well-known brands is ManageEngine that is on the management space. And there are other brands like, say, Jambav that is for kids and education for kids. We also have other brands like SwisSQL for database migration. We have others as well, like vtiger. It is an Open Source CRM application that is another brand of AdventNet. So AdventNet is officially like a venture capital (VC) company listing in different areas and different markets, primarily focused on software or developing software.

The headquarters are located in Pleasanton, California. All of our development is in India. We have offices worldwide in London, [England]; Beijing, China; and Tokyo, Japan.

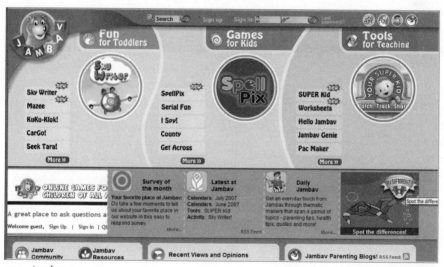

www.jambav.com

You mentioned AdventNet. Does AdventNet focus on software in general or software on the Net?

Software in general. Zoho is the only division that is focused on online software. All of the other divisions of AdventNet primarily sell software. In some cases Open Source software like vtiger, but primarily software.

So, jumping to the key question: How would you define Web 2.0?

Well, Web 2.0 is just a buzzword; we really don't believe it. But what we really like is the movement that's happening at the grassroots level where control is given back to the users. That is the key thing and if you want to have a term, then yes, that is probably where Web2.0 is a good marketing term.

The grassroots movement is what I would define Web 2.0 as. Prior to this one, all the web sites you [saw] out there were like brochure ware; it's like putting your brochure on your web site and more like marketing collateral. There's no interaction. It was kind of a "read-only web" prior to this movement. But with Web 2.0, I think the movement is coming to the bottom level, and it's becoming a really great web where the interaction is two-way. Now the users are communicating with the content publishers, and the users are part of the content publishing. That, in general, is Web 2.0.

> *"Wikis are going to die and merge with online word processors."*

Now, most of the movement primarily started at the consumer level, so you see many consumer applications are taking this direction we started with del.icio.us and similar applications. But, it is essentially moving to the business level as well, and then it is often referred to as Office 2.0, Enterprise 2.0, or Business 2.0. There are several terms that are coming for the same Web 2.0 concepts ported to the business market.

Can you talk about how Zoho fits into the Web 2.0 world?

Zoho really fits into the work side. Our tagline is "Work. Online," so we provide a set of tools that enable an individual or business user to do the work online. We have a broad set of applications that we offer, like say, a word processor, spreadsheet, presentation, and all of that, and eventually we plan to offer an essential set of tools that you may need to do your work online with a browser, without having to depend on a personal assistant.

When your work is online, there are a lot of advantages, like mobility, collaboration, and what not. We plan to take advantage of those applications, or those concepts, like mobility and collaboration, and build on top of them.

Earlier, it used to be work focused on an individual, but at work today it's collaboration that's important. You don't create a document just to keep it to yourself. You create a document, and you share it with other people. Online applications simplify collaboration. We plan to enhance the productivity of the users offering collaborative features.

We have about 16 applications along these lines, providing the infrastructure of the basics of the applications that the user needs. We primarily focus on two divisions or markets; we have something called Zoho Personal, which has a set of apps to be used by individuals. For the personal user, these are free, and they will remain free. Then we have something called Zoho Business that is for business users. There are two versions—a free version and a pay version—but those sets of tools for business users include applications like CRM project management, web conferencing, etc.

So essentially again, we divide our applications into two buckets for now: Zoho Personal and Zoho Business. Eventually we plan to have other offerings such as Zoho Education for students, and then Zoho Enterprise for enterprise deployment.

It is good to see that collaboration is going beyond just the commonly known Wiki on the Web.

Wiki is just one concept. Personally, apart from Zoho, I think wikis are going to die and merge with online word processors. You can see today there is about 60 [percent] to 70 percent overlap between the online word processor and a wiki. For the next maybe two to three years I would guess that these two will come together.

The good part about wikis is that there are no formats there—everything is on the Web; everything is a web page. If you look at online word processors, they're all pretty much the same. If all of us use the same web-based word processor, then formats don't matter; it's all there on the Web. That's the concept of wiki anyway. If the concept of linking comes to the web-based word processor, then pretty much you have the same functionality as the wiki word processor. So, I see those two coming together. You should be able to create a spreadsheet inside of a wiki. The same is the case of what you can do inside of a word processor. These are all possible.

When I think of a wiki, I think of collaboration first, so once you bring collaboration to word processors...

If we look at the word processors today, we can edit the same page or the same document at the same time. I'll see your changes, and you'll see my changes. While we're doing that, I can chat with you. So real-time collaboration and real-time communication is what is enabling the web-based word processors. And in fact, some of the wikis are supporting this—we are also doing that.

I personally think that the gap between the word processor and wiki is coming down. Eventually you may not see a specific wiki out there. We'll see how that moves.

You have mentioned user collaboration as being one aspect of Web 2.0. What other aspects of Web 2.0 do you see happening?

There are other things like "wisdom of the crowds," where the crowds define what you'll see. There are some good Web 2.0 applications, like Digg, where the content is given to the users to vote which is the best.

> *"Web 2.0 is not AJAX."*

The same concept applies to Wikipedia. That's the best example: The wisdom of the crowds updating the content so you always have the best content out there—and a huge set of content out there. The Read/Write Web concept comes into Wikipedia. When combined with the wisdom of the crowds along with some of regulation and moderation, we can really combine these two. I think that's what Web 2.0 is—a combination of the wisdom of the crowd and the Read/Write Web.

There are technologies like AJAX, JavaFX, Silverlight, and AIR...

Many people consider that Web 2.0 is AJAX. That's not the case. AJAX is just a technology, but again, AJAX does play an important role in Web2.0. But AJAX is not Web 2.0

Ignoring Web 2.0 being hype, what are people misunderstanding about Web 2.0?

Many people are getting a wrong impression of Web 2.0. I recently saw a video talking about Web 2.0 saying that it is AJAX. That's a different perspective. My perspective is that Web 2.0 is not AJAX. It is a concept of Read/Write Web. It is the concept of "wisdom of the crowds." AJAX is a technology, and you can't really define a movement that's coming at the grassroots level and label it a technology. The technology helped the momentum, and definitely AJAX did help the Web 2.0 concept, but Web 2.0 is not AJAX.

What other things are people getting wrong about Web 2.0?

People on a high level or broad level say they have a Web 2.0 site if they use one or two concepts such as JavaScript or AJAX. They say that's Web 2.0. That's really not the case. It really has to be community-driven; the community has to be involved there. There are different perspectives; I would agree with some and probably disagree with some. At the high level, everybody is trying to jump on and use it as a marketing pitch.

That's really hot-apparently, and everybody who has been there has been jumping on this. For example, Craigslist has been there right from Web 1.0 days, but the concept of Craigslist is Web 2.0. That's the wisdom of the crowds; that is the Read/Write Web. But they don't claim to be Web 2.0 but essentially they are providing good value.

> *"Security and offline are important aspects...they will be addressed in the next six months to a year."*

What other values do you or Zoho get from implementing the "wisdom of the crowd" and things such as that?

We are seeing lots of advantages. In fact, most of our development is primarily driven by our users. We made it very interactive between the feedback loop and the communication loop between us and our users. In some cases, our users drive the applications.

In most cases, we define the applications, but there are cases where our users force us to do applications. When we introduced word processing and spreadsheets, we never had plans to do a presentation application. People came to our blog and asked when the presentation application was coming out. They kept asking and kept pushing us to do a presentation application. To some extent it's driven by the community.

Similarly, looking at what you've done and what others have done, what are the coolest things you've seen done in regard to Web 2.0?

One of the best applications that I like is definitely Digg. Digg is an awesome idea: giving the power to the crowd and letting them decide what's good and what's not. That's a really cool application. Flickr is one; it's a great photo-sharing app. And YouTube, obviously.

Note that these are three different applications; Digg is mostly text-based, Flickr is image-based, and YouTube is video-based. So these are three highlights of Web 2.0 in different form. Obviously there are some other good applications, like del.icio.us, and others as well; I'm sure I'm missing a lot.

You didn't say Zoho!

That goes without saying. These are consumer apps, but Zoho falls into a different category of Web 2.0; maybe you can call it Work 2.0.

What do you see as the next big "hype" term or "hype" thing?

Probably "Enterprise 2.0."

> *"Security is not something that you address in a day."*

I think Enterprise 2.0 is a hype term; that's why I would prefer Office 2.0 or Work 2.0 to give a label to what all we are doing. "Enterprise 2.0" is at least a year or two away. Enterprises have some complex work flows, and I don't think online applications, including ours, are ready to really fit into to the complex workflows in enterprises yet. They'll get there someday, though. I think that is a hype term at this point, or is becoming a hype term.

"Enterprise Web 2.0" is a good topic. With enterprises I see security and offline access coming up as issues. Do you have any insights into these?

Security and offline are important aspects. It's not that they're not going to be addressed; they will be addressed in the next six months to a year, but they're not there yet.

In fact, we recently offered Zoho Writer in offline form so that your documents will also be viewable and editable when you are offline. They'll be synced when you go back online.

You'll see offline capabilities added to pretty much all of the Zoho applications wherever it makes sense. There are few times you might be disconnected and you obviously want access to those or your content, so the applications will obviously have to support offline functionality, and that's the reason we support that.

So, offline access in the long term I don't think will be a problem—even if it is one year from now. There are good technologies out there like Google Gears, Adobe AIR, and even Firefox is coming up with their own platform. Similarly, you'll see many along those lines.

Security is not something that you address in a day. It's a common thing that has to be addressed regularly. Currently, it's password protection, but that is not good enough. The user has to be given options to tell where the data has to be saved. He may, or may not, save to Zoho. We need to give him the option to save the data the way he prefers. It could be on Google or Amazon, so we have to give him the option to save his data there. That is number one.

Then while saving data, encrypting the data is important. We have to give him a way to encrypt the data on the server side so that he is confident that no one at Zoho will look

> *"I wouldn't define Web 3.0 anytime soon."*

into his data. Of course we don't do it, we don't ever look into anyone's data, but it is mostly a psychological comfort. And so, it has to be encryption of the server side, the client side, at the transport layer through SSL, and then he has to be given the choice on where he is to save the data. All four have to be addressed.

Are they being addressed? Yes.

Are they all addressed today? No.

But they are being addressed, and maybe six months down the road it may not be as big a concern.

Transitioning, you have Zoho Writer, which is text-based. Text leads us to the Semantic Web. What are your thoughts on Web 3.0, the Semantic Web?

I have no comments on that. That's been talked about for the last four years, and it will be talked about for the next five years, too. I don't want to comment on that until it is out or until there is more momentum on that.

The tools are starting to come out. Do you think that someday the Semantic Web will happen—that data will be given context?

Probably. It makes sense, but I wouldn't bet on it.

I wouldn't define Web 3.0 anytime soon.

Do you see Software as a Service (Saas) as fact or fiction?

Software as a Service is what we see today; for example, we at Zoho are 200 employees, and we don't have any software installed on our laptops. We just use online apps. Recently my Dell laptop crashed, and the good news is that I didn't lose any data, because all my data is on the cloud backed up. I know that everything is fine and safe.

So I just went out and bought a Mac. Why Mac? Because it really doesn't matter; all I need is a browser. It looks pretty, so I just got it!

> *"Software as a Service is the new model and that's the future."*

Software on a system doesn't matter. Now, software is in the cloud. There are lots of advantages. I don't bring my laptop to work. There is a desktop there that I use. If you're at a friend's place during the weekend, if you have to look at something, you just open a browser and do your work and sign out when you're done.

It's a convenience, and of course, it's also available on your mobile phone, and it's readily accessible. You can't imagine installing all the apps on your phone, but if it is web-based, then you have access to them anyway. Software as a Service is the new model and that's the future.

Microsoft does push Software *plus* Services (S+S), because they cannot push Software as a Service only; they have something to lose there.

What do you see as the next big change or revolution on the Web?

The operating system becomes a commodity. It's not something you would want to you pay for. It's like your device drivers or anything that is basic; you just take it for granted, and all you care about is your data and moving on the Web. That's the next paradigm; everything will be on the Web.

Apart from that, mobility will play an important roll eventually, in the next three to four years. The United States is unfortunately pretty slow in the mobility area. If you go to Europe or Eastern Asia you will see that many people have already abandoned their laptops and are using their mobile, portable devices to basically do their work. That will be within the next wave.

But to go there, the first step has to be Software as a Service. If all your data and all applications you need are online, there is no reason to depend on a particular system. Mobility will eventually follow.

We have been seeing that today. If you look at the demographics of Zoho users, 30 percent of all our users are students. Currently we have more than 600,000 users. Why students? Because students are living on the Web. And that is the reason—this is totally unexpected—but that's one of the reasons, is that they prefer Web-based applications. When they grow up, and when they go to work, that's when they will consider installed applications as the previous generation.

And that's the good news.

Sound Bites

Zoho is building online collaborative applications that allow users to use the Web in ways not available in the Web 1.0 world. In reviewing the Web 2.0, or Work 2.0, paradigm Raju Vegesna provides a number of interesting views:

- Users are communicating with the content publishers, and the users are part of the content publishing. That, in general, is Web2.0. Web 2.0 is also a combination of the wisdom of the crowd and the Read/Write Web.
- Wikis are going to die or merge with online word processors.
- Real-time collaboration and real-time communication is what is enabling the web-based word processors.
- AJAX does play an important role in Web 2.0, but AJAX is not Web 2.0.
- Enterprises have some complex work flows, and online applications are not really ready to fit into to the complex work flows in enterprises.

- Security and offline access will be addressed in the next six months to a year. Security is not something that you address in a day. It's a common thing that has to be addressed regularly.
- Software as a Service is the new model, and that's the future.
- All you care about is your data and moving on the Web. That's the next paradigm; everything will be on the Web.
- If all your data and all applications you need are online, there is no reason to depend on a particular system. Mobility will eventually follow.

Richard MacManus:
Read/WriteWeb &
Web 2.0 Workgroup

7

> *"Whereas the last era of the Web was people publishing
> things and you went onto the Web to read it, with the
> current era anyone can contribute, can write content, or
> can launch applications on the Web."*
>
> —*Richard MacManus*

R ichard MacManus founded and runs Read/WriteWeb (`www.readwriteweb`
`.com`). In September of 2005, he had also started the Web 2.0 Workgroup
(`web20workgroup.com`) along with Fred Oliveira (`www.webreakstuff.com`) and

www.readwriteweb.com & www.web20workgroup.com

Michael Arrington (www.techcrunch.com). He has worked for companies such as ZDNet, MicroMedia Corporation, and more.

Read/WriteWeb is a popular weblog that focuses on Web technology news, reviews, and analysis. It was started in 2004 and is now ranked by Technorati as one of the Top 20 blogs in the world.

Richard, along with Fred and Michael, is recognized as being in tune with Web 2.0 and the trends around Web 2.0. The starting of the Web 2.0 Workgroup is just one example of their early efforts to help bring attention to the topic. The Web 2.0 Workgroup site was originally an attempt to bring focus to the key blogs discussing Web 2.0 technology. As Web 2.0 has become more mainstream, the Web 2.0 Workgroup has become primarily a simple portal for some of the leading Web 2.0 sites.

Web 2.0 Has Come To Be a Marketing Term...

Richard has been involved with Web 2.0 since before the term Web 2.0 become mainstream. As one of the founders of the Web 2.0 Workgroup and as the proprietor of Read/Write Web, Richard has insight into what Web 2.0 has been, and into what Web 2.0 is.

Can you tell a little bit about yourself?

In about April 2003 I started to write about Web technology and the latest trends. At that time there was no Web 2.0 phrase. It hadn't been invented yet. It was kind of a down time on the Web at that time too. Things were just starting to build up among technologies. I started to get all these thoughts, and I like to write about stuff, so I jumped right in and just started writing about it.

I started to pull together people that were doing interesting things in technology and developing stuff. At that point, I was a Web manager for a corporate company in New Zealand. Then the Web 2.0 concept came along—that was about late 2004, early 2005. Now Read/Write Web is like a media publication, so now it is pretty much my professional job.

What is Read/WriteWeb?

Read/WriteWeb is a blog about Web technology and it covers news and analysis. We try to cover quality and the pulse. We have an emphasis on analysis and in explaining the latest trends around Web 2.0. If we write about a product, we make sure we compare it to other products and explain a little bit about the market segments. It covers the news and latest trends of Web 2.0. It is one of the most popular blogs in the world–certainly among the top three tech blogs. It is doing really well. We are building network blogs as well. We have launched one about search engines and another one about the digital lifestyle. So, it is an exciting time.

Are you still involved in the Web 2.0 Workgroup?

That is something I started back in around October 2005 with Mike Arrington of TechCrunch and Fred Oliveira from WeBreakStuff. At that point, TechCrunch and Read/WriteWeb were kind of at the same level. Now both of us are among the biggest blogs in the world.

At the time, not too many people knew about Web 2.0. So we wanted to get a lot of people that write blogs together and just try to explain it to people a little bit more, and try to link to each other a little bit, and basically just try to get the word out about these new technologies that were happening at that point in time.

Right now it is kind of like a portal. Not a lot of work is being done on it. We all try to keep in touch with each other, but it's not quite as formal as it used to be.

When you created the Web 2.0 Workgroup, did you have any long-term objectives for the site?

It possibly has served its purpose, because there is much more out there on Web 2.0 now. It kind of got to the point where there were so many sites and blogs talking about

> *"It is very hard to technically define it [Web 2.0]."*

Web 2.0 that it became difficult to keep adding more onto the site. In early 2005 or 2006 it was a great way for people to discover all the sites and all the people talking about Web 2.0. Now, with Techmeme.com, and all those aggregation sites that cover tech news, there is not so much a need for it as there was when we started it.

So let's ask the core question; how would you define Web 2.0?

It has come to be like a marketing term. In the old days, we used to call it the dotcom era. With *Time* magazine making Web 2.0 the person of the year [in 2006], everyone now knows the term, or at least recognizes the term. It is very hard to technically define it.

If I had to define it, then it would be social sites and software, and social networks such as MySpace and Facebook. But, also user generated content such as YouTube. It is all those things plus technologies like RSS and using APIs and Web services to hook sites and things together. It means a lot of things. In a nutshell it defines the era of the Web we are in right now, just like dotcom was used to describe the last era.

You mentioned several characteristics such as social aspects, mashups, and more. Are there any parts of Web 2.0 that stand out more than others?

> *"Because everyone can contribute content, it is hard to focus on the best content."*

The most important thing—just as I named my blog Read/Write Web—is the fact that the current era of the Web can be contributed to by anybody. Everybody can create content and aggregate content, and personalize their own content. Whereas the last era of the Web was people publishing things to the Web and you went onto the Web to read it, with the current era of the Web anyone can contribute and can write content, or launch applications on the Web.

That is probably the big main feature for me—that everybody can contribute. It is a read/write web basically.

Taking the opposite perspective, where do you believe there are misunderstandings about Web 2.0?

One thing that a lot of people are sort of tricked on is that because everyone can contribute content, it is hard to focus on the best content. A lot of old-school media people will complain about user-generated [content] to the effect that there is a lot of rubbish in there.

In terms of filtering technology, it is definitely something that is still being worked on. It is not quite there in terms of having the technology for filtering out just the good stuff and to mine for all of this information on the Web now.

It is kind of the next stage, when people are starting to think of "Web 3.0" now. They think of it as the Semantic Web, the intelligence web, where we can filter on information more so than we can at the moment. So, yes, I would say that this is one of the challenges of Web 2.0 at this time.

You mention the Semantic Web. Do you think that is even possible?

Yeah, I think it is definitely possible. Whether it will turn out like Sir Tim Berners-Lee had envisioned it is yet to be seen. And he's been talking about it for years.

A lot of companies are trying to incorporate Semantic Web features into their products. One of our writers here at Read/WriteWeb, Alex Iskold, has a company called AdaptiveBlue and they do a lot of Semantic Web technologies in their products.

So, yes, I think it is slowly coming, but it is bubbling up rather than being defined top-down as Tim Berners-Lee probably wanted it to be when he started talking about it a few years ago.

> *"AJAX made web sites a lot more interactive."*

Stepping back to the misunderstood areas of Web 2.0, what is your thought on the comment "AJAX is Web 2.0" or that "Web 2.0 is AJAX"?

AJAX made web sites a lot more interactive, and Google is probably the main proponent of that. On the other side of the coin, we have Adobe and Microsoft, which have RIA (Rich Internet Application) technologies. So desktop applications are kind of Web-enabled as well.

So there are two basic trends. One is the browser based, which Google is going with using AJAX and other technologies. The other trend is the web-ified desktop, which is Adobe and Microsoft.

In terms of the enabling technologies, they don't define Web 2.0. There is a lot more to Web 2.0 than just those enabling technologies. There is user-generated content, the social aspects of it and the read/write web nature of it. I don't see those enabling technologies as defining it.

Are there any cool Web 2.0 things you see out there by other sites or that you have done?

We are seeing a lot of activity in search at the moment. There are a lot of companies trying to be the next big thing in search. We've got a blog devoted to this called AltSearchEngines.com. That is one trend I've really been following quite closely.

Another is Web office. Yahoo! bought Zimbra in 2007, which is a web office collaboration suite, for about $350 million. And of course, Google released their PowerPoint application called Presentations and they added it to Google Docs. Zoho and ThinkFree are two other web office companies as well.

Those are probably the two areas I'm following the closest.

But also there are a lot of interesting things happening with mobile. With Apple having releasing their iPhone, that has made Web applications a lot easier to develop for the mobile phone. I think we'll see a lot more action on the mobile front in the next few years.

> *"Premium content is kind of a lost art on the Web."*

And Web Services as well. Particularly, Amazon has done a lot of great things with Web Services. I think we will see more on the Web Service front too.

And finally, the online video and Internet TV spaces are very hot right now with Joost, YouTube, and a whole lot of others. Again, we have a network blog called last100 that tracks those trends.

In the Web 1.0 world, it seemed like sites were financed by banner ads and other business models. Some say page views go down with AJAX sites and that this could affect such business models. Do you see business models changing for Web 2.0 businesses, and what models do you see?

Recently I heard something about Facebook adding more AJAX functionality to their site. A few commenters mentioned on my site that the page views don't actually go down. Even though the page is refreshed without the user knowing, it still transfers an extra page view. In general, at the moment, online advertising is the way that things have been monetized. There have been a lot of recent acquisitions on that area as well. Microsoft and Google have both acquired online advertising companies, so there is a lot more action to come on that front in the next couple of years.

On the other hand, I think that premium content is kind of a lost art on the Web. It didn't really work in the first era of the Web, but there are a couple of promising products coming on board now that might make premium content workable. One, which I reviewed recently, is by a company called Edgeio. It is a premium content product that makes it easy for bloggers and any small company basically to get in on premium content.

That is possibly one thing that might make a new revenue stream. There are some startups out there that make it easier to advertise on web sites. There is one company called Adicate which sells advertisement in one-hour blocks on a web site. So there is some innovation on that front as well—in how people advertise and how they combine advertising on the Web with applications. There is probably more innovation to come there.

You touched on Semantic Web. Let me ask, what's next? What do you see as being next?

Recently I wrote a post about future web trends. It kind of talks about things like the Semantic Web, artificial intelligence, and virtual worlds. I think the big dream will be that the Web becomes more intelligent, which is the Semantic Web vision. It will also involve more social software, filtering and recommendation systems.

I think the next step will probably be that computers can talk to other computers and understand other computers so that a lot of work can be done in the background for people, whether it be filtering of information or going out and finding products that people want to buy

> *"A lot of that stuff will hopefully become automatic in the future given Semantic Web technologies."*

and delivering it to people. Or, that computers will do a lot of background work for us rather than us trying to step through hundreds of hours of feeds, or go through tens of hundreds of web sites to find what we are wanting.

A lot of that stuff will hopefully become automatic in the future given Semantic Web technologies.

What are your thoughts on Software as a Service or Software plus Services?

Yes, I think the term is being used the most with office software. Google is coming out with Google Apps suite of office software.

Over time I definitely think that a lot of that type of software will be delivered as a service over the Web rather than being software that you install on the computer. The main benefit that has become enabled is that there is a lot more collaboration with approaches and workflows over the Web. Also, you can update software automatically over the Web; you don't have to install a new version.

Definitely, Google is providing a lot of oomph in that respect at the moment. Microsoft is a little bit fearful. They came out last week with reasons to not use Google Apps. In the next three to five years, I think we'll see most Microsoft software delivered as a service over the Web. I think that will happen to a lot of other types of software as well.

Is there anything you'd like to add about Web 2.0?

With Web 2.0 a lot of mainstream people are recognizing the trend whether they call it Web 2.0 or not. I started writing about these things in 2004, 2005 when it was kind of niche. Now everyone is using Google software as an example, and YouTube, MySpace, Facebook, and such. To sum it up, it is really an exciting time. It is great to see these Web technologies being used in the mainstream.

You mentioned the quality of content bothering old-school publishers. Do you see issues coming with the free flow of open information?

Definitely. YouTube is a prime example. Even in blogging, a lot of people copy my blog content without giving credit. There is a lot of this stuff happening out there, but there is not a lot you can do at this time. The most you can do is put your name on it and ask that each person using your material adds an indication that it comes from your site. And that is pretty much all you can do at the moment.

You get the feeling that there is a lot more to be played out. It is definitely an unsolved problem.

Using APIs and services from other companies, there is the issue of being disconnected. Do you have any insights into solutions to this issue?

I use Gmail as my main mail client and they don't have offline functionality at the moment. There are times when I want to use email offline. Having said that, there is a technology called Google Gears. It enables developers to create offline functionality for AJAX Web applications. I think that will reach Gmail pretty soon. Right now amongst Google properties it is only available in Google Reader. I would image that is coming in Google Apps as well.

I think parts of it have been solved and in the next few months we will see more applications having offline functionality. In Zimbra, for example, that has a large offline functionality and it was bought by Yahoo! Mozilla is working on offline functionality for Firefox as well.

So, it is definitely happening.

Sound Bites

Richard MacManus has been involved with Web 2.0 since before the term became mainstream. His observations and connections with the industry lead to a number of insights. From those insights are a number of notable observations that follow.

- Web 2.0 has come to be a marketing term. In a nutshell Web 2.0 is defines the era of the Web we are in right now, just like dotcom was used to describe the last era.
- Whereas in the last era of the Web, professionals published and people visited a site to read it, with the current era anyone can contribute and write content.
- Because everyone can contribute content, it is hard to find the best content.
- Semantic Web is slowly coming, but it is bubbling up rather than being defined top-down.
- We are seeing a lot of activity in search at the moment. In the next few months we will see more applications having offline functionality. We'll see a lot more action on the mobile front in the next few years.
- In the near future, we'll see more Microsoft software delivered as a service over the Web. This will happen to a lot of other types of software as well.
- Premium content is kind of a lost art on the Web.
- The big dream is that the Web becomes more intelligent.

TJ Kang:
ThinkFree

8

> *"We were about to change the way the software was used and distributed. We were going up against this 800 lb. gorilla in Redmond, Washington."*
>
> —*TJ Kang*

Online applications are gaining popularity. More important, online applications are gaining power and functionality. ThinkFree is a prime example of how much power and functionality a little Java can bring to the Web.

While companies like Microsoft and Google talk about online applications, ThinkFree actually is an online application suite that also happens to be Microsoft Office compatible. Although its origin predates the concept of Web

www.thinkfree.com & www.thinkfreedocs.com

2.0, it is in fact one of the early leaders in the online office application space. Being an online web-based application, ThinkFree is also compatible with Windows, Macintosh, UNIX, and Linux.

Using ThinkFree, you can create a number of different types of documents, including word-processing documents, presentations, and spreadsheets. You can also edit existing documents. As an example, ThinkFree online will let you edit existing Microsoft Office 2007 Word documents (.docx files).

In addition to ThinkFree, there is also ThinkFreeDocs.com. ThinkFreeDocs .com is a site where you can share your various documents with the community at large. You can find documents that others have chosen to share as well. If you are looking for an example document or a starting point, then ThinkFreeDocs is likely to have them. For example, if you need an invoice document, you can search ThinkFreeDocs to see what others in the community have posted. You can then use these documents. Ratings, groupings and other features make finding the right documents a little easier.

Where do ThinkFree.com and ThinkFreeDocs.com fit in the grand scheme of Web 2.0? The best way to find out the answer to this question is to ask the person running the company.

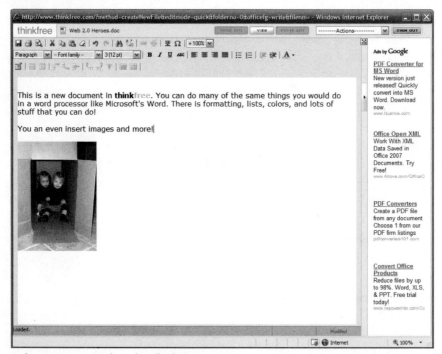

A document created on the ThinkFree site

We're at the Inflection Point

TJ Kang is the CEO of ThinkFree, where he leads the strategic direction of the company. He has worked with ThinkFree since 1999, when he founded it. Like many people in the Web 2.0 world, TJ has a background that helped lead to what is now considered a prominent Web 2.0 site. TJ talks about his background, about ThinkFree, and about technology.

Tell a little bit about yourself and about ThinkFree.

I started this business in my last year of college, while I was a student at a University in Canada. I came across an algorithm with some friends that could be used to automate Korean language input.

Although I was living in Canada, I grew up in Korea, and the Korean writing system is different from other East Asian writing systems in the sense that it is an alphabet. It only has twenty-four letters, but you arrange these letters in a two-dimensional space, rather than in a single dimension, as in English, to compose a syllable block.

In English, if you want to divide words into syllables, you actually need a hyphenation dictionary to do it properly because there are no simple rules for this. In Korean it's fairly easy. There is a well-defined orthographic rule that every Korean writer understands. The letters are composed so that each syllable forms a visible whole distinct from each other. Even if you don't understand Korean, you can always tell where one syllable ends and the new one begins. The alphabetic letters comprising the syllable block may change their shapes depending on what other letters are present in that block. If the same rules were to be applied to English writing, the letter "K" in "King" would look different from the same letter in "Kong." This obviously made Korean typewriting a difficult process. The typist often had to use two or three different shift keys to select the correct instance of the same letter depending on the context.

When computers came along, I figured that with the intelligence that a computer CPU can provide, that perhaps we could automate this. When I looked at this problem with some friends, we found a simple but elegant rule that can be programmed into a computer. So, back in 1982, we created the software for a demonstration on our Apple II computers. And it worked. One thing led to another and we started developing a full-fledged Korean word processor.

In 1983, we had created the very first Korean word-processing software. I'm known as the co-inventor of the Korean Word Processor. This actually led me to create a software company that developed personal productivity tools. Originally, I developed for the Korean language market, but eventually I also did work for the Silicon Valley companies. In 1989 I relocated to Korea and started a company there with the idea of creating personal productivity software for the then-fledgling Korean software market. I stayed there until 1999—just before the dotcom boom—and I began to have an idea.

> *"Competing against Microsoft, which…I've been doing all my life, was becoming more and more difficult."*

In 1997 Scott McNealy of Sun and Larry Ellison of Oracle went around the world preaching this network computer gospel—that people will not be using desktop PCs anymore. The computer will become a thin client. The software and data will live on the server, and everything will come down over the network. You will use these thin clients to access your applications and data, and Java will power these thin clients.

I liked the idea, mainly because I felt that competing against Microsoft, which, I guess, I've been doing all my life, was becoming more and more difficult. And I felt that a network computing platform would provide a more neutral battlefield. So I began developing an office suite for the network computing platform, and I wasn't the only one. Corel in Canada were doing Corel Office for Java. They were the best known at the time, but there were others. IBM/Lotus, Star Division in Germany, and JustSystems in Japan, who all had a big market share at one time in their respective markets, were all working on the Java version of office suite. And I was doing this in Korea. But as with any new technology, desktop Java had many problems in the early days. Corel, who started before anyone else, suffered the most and gave up their effort in early 1998. And I found myself leading the most fully developed Java-based office suite project in the world and as a result fielding calls from many hardware manufacturers with network computer plans.

Many of these hardware vendors were in Japan. I met with Toshiba, Fujitsu, Funai, and NEC. We had network computer prototypes from the manufacturers around the world in our office. I still have some of these machines in my office bearing IBM, LG, and Sun logos. However, the more

I talked to these companies, the more I began to suspect that the network computer market was not going to happen. This was a classic chicken-and-egg problem.

The hardware vendors were reluctant to start mass-producing the network computers because they felt there was no market for it. There was no market or customers for network computers because there weren't any applications that ran on them. There weren't any applications, because developers were reluctant to port their applications to where there are no customers. This was a vicious cycle. I found it hard to see how this cycle could be broken.

In 1999 I was coming to Silicon Valley a lot to talk to Sun. When I visited Sun, I had the sense that Sun was also dropping their plans for their Java Station 2 that was scheduled for release in the spring of that year.

> *"My business model had been to create the software and to sell it to hardware vendors for bundling…I changed [this] to provide office productivity as a service."*

I felt that I had to find a new business model very quickly. Up until then, my business model had been to create the software and to sell it to hardware vendors for bundling. But when there isn't any hardware…

By this time, it was clear that the Internet was big, huge. There was a lot of money being invested in dotcoms. I realized that people already had network computers sitting on their desktop! They were PCs and laptops running web browsers. This was before Sun picked a fight with Microsoft on their Java licenses, so every copy of IE (Internet Explorer) on a Windows PC shipped with Java. I already had a suite of applications that run on Java, so if I modified them a little bit, I would have this ready-made platform that would work with what is on most peoples' desktops. I changed my business model, to provide office productivity as a service to users who use browsers to do most of their work.

This was back in 1999. The Application Service Provider (ASP) business was becoming pretty hot. There were companies who had an IPO with the idea of providing applications as a service. We are now calling it "Software as a Service" (Saas), but back then it was called ASP. So I married the ASP model with the model that most of the dot coms had. I was going to offer the personal productivity software as a free service and make money by running some banner ads. When people used the word processor or spreadsheet, the ad would be shown. With that idea, I was able to raise about 24 million dollars from the venture capitalists. So, that's how ThinkFree was born in 1999.

So you were doing Software as a Service and Service Oriented Architectures (SOA) to some extent before the jargon really became main stream?

But I think we were a little too early. We launched the very first version of our online office service in February 2000, at an IDG Demo conference in Palm Springs, and we actually generated quite a bit of buzz from the media because we made some bold claims. We were about to change the way the software was used and distributed. We were going up against this 800 lb. gorilla in Redmond, Washington. This was a time when the U.S. Justice Department was locked in a battle with Microsoft. I think the media liked that angle so we were covered by major media interviewers.

> *"'These guys are not very good right now, but if they keep trying...'"*

I had my picture in *Fortune* magazine in 2000; however, my favorite article was actually in the March 2001 issue of *Fast Company* magazine. It was an interview of Steve Ballmer. The interviewer asked him what were the potential threats for his company. The interviewer wondered if Microsoft was vulnerable to the disruptive changes described in Clay Christensen's book *Innovator's Dilemma*.

Ballmer initially replied that Microsoft is so different that it is basically immune to these disruptions. Reluctantly, when pressed by the interviewer with, "*But there must be something that keeps you up at night, right?*" Ballmer acknowledged that Linux is his number-one concern. And then he went on to say something that surprised me, "Take companies like ThinkFree, for example. These guys are not very good right now, but if they keep trying to provide a subset of Microsoft Office functionalities in a convenient manner, then I can't be 100 percent certain that businesses won't move to that." So, he has to watch out for guys like us.

That seems like a complement to me!

We definitely were on their radar, but I think we disappointed Mr. Ballmer. After the dotcom bust, investors became uneasy about funding the company. In the market we had hoped for, we were actually a consumer play in those days, and the consumers that we were targeting didn't really have broadband connections, not in the U.S., anyway. So even though our code size was a lot smaller by an order of magnitude than Microsoft's, it still took 20 to 30 minutes to download our application software over a dial-up connection.

If you remember, back in 2000, even 2001, the biggest Internet company in the U.S. was AOL (America Online)—and AOL was by definition a dial-up service provider. AOL's home page didn't have any graphics whatsoever because of bandwidth issues.

I think we were a little early. The network infrastructure that we were counting on wasn't there. Plus, the business model of advertising using the banner ads didn't really work. Lots of dot coms bottomed out. Things have changed quite a bit since then.

Wouldn't you say that in 1999 or 2000 to as late as 2003, the idea of creating documents online was a paradigm that the average person wouldn't accept because of concerns with security and trust that the document would really be out there accessible to them?

I think that might have had something to do with the failure for our service to catch on, but the biggest reason was the infrastructure issue. I think these security concerns still exist today, regardless of what we tell people. I personally believe that your data is more secure on our server than it is on your desktop.

> *"Your own system administrator might sell the customer data."*

You read about these reports on data theft. Most data theft—65 to 70 percent—is due to lost laptops or misplaced USB drives. People store customer and credit card data on these things and they leave them on the train or in the restaurant. Or, they get stolen.

Another 20 percent of data loss happens because the information was stolen by insiders. Your own system administrator might sell the customer data. These are the guys who know which of the data they manage is attractive to buyers.

But when we leave the data to a company that actually stakes their future on safe-keeping these, things are different. There will always be people who are concerned about security, especially those enterprise costumers. For these, we actually provide on-premise hosted solutions so that they can manage all the data themselves without having to worry about someone else managing their data. We are now a lot more flexible in the way we go about doing this and I think that enterprises appreciated it.

Let's jump into the topic of this book. How would you and ThinkFree define the term Web 2.0?

To me, Web 2.0 is an application platform, and a vendor- and device-neutral one at that. I think this is probably a different definition than what most other people give. From my point of view Web 2.0 revolution is the platform shift that I've been waiting for all my life.

Microsoft Office has been so dominant and it has been dominant for so many years that most people don't even remember there were other office productivity solutions. In the IBM PC days it was WordPerfect and Lotus 1-2-3 that reigned supreme. If you go back even further to around the Apple II days, on the Apple II platform was actually Word Star and VisiCalc. VisiCalc was the very first spreadsheet, invented by Dan Bricklin. These two probably had more than 80 percent of the market respectively. When the IBM PC came out, it was Lotus 1-2-3 and WordPerfect. They dominated the market for seven or eight years until Windows became the major platform choice for most users.

> *"When the computing platform itself changes, then people are forced to change the way they work."*

When Windows 3.1 came out, (not with Windows 1 and 2, not Windows 3, but Windows 3.1), the majority of people started to adopt Windows as their main operating system. Along with it, Microsoft Office became the main dominant force. Some people argue that it's because Microsoft created these applications that people became enamored with them. They say if Microsoft Office had come out before Windows came out they would have been popular. But that's not really true.

When the very first version of Microsoft Word came out in 1982, I started using it just to see what it was like. It was an "OK" software—very different from WordPerfect.

Microsoft actually had a very good spreadsheet called MultiPlan that came out in 1983, and it was much better by an order of magnitude than Lotus 1-2-3. It supported some graphical user interface, and this was before Windows. It ran in MS-DOS and it supported mouse and pull-down menus. But even though the software was revolutionary by the standard of the time, it never caught on. Market share for Microsoft Word and MultiPlan never exceeded more than five percent. It was only after Windows became the dominant operating system that these applications began to see the light of day. It was then that people began to look for applications that ran best on the new platform.

Because people invest so much of their time getting used to these applications, and because they accumulate so much data with these applications, the switching costs become prohibitive. So just because somebody comes out with an application that does some things better and at a little bit cheaper price, that's not going to make users switch what they're used to the latest or "best" software, because the cost is so high. But when the computing platform itself changes, then people are forced to change the way they work. They begin to look for things that are out there that make use of the new way of doing things. I do think we're at the inflection point. I've been seeing this for the last four or five years. I think for sure now—it took a little longer than I expected—but the momentum has gathered enough, (so now we are calling this Web 2.0). Now people see this as a real, serious alternative to the way they've done things.

Office workers, pretty much, now live inside a web browser. They come to work, and they fire up their favorite browser. They do most of their work inside the browser, except when they have to use their Office software that they run on their desktop.

I think there is something wrong with this picture, but there just hasn't been a solution that's good enough for people to make the switch to allow them to take advantage of the power that browser-based or server-based computing gives

> *"I don't think there's any one, correct definition of Web 2.0."*

them and at the same time, allow them to leverage the investment that they have already made—the thousands of documents that they have already created and stored on their desktop and the skills that they have spent so much time mastering. At ThinkFree, we do have a solution that actually does this—that gives them the power and convenience of web-based computing, but at the same time gives these users the familiarity, the compatibility that they need to make the transition as painlessly and as smoothly as possible.

Web 2.0 is being used in a lot of ways. Is there anything you see that people are getting wrong or misunderstanding about Web 2.0?

Web 2.0 means many different things to many people. I don't think there's any one, correct definition of Web 2.0. I'm more excited about the variety, the diversity of the ideas about what the term means to a lot of people. As an application developer, I'm always trying to see ways to leverage some of these cool ideas that different people bring to Web2.0 space.

I mentioned that as far as I'm concerned, Web 2.0 is an application platform. The other aspect of Web 2.0 is that you have this idea of "wisdom of crowds." We have a sister site called ThinkFreeDocs.com where we allow people to upload any documents they have—could be a PowerPoint Presentation or a spreadsheet that they have that they want to publish and share with other people. There is all kinds of stuff that people post there— some of it is entertaining, some is actually useful as a template for studying or for business…it is sort of like a YouTube for documents.

But unlike YouTube, I don't think people go there just to kill time. People go there to find useful information. For example, there are all kinds of lessons/instruction by teachers; there is this project going on between a school in the U.K. and a school in some African country. They have kids across two continents creating poems on the same subjects. They are posting this to the ThinkFreeDocs site. So the UK kids can see what their friends are doing in Africa and vice versa. I think it's kind of amazing that you don't have to create your own web site—you can just go in and use the tools that are available and do this.

In looking at ThinkFreeDocs, you are right—it looks like a YouTube for documents!

If you have a presentation that you want to share with blog readers, you can post it to ThinkFreeDocs, do a copy and paste, and create a blog. People who come to your blog can see your presentation without leaving your blog, and you can use Flash animation if you want.

Transitioning to another area, ThinkFree is doing a lot with documents. What are your thoughts or opinion on the Semantic Web, Web 3.0?

I think it's very interesting and I think it will probably be very helpful in the future—hopefully the not-too-distant future. Right now we just offer a full text search on the text that you have either in your own private storage or in the shared area in your storage that you have given access to your colleagues, as well as ThinkFreeDocs. When you do a search in ThinkFree in your account, you find documents that are in your private area, and also documents that are in your friends' ThinkFree accounts that you have access to. The search is based on simple keywords and tags and comments. Once we could add intelligence to the structure of the documents, the discovery process, getting more relevant information, maybe in some cases automatically into the documents, would be very powerful. But we haven't gotten around to incorporating the latest ideas coming from this Semantic Web research.

Do you think that the Semantic Web is just a research thing, or do you believe it will happen?

I think it's quite promising—I'm not an expert in this field, but we talk about this within the company and we have some people on our development team who are experts on this. They have all kind of interesting ideas that hold great promise, like classifying and searching documents based on meaning rather than matching keywords. However, the reality is that we have many things on our plate that require immediate attention. It will probably be a while before we incorporate some of these ideas.

> *"Five years is an eternity."*

You were ahead of the game with Software as a Service and online applications. Looking forward, what do you think the next revolution on the Web will be? What do you think will be the big thing in five years?

To be really honest, I really can't see that far ahead. Five years is an eternity; however, I will tell you what I think the important thing is regarding office 2.0 space—seamless support for transition between offline and online. This is something that I've been saying for the last year or so, and now

Google has come out with Google Gears to support offline use of a lot of the applications that they are building. It is currently only supporting a limited number of applications, but I'm sure they are also moving towards providing some way for people to get some useful work done even when they are not connected.

As you touched upon earlier, there are two main issues or barriers that keep people from moving from desktop to Web: security and the offline issues. Because we are still living in a world where connectivity is not ubiquitous, people worry—rightly, "What happens when my network goes down? Or I find myself in a place where I can't get access to the network?" You need to provide a way to cache the data and the application so that they can continue using it when they're not connected. We are doing this with our ThinkFree Premium product. I think it's really cool that you could run the applications when you don't even have a connection. You could work on your PowerPoint presentation. You could work on your expense report on an airplane. When you touch down and you link back in, everything is synchronized so that you have a backup, or you could access it from other places, or you could share it with other users.

We are talking to some mobile-device vendors who are creating the next generation of mobile Internet devices. Intel is really big on this now, so they will be coming out with the first generation of these devices. Intel creates the reference platforms, so they have some five or six vendors signed up so far, who will be manufacturing and distributing these devices in the first half of next year. We are also talking to another large company who is creating another device platform to compete against Intel's MID [mobile Internet device] or Apple's iPhone. A little bit bigger than a phone, but gives you the full web-browsing experience.

But even on these devices whose primary goal is to access the Web, they all say that they would like to have some applications installed on the device so that they could actually do some of the work when the connections are not stable. That's why they come to us, so that we can give them our Premium edition that could actually be installed on these devices. We also handle the storage in the cloud, and data synchronization for documents that they create and edit.

They have a small device that you could use to check your email and even view the attachments that come with the email. You could view a PowerPoint presentation or a spreadsheet—even make some changes to it if the changes are simple enough. If it requires maybe a half to one full hour of work making these modifications and you'll probably want to sit down in front of a real computer and do it—it would be much easier.

When you do that, our Premium edition would have synchronized the document you viewed on the small mobile Internet device to your desktop computer via the online storage. You'd actually have the same document on your PC. If it was edited a little bit on the mobile device, you'd see that. You could then edit and perfect the document on the desktop. The synergies between the offline and online transition and the synchronization of different devices—people like this idea. We'll begin to see more and more of these hybrid solutions in the next couple of years.

These applications are what will be brought up in trying to address the real-world needs. Last year and this year it was all about proving that you could do these things in the cloud and in the web browser. I think in the next couple of years we will see more vendors trying to convey that you could really do your work anywhere on any device and do it without Microsoft Office.

> *"[Everybody having access to broadband] took a lot longer to happen in the U.S. than in other parts of the world."*

So based on what you've said, do you believe the big issue is connectivity? Will the day come when connectivity is no longer an issue?

Yes, definitely, four to five years from now, especially in smaller countries. I've been through this before—in 1999–2000, my business model was predicated on the premise that everybody will have broadband. That took a lot longer to happen in the U.S. than in other parts of the world.

We'll probably see the same thing. The U.S. is such a big country. In most metropolitan areas, I'm sure we'll have this ubiquitous connectivity. In rural areas, you may never get that; I don't know. I think you still need some type of insurance point, which is why many of the key Internet players are now concerned about support of offline solutions. Connectivity is one concern, security is another concern.

There is a lot of education and trust-building that the vendors need to do. I'm sure a hundred years ago, people thought that the safest place to put their money was under the mattress; I think we need to build the same kind of trust that the banks now have with the customers. You can't do this alone, but I think that we will get there.

It seems to be happening. I used VisiCalc, and the world of applications has changed quite a bit since then. But as you stated, four or five years is a long time out to predict. To somewhat conclude, is there anything else you'd like to add or comment?

As I said, this is the official beginning of the market. I saw a Gartner report that came out last month that had all these predictions for the Software as a Service (SaaS) market. They've been tracking this for a few years and they had the usual categories such as CRM, ERP, and such. For the first time, they added office suite as a category to the SaaS market so for them, this is the beginning—the first year they started to track this market as a separate category.

The market is small right now, and they are predicting that it will grow to $1.5 billion in 2010–2011. The compounded annual growth rate that they are predicting is 95 percent over the years, every year. This is a very exciting market and I think we'll actually see some real traction next year.

> *"We'll see some real changes taking place in an area of the market that had been stagnant for the last 15 years."*

We are talking to some large enterprises, which surprised me. As I said, when I first started this in 1999–2000 my initial target customer was consumers because I thought that the enterprises were big and not as subject to the cost pressure as much as the consumers or the small businesses. With our ThinkFree service, our intended market was the SMBs (small to medium businesses). We do have a lot of small companies as our customers, but we are actually getting a lot of calls from some really, really big companies. I hear the same story, over and over again. They are all concerned about cutting costs and they are finding it increasingly difficult to justify paying hundreds of dollars to Microsoft every year. With volume licensing, they pay something more like $70 or $80 per seat—higher, if they then have something like SharePoint for collaboration, which comes free with the online office such as ThinkFree.

Cost is a big issue, but also the convenience and the freedom that it gives them—they are very interested in that. I think we'll see some real changes taking place in an area of the market that had been stagnant for the last 15 years.

That's exciting; I think that's good for everyone.

Sound Bites

TJ Kang has been in the computer industry for a lot of years. While his focus is online office applications, it is obvious from his experiences that he is also aware of what is happening with Web 2.0. The following are some notable comments from TJ regarding Web 2.0, online office suites, and more.

- We are now calling it "Software as a Service," but back then it was called ASP (Application Service Providers).
- There are two main issues or barriers that keep people from moving from the desktop to the Web: security and the offline issue. Security is more an issue with enterprise customers.
- People do most of their work inside the browser, except when they have to use their office software that they run on their desktop. You, therefore, need to provide a way to cache data and the application so that they can continue use when not connected.
- Web 2.0 is an application platform, and a vendor-neutral one at that. This is probably a different definition than what most other people give. The other aspect of Web 2.0 is that you have this idea of "wisdom of crowds."
- Microsoft Office has been so dominant for so many years, that most people don't even remember there were other office productivity solutions. We'll see some real changes taking place in an area of the market that had been stagnant for the last 15 years (online applications).
- Just because somebody does come out with an application that works better and at a little bit cheaper price, most users won't switch because the cost of converting is so high.
- When the computing platform itself changes, then people are forced to change the way they work.
- In the next couple of years we will see more vendors trying to convey that you could really do your work anywhere on any device, and do it without Microsoft Office.

Patrick Crane:
LinkedIn

9

"*I see Web 2.0 as a course correction…[that] weaves the social fabric back together again…You can now consume and share things, and discuss them, interpret them, and ultimately get that lens on the world, and it's not just your own individual perceptions and observations anymore; it's back to the old way.*"

—Patrick Crane

everal years ago, the phrase "six degrees from Kevin Bacon" became popular. It was theorized that everyone is within six people of knowing Kevin Bacon. As an example, if I know you, that is a first-degree connection. If you

know someone famous and I know you, then that would make me two degrees from knowing that person. So it is hypothesized that everyone in the world is within six degrees of knowing Kevin Bacon.

This same premise has been applied to a web site, LinkedIn. LinkedIn is an online network of more than 17 million experienced professionals from around the world. Within LinkedIn, you can connect (link) to other people you know. Those people can also connect to people they know. The end result is a giant network with everyone linked together.

The LinkedIn network can be searched and used to extend your network. You can search for clients, consultants, subject-matter experts, friends, family, old acquaintances, jobs, business opportunities, new hires, and much more. You can use it to do everything you would want to do with the professional network that you would previously have created with a Rolodex and lots of business cards.

The difference is that you have the power of the computer and of a very large network helping you. One other difference is that if you find someone with whom you want to connect, you can see how many degrees away you are from them. For example, I interviewed Patrick Crane for this chapter. Patrick and I are three degrees apart. That means I know someone that knows someone that directly knows Patrick. Having discovered this tidbit, I could actually use the LinkedIn system to connect with Patrick through the chain of people.

It's a Fascinating Era That We're In

Patrick is the vice president of marketing at LinkedIn. He also has more than a decade of high-tech, world-wide business experience. A lot of this comes from having worked with organizations such as Vodafone and Yahoo!. Rather than detailing his experience here, it makes sense to suggest you take a look at his profile on LinkedIn (www.linkedin.com/in/patrickcrane). Patrick had a number of insights to share.

Can you tell a little about yourself and about LinkedIn?

I have been in B2C marketing for about 13 years. I have worked on trying to make sense of new and emerging technologies for the consumer for pretty much my whole career. I've done that in a number of different countries; first on the wireless side for Vodafone, and then more recently, four years at Yahoo!.

It was actually the four years at Yahoo! that got me absolutely intrigued by the Web 2.0 space when I ran all the go-to-market efforts for Yahoo! Answers, which became the world's largest Q&A site. That kind of made me truly fall in love with Web 2.0, and then the LinkedIn opportunity came along, which was the opportunity to live and breathe it every single day, so I took it. Now that I'm here, I'm responsible for marketing, public relations, and I also run the ad-sales business.

For those few that might not know, what is LinkedIn?

LinkedIn is a *professional* networking site. It uses many of the core technologies and capabilities of the social networks, but is exclusively for connecting professionals together, and through those connections, enabling them to accomplish tasks, get information about their market and their industry, do research, and ultimately get things done.

> *"Web 2.0 is the advent of the individual publisher and the advent of the group consumption and interpretation of media."*

I'm a member of LinkedIn and you and I are three degrees apart, so I know people, who know people, who know you. LinkedIn seems to center on the "six degrees from Kevin Bacon" idea, except everyone seems to be fewer than six degrees.

You're absolutely right. The whole premise of LinkedIn is based on that six degrees of separation, but it's geared exclusively towards, "What does that inter-connectedness of the professional community do for you? How can you use that to get things done?"

How would you and LinkedIn define Web 2.0?

I describe Web 2.0 as a fundamental course direction for the Internet. Let me explain what I mean by that.

Web 2.0 is the advent of the individual publisher and the advent of the group consumption and interpretation of media.

In regard to group consumption, I believe the way that we all used to consume media and the information coming at us was as a group. From my own experience, we as a family would all sit and my dad would read the newspaper or yell at the television about a particular news article. We would, as a family, as a group, then sort of process it, interpret it, and then derive meaning from it. But we'd do it as a group, and that's how we sort of had a lens on the world.

Then over the past 20 years, technology accelerated at an incredible rate, but people's available time reduced at an equally accelerated rate. Media consumption, up until the advent of Web 2.0, became a pretty solitary experience. You would read the newspaper alone, try to digest something; read something on your cell phone, you'd grab a clip on the Internet…but it was just *you*.

I see Web 2.0 as a course correction. The reason I don't believe that it is a fad is because it weaves the social fabric together again. It re-establishes the relationships we have in the offline world, puts them in the online world, and enables that group consumption to happen again. You now can consume and share things, and discuss them, interpret them, and ultimately get that lens on the world, and it's not just your own individual perceptions and observations anymore; it's back to the old way.

That's why I see it as a course correction for the Internet and why I don't see it going away. I don't see the whole advent of social networking as something we look back on in history and say, "That was interesting." I just don't think that will happen.

The thing that I've found particularly interesting about LinkedIn, though, and one of the main reasons I decided to jump in and really place everything I had behind it, was that this isn't any kind of relationship that you have. LinkedIn, for most members, is not a popularity contest. It's not a game. You don't connect to everybody you possibly can. The relationships that you form in the first-degree connections that you create are based on respect, based on a track record with someone, based on trust, or based on a working relationship. What we've learned from talking to our members a lot this year is that what they see is a true reflection of themselves and a true reflection of their own personal brand. So, the relationships that are formed are very important to people.

What I did one day when I first joined LinkedIn as a way to prove to people [working at LinkedIn] that the brand was important, was to ask, "With a

show of hands, let me see all the people who are not very good at golf."
Half the hands went up. Then I said, "Now give me a show of hands of all
the people who are prepared to admit that they are not very good at their
job here at LinkedIn."

No hands went up.

It matters hugely to people that they do well and that they are seen as doing
well in their chosen pursuit. LinkedIn's unique take on Web 2.0 and on
social networking is such that those relationships that are formed are a
reflection of you, and you need those relationships for life.

So you don't find that there are people trying to do "connection collection" on LinkedIn? Are there people who are just trying to get the highest number of connections?

It is very low. You do see them, and you may even receive requests from
them if you are a member. There are people out there to whom it is a game.

In fact, it worries me when I see that kind of behavior because they're not
helping themselves. The more people they connect to, the more people
who accept their invites, as opposed to saying "I don't know this person,"
and then the fabric of their particular network on LinkedIn is weakened a
little bit.

If you think about how you typically use LinkedIn, what happens most
often is that you're trying to find the right person in an industry or company to deal with. Whether it's because maybe you want to work with
them, you want to do a deal, you want to purchase something from them,
or something else, then you want an introduction to them. If the person
that you mutually "know" is a person that neither of you *really* knows, or
respects, then the fabric is weakened a little bit. You might get a referral,
but what, ultimately, does that referral really mean if it's someone who con-
nects just for the sake of it?

We encourage getting guidance on how and why you should connect to
certain people. That's also why we encourage people to only connect with
others that they really trust or with whom they've already got a track record
or a relationship. That's when the fabric of their network can stay strong.
When it's someone I've only connected with once, and it was six months
ago, I click the "Archive" or the "I Don't Know" button.

I don't know whether you realize this; when you say you don't know a person, then that goes against their account. If three people say they don't know a person, then the unknown person's account gets suspended. So, we take this really seriously; it's not just guidance and encouragement—we act on it. We don't like it when there is what we call "promiscuous linking." We don't like it and we take steps to stop it.

You mentioned that you worked with emerging technologies back at Yahoo! and such. Do you consider Web 2.0 a new thing?

I consider it a new technology that solves an age-old problem, which is maintaining and keeping alive human relationships that matter to you, in my view, towards a specific end. There have been multiple attempts to do it—like the Rolodex, the little black book, the SIM card, and those types of things. That is one of the age-old problems that Web 2.0 attempts to solve, but the technology that Web 2.0 uses to solve this problem is a new thing.

You've mentioned technology a couple of times. Are technologies such as AJAX, Adobe AIR, or Microsoft's Silverlight Web 2.0?

They're all just small components of it. In my opinion, those technologies help with the publishing component. We haven't talked a lot yet about the incredible phenomenon where people publish things about themselves, and that is a fundamental part of Web 2.0. Those technologies enable people to publish. One of the foundational components of Web 2.0 is extremely advanced database technology.

The fact that you and I are connected through you knowing people who know people who know me, and the fact that millions and millions of computations are being been done in a few seconds in order for the web page on LinkedIn to show our connection so that we can see and know how we fit together—all of that entails some pretty heavy lifting.

You mentioned foundational components of Web 2.0 such as people publishing. Are there other things you would say are foundational components? You mentioned social networking and relationships as well.

The social networking is one, the publishing component is two. Another one is the sharing aspect. It never really existed before. You could go into this mode of cutting and pasting URLs and saying, "Hey, look at this!" but it's not the same as being able to effortlessly share something with your whole network.

You look at this with any of the major media sites, *The New York Times* being a good example, and you'll see an article and about eight different ways that you can share it. You can Digg it, save it on del.icio.us, share it with your Facebook network, and soon there will even be a particularly interesting way of sharing with differ-

> *"There is this pent-up desire among everyday people to say, 'Hey, I'm a bit tired of being told what to think.'"*

ent subsets of your LinkedIn network. That's an interesting thing, too, because it goes back to one of the things I was saying earlier about group interpretation of media, of stimulus and information, and that's another foundational component of Web 2.0.

Anything else?

I will just touch on one thing, and it's kind of implicit in the self-expression piece. One of the things I've noticed ever since I started working in this space is that there is this pent-up desire among everyday people to say, "Hey, I'm a bit tired of being told what to think, of being shaped this way, and of reading newspapers that have a particular political bias or an agenda. I'm not stupid and I will decide for myself and I will publish my own stories, thank you very much."

I think that's one of the reasons why we've seen the blogging sites go crazy; you can self-express and you don't have to just sit there and be told what to read.

So then do you believe in the long run that things such as television news are in trouble?

Television is just one way to get something, so I'd like to break the question into two parts.

I think of the media and what the Web 2.0 people call "head content" as opposed to "tail content." Head content will always be incredibly important, you can have all of these millions of people publishing their own points of view, but there will always be a major role for well-qualified, well-written research; good objective analysis and coverage and that will always be important. That need, among people, I see as continuing to be very important.

Do I see it in the future being delivered via television all the time? No, I do not. Absolutely not. Look at the usage and the time spent; more and more demographics are spending more and more time on this interconnected web thing than they are watching a flat screen.

Can you define head content versus tail content?

My interpretation is that head content is produced by the great publishing houses: it's well-researched, it's done by trained and skilled people who know how to do that, and it's fairly general in its scope, i.e., the news of the world, that kind of thing. A television show that's being produced by qualified producers and writers for 6 million people.

> *"One of the interesting things…is the ability to mix and remix."*

Tail content is generally not well produced (example: I'm a producer now, too, and I have a little show called *The Santiago Show*) not well produced, not well edited, is highly specific, and it's for an incredibly niche audience. In my case, it's specifically the 11 people who love my son enough to watch clips of him on the Web. That is a very, very far-end example of tail content.

In looking at Web 2.0, what would you consider the important features? Is there any feature that rises above the rest?

We've covered a lot of the features of Web 2.0, but one of the interesting things that we haven't covered yet is the ability to mix and remix; however, I wouldn't say that it's everywhere yet.

There is a company called JumpCut that Yahoo! bought last year. They are one example of a site where you can tap into people's consciousness and their points of view by the little shows that they produce, whether in the form of a blog or a video. The other interesting thing is the ability to take that, modify it, and apply your own point of view to it, and "mash it up," and then republish it. Some of the big producers, even the big television networks, have reacted in varying ways to that, ranging from the extreme of, "Take that down or I'll fine you 100 millions dollars" to saying, "You know what? This is our future and we need to be comfortable with letting people do it."

Another example is that when I was at Yahoo!, we ran a project with Doritos, which was to invite kids with camcorders to make Doritos' next Super Bowl television commercial. We worked with Doritos to design a program, and then ran the online component for them. A bunch of basic Doritos digital assets were given to these young tail-content producers and we said, "Have at it! Make an ad about Doritos based on anything you want to make it on."

There were 1,100 commercials that were produced, six finalists had a great time, and in the end, the parent company of Doritos was so happy that they purchased two Super Bowl commercials at millions of bucks each and they aired two of these creations. This showed great courage on the part of Doritos, [which is] an old and established brand that has not grown up in the online world. They took and risk and it paid off in spades. So, the ability to edit, mix, and re-produce, is another interesting feature that we haven't talked about, and it's something people clearly want to do!

The fact that they got that number of entries is also indicative of the power of Web 2.0 sites.

Yeah. You have to remember that these were scripted, wardrobed, produced, filmed, and edited. It wasn't just a guy with a webcam pulling a funny face. A lot of work went into this. These were such savvy young people, that they then embarked on their own marketing

> *"Recently, we had more professionals joining [LinkedIn] than there are seconds in the day."*

campaigns using Web 2.0, to make sure that the community picked *their* ad to go on the Super Bowl. They would record themselves handing out coupons to say, "Vote for me, vote for me" and put that recording on YouTube. They'd be doing street-level viral marketing. They'd have that whole production put on YouTube, have their friends distribute that out, and therefore they were being very entrepreneurial, using all of the capabilities of Web 2.0 to win.

When people refer to mashups, it often is mentioned in the context of APIs or Web Services on a site. Is LinkedIn doing anything with APIs?

We have a fairly interesting perspective on that whole area. What we're increasingly focused on at LinkedIn is enabling people to make use of these professional networks that they've built up. We've spent the last three years making sure that people could connect and reconnect and re-establish their offline professional network *on*line. I think we've done a pretty good job of that; we're 17 million members as of now, and as of this month, we're growing at 1.1 million professionals every month. Recently, we had more professionals joining than there are seconds in the day, which is incredible!

That's been our past, but our future is very much about enabling you to make better, more effective use of your professional network, in more of your daily tasks. With that context in mind, we're doing a few things.

First, we're enabling people to access their LinkedIn network anywhere on the Web, and take action with it. Let me give you an example: On *Business Week*, you'll be able to read an article about a particular company, and then right there, you'll be able to access your LinkedIn network, find out who you know in that company or how many degrees away you are from someone you *want* to know in that company. You will then be able to take action on that article—whether you want to do a deal with them, work for them, research them, or whatever it might be. You can find a company insider on any article that's been written.

> "Web 2.0... [makes] that whole process a lot more precise."

That's an example of LinkedIn's API strategy being about giving you access to your network so that you can actually make use of it anywhere on the Web. That's very different from the Facebook approach, which requires people to build things on Facebook and the end user to be on Facebook exclusively. That's part of our API approach—being able to combine publishers' content with Web 2.0 sort of network of people technology that LinkedIn has.

The second part is that we will be doing the kind of Facebook approach in terms of having third-party application providers and publishers launch applications on LinkedIn, but again, we're 100 percent professional—that's all we do. We won't be letting just anybody launch things; we'll do so on a very selective basis.

We were recently talked about for Google's Open Social platform. Our role in that will be to partner with proven publishers and proven productivity application providers to use Open Social, use some of the LinkedIn APIs and to then build applications that millions of professionals can use on LinkedIn. The one that we demo is based on what your profile says about your profession, your position, and the industry you work in. It tells you the kind of events, conferences, and such that you should think about attending. It mashes that together with the knowledge about your network and tells you who else in your network is going to that event. It then tells you who's not in your first degree, but based on your profile and your second degree, interesting people who are going that you should reach out to while you're there.

So what it does is it mashes together a bunch of content about the conferences you plan to attend with a bunch of information from your network. The output will be a completely different conference-attendance experience. It won't be go to the web site, sign up, get on the plane, and go to the conference. Rather, it will be an entire sort of professional social event where you'll get so much more out of that conference than you would have without it.

This seems to be a way to enable people to get more value.

This is another way of sort of categorizing Web 2.0. Prior to this technology, what could you do? You could book the conference, but it would be a hit-and-miss thing. You'd *hope* to meet the right kinds of people. Maybe you would, maybe you wouldn't. If you did, it was a quick conversation that you didn't know would happen because you didn't know ahead of time that they'd be there.

What Web 2.0, and LinkedIn especially, does, is to make that whole process a lot more precise. It maps out for you, in black and white, what the professional environment looks like—who is where, who's connected to whom, and shows how you fit into that and how you can

> *"If you make a Web 2.0 consumer, or anybody, feel exposed, there will be a nasty backlash—quickly."*

make use of that. And it's all databased; and it introduces much more precision into going to something like a conference and getting a lot out of it.

This seems reliant upon people to put the information into the system for it to work.

Absolutely. But if you were a conference organizer, there is no reason why you *wouldn't* do this, either in the signup flow or in the email that you send out to the attendee. You would say, "Thank you for signing up. Would you like to notify your LinkedIn network that you'll be there?" You'd be crazy if you were a conference organization not to do that.

This raises the question of security and of privacy. If you are sharing information with others going to a conference, then how much information is going to be secure?

The answer is, the moment you do something that isn't transparent and doesn't give the user 100 percent choice, you'll get in trouble.

So then where do you think security stands in the industry today?

I think it is a much bigger issue than all the Web 2.0 proponents perhaps realized. We talked earlier about basic human emotions, and one of them is to express, but another one is to protect oneself. That's a raw thing.

Everyone got so wrapped up in this self-expression, and "The world's free," "The world's open," "Everything should be completely transparent." There was recently an assumption in the pure social-networking space that people would be okay with their online purchases being broadcast to lots and lots and lots of people they may or may not know.

I think perhaps this was too much too soon.

It's a great idea, if you give the consumer the choice; at certain times they'll say, "Yes, that's great! I will tell my friends I bought this book or this DVD." But if you make a Web 2.0 consumer, or anybody, feel exposed, there will be a nasty backlash—quickly.

You have to protect your users or they will leave.

That's another thing about Web 2.0; the switching costs are definitely higher than they used to be. Where you are is a function of the people that you're connected to, and if you get so annoyed with a particular provider or brand, it's quite a bit of work to go somewhere else, because you've got to persuade everyone else to come with you.

So the switching costs are higher, but you have to realize that people *will* do it if you don't protect their rights, privacy, and needs.

We've talked a lot about information. Do you believe that the Semantic Web is real and will it happen?

My tendency is to think that, yes, it will happen. I'll be honest in saying that I don't have as much understanding as I'd like, but I look at things like

TripAdvisor. I didn't intend to use it, but I found myself acting upon it. With Web 1.0, TripAdvisor would have been "Go to this hotel because we, the hotel owners, think it's great, and here's why." With Web 2.0, it would be, "Check me out at this hotel," "Check me out at the beach," "Check me out at the Fairmont in Maui."

Now, let's say Web 2.5 or Web 3.0—why TripAdvisor is compelling is, you truly get to find out and take action based on the perspectives, experiences, and content published by people. If you use TripAdvisor, you say, "Well, I'm interested in going to Santorini," but you don't consult your social network, necessarily. You certainly don't consult

> *"The way that you consume, ultimately the way that you publish, promote, and post is all going to change pretty dramatically."*

the hotel's web sites. TripAdvisor says, "Here are the people who've gone there; here are some non–hotel-approved pictures of the hotel. Here are the experiences and ratings and references from people who've been there." And, you find yourself acting on it. It's a super, super early example, but an interesting one. When the whole web behaves like Trip Advisor does, and maps together content, links and transactions between people, the process of discovery will take another quantum leap forward.

Then looking forward, what do you see as the next big wave or revolution on the Web?

Part of it is just going to be access to it. I've got my iPhone, I've got my Apple TV, and I'm consuming more and more Internet content on my 60-inch projection television. So the way that you consume, ultimately the way that you publish, promote, and post is all going to change pretty dramatically. All you have to do is look at the Japanese market to understand that. I worked there for a little bit, so I've got some firsthand experience with it. I think that's a big one.

Another change that is going to frighten some of the news providers quite a bit is that the way that information is distributed and shared is going to change dramatically. Some of that's going to be brought about by the social and professional networks. For example, consider what some of the big media providers could do with LinkedIn. What if they knew that you were there, on their page? What if they knew what you did? What if instead of the main headlines, you were given items related to the stuff that we know that you're interested in based on what you've told us about you, on what information you've put on your LinkedIn profile, and based on what the professionals in your first degree have been reading? What if it were even based on what professionals like you have been reading, even if they're not in your first relationship degree?

> *"There could be very unexpected and hard-to-imagine flows of money moving back and forth across the planet."*

Basically, the whole static structure of how information is presented could completely change, powered by this network of relationships that you have. It will be interesting to see how it goes, because it's hard to do. But the way that stuff gets programmed to you, whether it's a television or a computer screen, what you see will be completely a function of the relationships that you hold dear.

That seems very similar to some of the concepts with the Semantic Web.

Absolutely. It's so much more relevant.

Any other ideas you think are going to be revolutionary?

There's also this whole concept of what Web 2.0 and its evolution will do to our economy. We're seeing some pretty amazing things happen with micro-lending, for example. What the Internet does, and what Web 2.0 increasingly does, is enable you to find the most unlikely people and form some kind of connection with them based on some kind of business or personal goal.

Could you imagine if micro-lending became able to permeate—at least more than a few isolated examples of people winning, deservedly, Nobel Peace Prizes for it? Could I receive a business pitch from somebody in Somalia who needs to borrow $50 and will give back $75 in two years? Yeah, I could do that. Yeah, I could provide/distribute that money, and I could watch how the project is going and all those kinds of things.

It sounds kind of unlikely, but there are web sites springing up that are doing exactly that. There could be very unexpected and hard-to-imagine flows of money moving back and forth across the planet because of this stuff.

The world has gotten smaller as a result of the Internet.

Reed Hoffman is our chairman, and he's also an official lender on Kiva.org. That actually does let you lend to a specific entrepreneur in the developing world.

You look at some of these guys who've done fantastically well already, and they don't need to work. But they do things like this, not necessarily because they're looking to make a ton more money—because there comes a point when you've got

> *"We might be able to ultimately create a better business ethic in the world."*

enough—but they do it because they think this stuff is going to change the world for the better. When Reid looks at LinkedIn, he sees that if this thing keeps growing the way it's growing, it will be the professional directory, at least of the developed world, and there will be this transparency through the business world that will enable all kinds of things to happen, from increased productivity and information flow, to what he likes to describe as a better business ethic. If everything is transparent, and your accomplishments are up on LinkedIn, and affirmed and recommended by other people, then you can rightfully take claim for something that you did, and you can also be found for something that you did that was bad.

When Reid looks at the LinkedIn component of his life, he thinks that we might be able to ultimately create a better business ethic in the world; good people will be rewarded and bad people will be punished.

Thinking about the fact that he's obviously done very well already, he's associated with Kiva because he wants to use his pretty unique perspective on Web 2.0 to do some good in the developing world, too.

Does LinkedIn emphasize the negatives?

It absolutely doesn't emphasize negative, because it's a positive construct. You're out there promoting yourself, your own professional brand, you're helping other people in their professional tasks and challenges and that kind of thing. This may be because you're answering questions for them, or because you're referring them to other professionals who need that introduction.

But of course, let's suppose you're an ass; you don't have good ethics and you go out there on record on your LinkedIn profile saying that you did this or you did that. All kinds of other Web 2.0 activity could take place saying, "Look at his LinkedIn profile—look what he's claiming! What a liar!"

So it is social regulation

Exactly!

Is there anything you would like to add about Web 2.0?

It's a fascinating era that we're in.

Sound Bites

LinkedIn is likely one of the most referenced Web 2.0 sites due to its ability to connect people together and provide social interactions among them. While some of the conversation with Patrick swayed a little off the topic of Web 2.0, there were still a lot of insights to take away. A few of those insights follow.

- Web 2.0 re-establishes the relationships we have in the offline world, puts them in the online world, and enables that group consumption to again happen. Web 2.0 and social networking is not a fad.
- It matters hugely to people that they do well and that they are seen as doing well in their chosen pursuit. LinkedIn's unique take on Web 2.0 and unique take on social networking is such that those relationships that are formed are a reflection of you, and you need those relationships for life.
- I consider Web 2.0 a new technology that solves an age-old problem. The age-old problem is maintaining and keeping alive human relationships that matter to you.
- One of the reasons why blogging sites go crazy is that people can self-express and they don't have to just sit there and be told what to read.
- The moment you do something that isn't transparent and doesn't give the user 100 percent choice, you'll get in trouble.

- Sites must be really obvious, transparent, and front and center on the choices they give to a Web 2.0 user about what is broadcast about that user.
- The way that you consume on the Web, and ultimately the way that you publish, promote, and post is all going to change pretty dramatically. Additionally, the way that information is distributed and shared is going to change dramatically. This will be brought about by the social and professional networks.

Shaun Walker:
DotNetNuke

10

"Web 2.0…was sort of the best attempt at coming up with a nice buzzword for a whole lot of new technology and innovative ways that people are using the Internet."

—*Shaun Walker*

There are web sites; then there are platforms for building web sites. DotNetNuke (DNN) is both. It is a web site for a platform that can be used to build projects such as commercial web sites, portals, and vertical applications.

DNN is available for free. Additionally, it is licensed under an Open Source agreement that allows people to do whatever they want with the platform.

www.dotnetnuke.com

These characteristics have resulted in over 440,000 people using and support-ing DNN. As a framework, it has been downloaded millions of times. The end result is that it is the most successful Open Source community project on the Microsoft platform.

In 2006, DNN was formed into a company, DotNetNuke Corporation. This was to allow for a focus on the management of DNN and to provide a solid foundation for future support.

What is more important about DNN in regard to this book is the number of sites that have been created using DNN as their foundation. Such sites include YouthRoots.com, EarSinus.com, WineAustralia.com, Q107.com, Franchise .LittleCaesars.com, Shop.volleyball.com, SnapForSeniors.com, Nuvision.com, AirfareWatchdog.com, HomeFree.com, Can-Trace.org, NYSEData.com, WildVoice.com, NRL.com, TrueLawyers.com, and thousands more.

A Lot of the Players Will Need to Evolve with the Technology

Shaun Walker is the president and chief architect for DotNetNuke. He is the creator and continues to be its key spokesperson. Having been involved with DNN and having seen the sites that have evolved from the framework have given Shaun a number of interesting insights into Web 2.0 and more.

To start, can you tell us about yourself and about DotNetNuke?

I'm Shaun Walker, and I'm the president/xhief architect of DotNetNuke Corporation. I was the original creator of DNN, which was released December 24, 2002; so about five years ago now. It's an Open Source web application framework that runs on the Microsoft technology stack—SQL Server, Windows Server, and the .NET Framework, ASP.NET.

It's got two parts to it. You can use the web application framework for building web applications, and then it comes with a fully functional con-tent management system as part of the package, which allows you to basi-cally build your own web site very easily using a web browser.

Let's jump right in; how would you and DotNetNuke define Web 2.0?

I break Web 2.0 down into a number of different quadrants in terms of functionality and user expectations. One aspect of that is user-generated content, where the public is now interested in contributing content to the Internet as a public good, which is different than in the past when consumers were just consuming content. They want more ability to interact, more ability to express their opinions, and that all becomes part of a greater repository of knowledge in the web sphere.

I also see social networking as another important part of Web 2.0, which I guess somewhat ties into user-generated content. It also ties into the association of different users to one another in the web environment.

We have the big players like MySpace and Facebook, which have really pioneered this area, but there are a lot of smaller players that are also tapping into the social networking

> *"It's becoming more difficult to find what you're looking for."*

aspect to basically allow people to interact over the Web. It's becoming a new communication media, much like the telephone was one of the originals, and then it moved on to email, then IM, and now interacting through web sites. It's becoming very common.

Another part of Web 2.0 would be a search and syndication of content. Because there's so much more content out there, and it's becoming more difficult to find what you're looking for, you need more advanced search capabilities, and syndication of content—so sharing content between sites is becoming more of an issue and is something that Web 2.0 tries to address. Some of that is in regards to tagging and taxonomy.

The last thing I see is the rich user interface, which really kind of exploded onto the scene with the adoption of AJAX technology, Flash, and Microsoft Silverlight (although that really hasn't proven itself yet)—I mean that rich user experience where users are expecting to interact with web applications, similarly to the way they did in the past with desktop applications.

Do you have features built into DNN to support the Web 2.0 features you just mentioned?

In terms of the DNN framework, obviously its fundamental benefit is in the area of user-generated content. It allows users to build their own web sites, but it also has a modular architecture where you can plug in features such as discussion forums, blogs, and wikis—all of which revolved around user-generated content.

As far as social networking is concerned, DNN can be used to build a large community web site. Each user can have an account on your site, and they can associate with one another through various modules such as the ones I mentioned earlier, such as forums, wikis, and blogs. Going forward, we plan to add a lot more social networking functionality to the platform as part of the Open Source product, so that module developers can use the social networking APIs to build more advanced functionality for consumers.

Of the things you've mentioned, what would you consider the most important feature of Web 2.0?

That's a tough question, because I think that all of these things are intricately linked together. I don't think that there's one feature that's more important. Possibly from a media perspective, in terms of consumer acceptance of Web 2.0, I would say that social networking has got the most hype behind it. From a software-developer perspective, AJAX and Flash have the most hype around them. And I guess from a busines-model perspective, search, syndication, and content management would be the leaders. They all fit together.

Flipping the question around, what do you consider the most misunderstood thing about Web 2.0?

I think that the term itself is the most misunderstood thing, because it can mean so many things to so many people.

You mentioned many of the aspects of Web 2.0 in the product you have created. What benefits do you see from using Web 2.0 technology?

> *"To categorize things as Web 1.0, 2.0, 3.0…it's pretty difficult."*

In the area of the rich user-interface experience, traditionally—especially in ASP.net applications—there were typically a lot of post-backs, page refreshes that would occur whenever a user would take an action within your application. That would lead to a poor user experience, and people would be left waiting, especially if network latency was involved in the operation. So, consumers could be waiting a long time to get some response out of the server. With new technologies, like AJAX, it really improves the user experience so that they're not constantly waiting for things to happen.

Is Web 2.0 AJAX?

AJAX is just one of the building blocks of Web 2.0. You couldn't exactly just point to AJAX as a technology comprising all of what Web 2.0 has to offer. It becomes part of the fundamental infrastructure behind Web 2.0, but there are a lot of ideas around 2.0, which are more network-oriented, human-oriented, rather than just pointing at a specific piece of technology.

Do you see any issues with Web 2.0 or with where Web 2.0 is headed?

There are problems in "versioning" anything. To categorize things as Web 1.0, 2.0, 3.0…it's pretty difficult unless there are pretty objective criteria to measure things by.

The Web 2.0 technology was sort of the best attempt at coming up with a nice buzzword for a whole lot of new technology and innovative ways that people are using the Internet.

> *"[It would've been] hard to imagine five years ago that we were going to be here today."*

There's no doubt that technology is going to continue to advance, so does that mean that it's going to be called 3.0 at some point? I hope not, but I know that as consumers we need simple ways to categorize major advancements in technology.

Ironically, Web 3.0 is a term being used in reference to the Semantic Web. Do you think the Semantic Web really is Web 3.0 and that there is validity to it?

At this point I think that it's too early to tell. The Semantic Web as a concept might represent a whole new paradigm shift, but there are going to be a lot of other supporting infrastructure, technology, and ideas that have yet to emerge as part of the Semantic Web, so I don't think it is well-defined enough yet to call the Semantic Web on its own Web 3.0.

When it comes to Web 2.0, what do you think is the coolest thing you've seen done or that you've done with it?

One of the things I find really interesting is the mainstream consumer adoption of web technology, which is represented by some of the larger players, like Facebook and MySpace. Just the sheer number of people that use those web applications on a daily basis is something that I never would have imagined five years ago.

The traditional search engines of the past have a large number of users that were constantly using those applications more as a utility to find information. But some of these social networks—people are using them as a day-to-day communication mechanism to keep in touch with friends and family. [It would've been] hard to imagine five years ago that we were going to be here today.

It's interesting—I actually wrote an application about five years ago using classic ASP, and it had many of the same characteristics that Facebook offers today. It was completely user-driven, and it was designed for me to keep in touch with members of my family. At the time, there were so many infrastructure constraints around technology that there was no way you could have scaled something like that to the extent that some of these Web 2.0 companies have been able to do.

Scale was a problem back then. Do you see it as a problem today or something that will be a problem going forward?

> *"It's becoming part of your every day life to be connected all the time."*

When you look at the numbers—the millions and millions of users that are using some of these services seem like a lot. However, if you look at the grand scale of things, there is still a lot of untapped potential in the world. There are a lot of countries that still don't have very good Internet access, so as more and more consumers start coming online and using these services, I think scale is going to be a constant concern. The fact that we've come this far in terms of being able to scale it and provide decent performance means that we'll be able to continue to adapt to the added load in the future.

It is an interesting example to look at social networking sites like MySpace and Facebook and realize that anyone using the Web is a potential users, yet only a small percentage of the overall Internet population is using them today.

Those sites get all of the hype because they cater to a certain demographic, which gets most of the marketing messaging directed at them. But there are a ton of other social networking sites that cater to different demographics today, which are probably not represented in those types of surveys.

Adobe AIR and Google Gears are examples of applications trying to take online applications back offline. What is your thought on this?

Well, there are certainly some advantages to having offline applications, although, with the availability of broadband, at least in North America and I guess in most of Europe, it's becoming part of your every day life to be connected all the time.

There are advantages to having some things offline. Certainly you could take advantage of the computing power of the individual machines when you take things offline and work in a desktop environment. I'm not sure there's a huge advantage there; it's an advantage for a particular demographic of users that need that offline functionality.

To use Facebook offline—is that something that people are going to want to do? I don't think Facebook was really built for an offline experience. I have a hard time imaging how you would integrate that. Along with offline come a lot of other technical problems.

Drilling into that, can you give examples of other technical problems?

Synchronization of data would be the big one. So, if you're working with an application offline, and then you hook up online, then your offline application has to synchronize with the online application. That has a lot of technical challenges around it.

Talking online versus offline, do you see a day when connectivity won't be a problem, or when there will always be connectivity available?

Yes, I think that's already becoming a reality in some areas today. I actually live in Canada, and we have very good infrastructure in Canada, and I'm connected all the time. It's become part of my life.

Email everywhere! Switching topics, Software as a Service (SaaS) or Software plus Services: fact or fiction?

They're definitely fact; it's a business model, and a business model that's become more viable because of the fact that technology has become a lot more scalable now. Even five years ago we were talking about ASPs (Application Service Providers) and it's not so much different than what a SaaS provider would be today, although there were some inherent problems with the ASP model.

> "There's going to continue to be a need for desktop applications."

It was difficult for those companies providing those services to scale. Definitely SaaS is real. A lot of people are actually using the DNN applications for SaaS implementations. Basically they would use our base platform and build a very specific vertical application on top of it. Then they would host that application and have customers pay them a monthly fee in order to use that application, and that's a good example of SaaS.

Do you think that desktop applications are going to go away?

No, I think there's going to continue to be a need for desktop applications. The computer power of desktop machines is not plateauing any time soon. It is continuing to advance, and the applications that are built on desktops are continuing to get more and more rich in terms of their functionality. A lot of that functionality can't be duplicated in a web environment.

There will continue to be a need for desktop applications. Perhaps for certain types of applications which are less demanding on system resources, some of those will shift more towards the Web. You'll still have a hybrid model where there will be plenty of desktop offerings in addition to web offerings.

If Web 2.0 is the big thing today, then what do you see as the next big thing or revolution on the Web?

One thing that's for certain is that a lot of the players that are large today in terms of the Web 2.0 world will need to evolve with technology. I have a hard time imagining some of the large social network sites like MySpace or Facebook continuing to have the same amount of hype around them in the coming years.

Basically there will be a new social network every year that comes along with some new, innovative feature. Because there's no lock-in to a lot of these social networks, consumers are free to move to the next flavor of the year—and they will do so. It'll be interesting to see how some of the large social networks will adapt to change.

What would you like to see as the next big thing?

I think that there will be more availability of devices that will have the computational power behind them to provide a decent user experience. The cell phones that we have today have come a long way, compared to where they were four years ago, but they still have a ways to go before they provide the kind of power that's necessary to run real applications.

I see that definitely happening. Cell phones are just a micro-example, but there will be a proliferation of other devices, some with small canvas sizes like we have today and others with rich, large canvas sizes.

> *"I just see the Internet becoming more and more an embedded part of people's lives."*

Some of the concepts we've seen lately, like tablet and tabletop user interfaces, will definitely play a part.

And probably even more accessibility to the Internet through kiosks and other mechanisms. For a long time we've had coffee shops providing access to connected PCs, but I see more devices becoming available, connected to the Internet so that you can get online at anytime so that you can interact with your peers as well as manage your life through the Internet.

I just see the Internet becoming more and more an embedded part of people's lives so that it's basically a fundamental rather than an optional thing.

Sound Bites

More than just a web site, DotNetNuke is also a platform. DNN's Shaun Walker provided a number of interesting insights from his experience with DNN and the DNN community. Some of the key insights follow.

- Web 2.0 can be broken down into a number of different quadrants in terms of functionality and user expectations: user-generated content, social networking, a search and syndication of contents, and the rich user interface, which really exploded onto the scene with the adoption of AJAX technology, Flash, and Microsoft Silverlight.

- In terms of consumer acceptance of Web 2.0, social networking has the most hype behind it. From a software-developer perspective, AJAX and Flash have the most hype around them. And from a business-model perspective, search, syndication, and content management would be the leaders. They all fit together.
- There are a lot of ideas around Web 2.0 that are more network-oriented, human-oriented, rather than just pointing at a specific piece of technology.
- The Web 2.0 technology was the best attempt at coming up with a nice buzzword for a whole lot of new technology and innovative ways that people are using the Internet.
- When you look at the numbers, the millions and millions of users that are using some of these services seem like a lot. If you look at the grand scale of things, there is still a lot of untapped potential in the world.
- There's going to continue to be a need for desktop applications.
- A lot of the players that are large today in terms of the Web 2.0 world will need to evolve with technology.

Biz Stone:
Twitter

*"The Web is increasingly a social environment and...
people are using it to communicate with one another, like
they've always done—but now in such an open way."*

—*Biz Stone*

What are you doing right now? What are your friends, co-workers, family members, or the guy down the street doing? If they belong to Twitter and are posting, you can likely find out.

Twitter is a worldwide community where members send updates about what they are doing or thinking at any given moment. These updates are sent via text messages from the Twitter site or from a mobile phone, or via instant messages (IM) from Jabber, AIM, LiveJournal, or Gtalk.

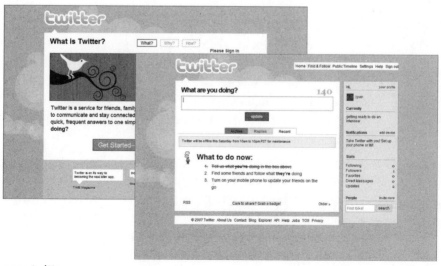

www.twitter.com

As a member, you can post short (140-character) messages about what you are doing at any given time. All the other members can be doing this too. Of course, if you try to read all of these messages, it could get very noisy. However, if you subscribe to people that are interesting to you, then you can keep up with what they are doing by seeing what they post to their Twitter feeds.

Of course, you don't actually have to go online to use Twitter. You can send text messages from your phone as well as receive updates from people you are following on Twitter. In addition to the mobile-phone support, there are also desktop applications you can use to send and receive information from Twitter.

Twitter is often described as a micro-blog because of its short-message format and its ability to follow what a person is doing. Regardless of how you describe Twitter, it has struck a chord with the worldwide community.

People Find Value in Openness

Biz Stone is the creator of a number of web sites. In addition to co-founding Twitter, he also helped with sites such as Xanga, Blogger, Odeo, and Obvious. He has shared his insights offline as well in books such as *Blogging: Genius Strategies for Instant Web Content* and *Who Let the Blogs Out?: A Hyperconnected Peak at the World of Weblogs*.

Can you tell a little bit about yourself and about Twitter?

I started a web service called Xanga.com. It's a Web log-in community that I started with some friends in New York in about 1999, and it's still pretty popular. It was kind of the predecessor to MySpace, except much more focused on blogging and catching up with your friends. I stayed there for a couple of years, then left and started doing a lot of thinking about social media and blogging, and wrote a couple of books.

In 2003, just after Google acquired Blogger, Evan Williams sent me an email asking if I'd be interested in joining the Blogger team to help Google. I accepted, and worked there for about two years before leaving in order to continue working with Evan Williams, because he wanted to try starting another company called Odeo, a podcasting company. It was while I was at Odeo that we created Twitter sort of as a side project.

Basically, Twitter was a simple idea that my friend, Jack Dorsey, had. He loved web-blogging, but he wondered if there was a very, very simple kind of stripped-down way to do that. He was kind of inspired by the concept of the status message, the instant-message application, kind of like AIM. The idea that you would say something very simple like, "I'm not feeling very well today," or, "Unavailable," or, "In a meeting," and that all your friends would know that and know that's what you are doing.

So he thought, what if you could merge that; take that simple concept of status, and make it much more social? He brought up the idea to Evan and me. We had been mulling over ways to merge SMS technology with the Web, and this seemed like the perfect thing. If you wanted to update your status, you could do that with a simple SMS; likewise, you'd get an SMS if one of your friends changed their status.

> *"Suddenly, you're having a more meaningful [event] occur because of a seemingly valueless update. It's kind of like…turning lead into gold."*

All of that together sounded like a compelling little project to spend some time on.

So Jack and I went off in a little corner and built it (while still at Odeo) in two weeks' time, just to have a prototype to share with the rest of the team. Everyone was compelled by it, they thought it was fun, and they really wanted to use it.

What ended up happening then was that we formed a new company called Obvious. Obvious acquired Odeo and Twitter, and then separated them into two entities. We sold Odeo and its assets to another company. We were therefore able to focus all of our efforts on Twitter. We then spun Twitter out into its own company called Twitter, Inc.

Twitter is now growing based all around this concept of "What are you doing?" to which you answer—in 140 characters or less. This goes out to your friends so you all stay connected.

Do Twitter messages go to only your friends, or to everyone in the world on Twitter?

It's basically up to you when you're using the service; when you sign up for Twitter, you create your profile and there is a check box that says, "I want to protect my posts or my updates," or, "Don't check it if you don't want to protect." Around 90 percent of the people do not check that box; they want that public.

That's something that is not entirely unique to Twitter; it's something that's happening in blogging, MySpace, Facebook, etc. People are increasingly okay with others knowing what they're up to and hearing what they're saying. There seems to be a lot of value in keeping that openness out there on the Web because you never know when someone is going to come along and say, "I really like what you're doing; how'd you like to work for my company?" or, "I really like your posts; how'd you like to hang out?"— anything like that.

> *"I would define what is being called Web 2.0 as the public acceptance of the fact that the Web is a highly social utility."*

It's something I've been calling "social alchemy" because you put out these mundane updates that you're shopping for a sandwich in Berkeley, and that seems of little value until it happens to fall into the SMS of someone else's phone. A friend of yours happens to be in Berkeley and says, "Oh, I'm in Berkeley, too! Let's get a sandwich together." Suddenly you're having a more meaningful conversation or meaningful events occur because of a seemingly valueless update. It's kind of like the idea of turning lead into gold.

Do you end up having people worrying about publishing something to the public, or having them come to you after they have done so to ask how they can secure their feed?

We don't get a lot of people coming back to us. People may, on their own. I still maintain that about 90 percent of the Twitter population keeps their feeds open—that's not changing. But people do sort of find their own way to determine what they do/don't want to share.

Of course, the same kind of thing happened with Xanga, Blogger, and others. You're happily Twittering along and you may forget yourself because all of this stuff has been updated by Google for the past year, and everything is available.

It would occasionally freak people out when they would say, "My teacher read my Xanga page! I can't believe it—he's such a jerk!" It's just a page on the Internet; you can't really get too mad that he went and read it! It's funny how they feel that it's more of a "between them and their friends" and that others shouldn't be snooping around. But, in most cases, people find value in the openness.

How would you and Twitter define Web 2.0?

That is a good question. I think people have very specific definitions of elements that go into it.

For me it's this big, growing realization that the Web is increasingly a social environment and that people are using it to communicate with one another, like they've always done—but now in such an open way. All of these tools that you see emerging, that you would associate with Web 2.0, like tagging, where you can easily categorize a piece of media, you do all of this in an effort to express yourself and to share your thoughts with other people—that is, communication and self-expression. I guess I would define what is being called Web 2.0 as the public acceptance of the fact that the Web is a highly social utility.

Technology helps make this happen. Are technologies such as AJAX, Adobe AIR, or Microsoft Silverlight Web 2.0?

A lot of what people talk about when they talk about Web 2.0 is openness; I think the tools mentioned are tools that are freely shared, or the codes and ideas behind them are freely shared among developers, as well as being publicly available for free on the Web. The idea is that the more open these technologies and services are, the better.

I don't think there's a fine line where you could show me a flash-card deck of different things and ask me, "Is it Web 2.0, or not?" It's more like a gradient where I'd say, "That's pretty much Web 1.0…that one's more 2.0, etc." It's just easy to say something's Web 2.0 because people can understand what you're talking about.

> *"The Web is a very highly social utility. If we create more open systems, it will be even more social."*

Is there a feature or something that stands out more so than others in regard to Web 2.0?

I think it would be the open factor; the idea that the more you can open up your platform, your idea, or your concept to invite other people to build on top of it, and work within it, the better. It all goes hand in hand, realizing the Web is a very highly social utility. If we create more open systems, it will be even more social. I would guess that this openness in general is really the broadest definition.

Is there anything you would say that people are misunderstanding about Web 2.0?

> *"We see 20 times the traffic through our API than we do the Web."*

For most people there is no Web 2.0; there is just the Web. So, I guess you're talking about a certain set of builders and people who work on the Web, who've decided to lump together a bunch of different aspects, trends, and technologies and say that they are Web 2.0 if they have these elements in them. I can't really think of something where there's a misconception right now.

It sounds like you are indicating that the term is a bit misunderstood.

Yes. It's easy to call something Web 2.0, but when you have to dig in and define the specifics of it, things get kind of murky.

Is there anything that you have seen or that you have done at Twitter that you would say is really cool?

The fact that we built an API very early on with Twitter is one of those things that people might associate with Web 2.0 and with openness. You have to provide an Application Programming Interface so that other developers can build on your platform, and we did that because we thought "This will be great; this is a simple service and it's easy to make an API; at the very least we'll garner some good will from other developers and other like-minded people."

At the same time, we had no idea that the API would end up being a very central part of our strategy and our growth. We see 20 times the traffic through our API than we do the Web. So, suddenly, this thing that we thought would be just a good idea to have becomes a "must-have." That's sort of a key driver of Twitter.

Out of curiosity, what is the business model?

Our focus right now is on reliability and user experience. Before we go to the revenue model we have to have a compelling product and service. If we focus all of our time designing the revenue model in the beginning, then we wouldn't be as concerned about the product. It would kind of be like putting the cart before the horse.

Twitter's business model is going to be pretty diversified, because of the fact that we as a company are on pretty diverse platforms. We're on SMS, we're on the Web, we're on instant message, and the mobile web. We want to continue to be as agnostic as possible with regard to how people interact with Twitter. That means adding email support—emailing in and out of Twitter. It means continued cooperation with other big social networks, like Facebook and others where Twitter can come in and out. The business model is going to be something that is as simple as the concept of Twitter.

Do you recommend to other people to focus on the core site and concept and not worry about the business model up front?

If you're talking about new technologies, new ideas, especially on the Web, then I think it makes sense to really work on the concept, the product itself, and the reliability. If you're talking about going out and starting a bookstore and buying a building and things like that, there are some proven models and you know exactly what you want to do, within reason if you're experimenting and trying to think.

If you've invented a communication technology that you're not even sure people are going to want, use, or need, then you first need to focus on the product. Then when it gets popular, you need to focus on reliability so that you don't base a whole revenue model on something that isn't going to work. If someone is

> "If someone is talking about Web 3.0, it means they're talking too much and they're not working on something."

going down an innovative technology path, I recommend that they make sure they have a compelling product before they invest resources into the revenue model.

Stepping back to the Web topics, what are your thoughts on Web 3.0, the Semantic Web?

If your head is down and you're really working on Web stuff and you hear people talking about Web 2.0, then Web 3.0, you do see a lot of sort of eye-rolling, because at a certain point, if someone is talking about Web 3.0, it means they're talking too much and they're not working on something. They've talked themselves all the way into a new term. So, I'm not entirely familiar with what people are associating with Web 3.0; I'm still catching up with what's supposed to be Web 2.0 and what gets added into that and what doesn't.

Some of the people talking the loudest are associated with publishing.

At least they're attempting to explain it to a bunch of people who aren't as familiar with it. It certainly helps to frame it. People are used to Microsoft Word version one as opposed to Microsoft Word version three....

> *"We're seeing a lot of fun, small, desktop applications that are interacting with the Web."*

The idea of clumping together all the iterations that are taking place over four years—design trends, new innovations—you clump them all together and say, "This is the next version." Even if it happened gradually, it helps to explain to people who weren't paying attention every single new turn in the road to say, "Here's where I'm marking Web 2.0 and Web 3.0, so that you can understand that there have been major accomplishments. It's not that I'm against the concept of doing it; I'm just not maybe zoomed out enough to think about what is being called Web 3.0.

Software as a Service (SaaS) and Software plus Services (S+S) are being talked about a lot. Do you think these are fact or fiction? Do you see things moving off the desktop?

I think everything is moving towards this idea that you can add a lot of value to the Web. You mentioned before, Adobe AIR; now we're seeing a lot of fun, small, desktop applications that are interacting with the Web, so I'm not going to say that desktop applications are going to completely go away. There's a desktop application that interacts with Twitter, and people love it.

It's just a growing awareness of, "We can connect, we can make this software a lot more social, and we can bring a lot more value to it if we connect it to the Web and thereby connect it to other people."

Do you see connectivity being pervasive—i.e., always available?

That's the hope; that's kind of why Twitter is on mobile. We started off from the very beginning on mobile. The idea of connectivity with the Web is not something that should have to be tied to the PC. We've shown with Twitter that just through simple SMS you can connect similarly as you would on the Web.

That means that we really are bringing the social connectivity web style to every mobile, SMS-capable phone in the world, which is very, very simple technology. The hope is that anywhere there is a simple glimmer of connectible technology, we'll tie it to simple messaging.

What do you see as the next big change or revolution on the Web?

I guess what I just mentioned with the mobile combined with APIs and openness is also increasingly important to companies. Right now, Twitter is mobile over SMS. You never have to go to the web site. We also have an API, which means you can write an application that works over SMS (Twitter).

It's possible that we may see in the future something like farmers in India interacting with an application over SMS that helps them get a better price for grain, or something like this. They wouldn't be able to do this otherwise because they wouldn't have access to a PC or a Web connection.

We've seen it already—someone wrote us and told us about a simple SMS application where you send a text like, "In 15 minutes call Mom;" and in 15 minutes you get an SMS back that says, "Call Mom." That's an application written on our API that works over SMS. So now it's possible to do computing over SMS. I think that concept is sound and I'd love to see that flourish around the world and just see what people can do with it.

Sound Bites

Twitter proves that simple concepts can result in big communities. There are a lot more insights that can be gained from Twitter's Biz Stone. Several notable observations follow:

- For most people there is no Web 2.0; there is just the Web.

- Around 90 percent of the people do not check the privacy box on Twitter. They want their posts public. That's something that is not entirely unique to Twitter; it's something that's happening in blogging, MySpace, Facebook, etc. People are increasingly okay with others knowing what they're up to and hearing what they're saying. There seems to be a lot of value in keeping that openness.
- Web 2.0 is this big, growing realization that the Web is increasingly a social environment and that people are using it to communicate with one another, like they've always done—but now in such an open way.
- If you look at a flash-card deck of different things and ask, "Is it Web 2.0, or not?" it's more like a gradient where you see things as, "That's pretty much Web1.0...that one's more 2.0, etc." It's just easy to say something's Web 2.0 because people can understand what you're talking about.
- The more you can open up your platform, your idea, or your concept to invite other people to build on top of it, and work within it, the better.
- You have to provide an Application Programming Interface so that other developers can build on your platform.
- If you're talking about new technologies or a new idea, especially on the Web, then it makes sense to really work on the concept, the product itself, and the reliability first.
- SaaS is just a growing awareness of, "We can connect, we can make this software a lot more social, and we can bring a lot more value to it if we connect it to the Web and thereby connect it to other people."

Seth Sternberg:
Meebo

12

"If you don't [innovate], then you'll lose market share and you'll wish you did."

—*Seth Sternberg*

Instant messaging (IM) has become a part of our society, and for many, a primary means of communicating. Like many types of software, there are many different companies that provide IM solutions. This includes AOL's AIM, Yahoo!'s IM, Google Talk, and even Microsoft's MSN IM. Of course, not all IM networks connect easily with others. Additionally, each IM network has its own desktop to use.

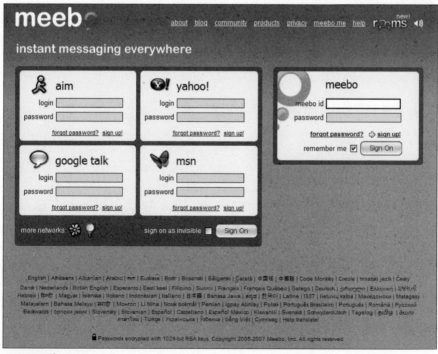

www.meebo.com

Meebo changed instant messaging by doing two key things. First, it provides a single interface that can be used to connect to all of the different IM networks. Second, and more important, Meebo removes the need to install software on your machine. Instead, you end up with the ability to access your IM networks via a web browser.

In terms of social interaction and Web 2.0, Meebo takes social networking to a whole new level. Six million unique people sign into Meebo every 30 days and the average person spends two and a half hours per day on Meebo. When you do the math, you realize that about 250 years of time is spent with Meebo every day. That is a lot of social interaction!

Along with Elaine Wherry and Sandy Jen, Seth Sternberg was one of Meebo's three cofounders. He was an undergrad at Yale before working with IBM. He then attended Stanford business school. A few weeks into his second year at Stamford, he left to work full-time at Meebo. The result of the work of these three heroes is a social network of millions of people.

I Don't Think There is Anything Right or Wrong About Web 2.0

Meebo is to instant messaging what programs like Hotmail and Gmail are to email. They bring the ability to socially interact with anyone else in the world with the only requirements being a browser and an IM handle. With growth from start-up to over a million users in the matter of about a dozen months, Meebo has shown the power of Web 2.0 and the community.

Can you tell me a little bit about Meebo?

There are three of us that started Meebo: Elaine, Sandy, and me. Elaine is the front-end tech guru, so she is like the AJAX person. Sandy is the back-end, "straight C, I can make it move across servers really, really fast" person. And then me. I'm the business guy.

> *"Now we have six million unique people who sign into Meebo every 30 days."*

The three of us worked on two projects before the Meebo that we released to the public. This is the third one we worked on, and the first we actually released. We put it into the public in September of 2005 and it got traffic very fast. Two bloggers wrote on it. That is how we got it out into the public. We then raised an Angel [financing] around a month after we launched. That was because we needed some help paying for the servers and stuff because we were getting a lot of traffic.

And then two months after that, so three months total, we raised a Series A. We recognized that we needed to add people to the team because we couldn't handle the traffic ourselves. Sandy was keeping servers alive rather than coding new features.

That is the quickie background.

Now we have six million unique people who sign into Meebo every 30 days. The average person spends two and a half hours with us per day. Most log into Meebo about twice a day. Not just office use and school use, but home use as well.

So is that about 15 million hours?

In term of years, daily we do about 250 years every day. And that is served up to our users. They move about 140 million messages a day.

We recently did this thing called Meebo Rooms. That creates a chat room that can live anywhere on the Web. It has very rich media associated with it. Sony is using it. Jive Records, a part of Sony, is using it when they launch new albums with an artist. If you go to CBS's site for *Jericho*, www.cbs.com/jericho, they use it for chat. The fans can take those chat rooms and put them on their MySpace pages. So, one chat room spreads across the Web. They serve over 16 million unique people monthly.

So these are embeddable chat rooms?

Yes, embeddable chat rooms that are media-rich. You can use them at Meebo privately, or you can use it outside of Meebo.

The whole goal of Meebo is that IM and the Web can be so much more than IM and software.

From your perspective, what is Web 2.0?

I think that at a very broad level, it is the interactive Web. There are a couple of really neat technologies that came out along with concepts that made the Web overall more attractive to people. You can break it down into certain buckets. One bucket is the whole AJAX thing. That allowed people to create much more application-like experiences on the Web, so things like Meebo and Writely are really good examples of that. Writely did a word processor on the Web and Meebo did instant messaging on the Web. Before AJAX, that would be much harder to do in a way that users would like the experience.

> *"Empowering the individual voice...let[s] any given individual become a publisher."*

That is one piece. Another piece is empowering the individual voice so that blogs, YouTube, Flickr let any given individual become a publisher. Not only does it make them a publisher, but it lets them become a publisher who actually has a reasonable chance of being found.

A lot of this had to do with the way that search evolved. For example, on YouTube, there are not that many videos on airplanes, but if you happen to have a quality video on airplanes, people are more likely to watch it. If you look at how blog searches are done on Technorati, you see that it is chronological. Right? It can also be done on relevance, but its default is chronological. So if you are a person who wrote a blog on SR22, then they will find you. So that is empowering individual publishing and giving it a reasonable shot of being found.

Another part of it, like another subdomain, so to speak, is the whole open concept such as open APIs. I will build my service in such a way from a business-model point of view and a technical point of view that I let other people integrate with me and I let others take my stuff and integrate it with their stuff. It is kind of a recognition that any given company is good at one thing, but not three things.

I'm sure I'm missing a couple of categories. Another area you should consider is the whole monetizing of things. In "Web 1.0" from a chronological perspective, it was very unclear as to how you could monetize the Web. There was not an efficient system to do so. In Web 2.0 there is. Advertising on the Web is now very, very efficient; an efficient, liquid market. It is much easier, if you have a site with a lot of traffic to make money on that. And so, that is another key element because that enables a lot of the investment that is going into this stuff these days.

Going after advertising isn't something the average site developer or creator necessarily does. Do you see other means of monetizing Web 2.0?

I would challenge that a little bit because I think that advertising is so liquid and so efficient that anyone can put it on a site now. It takes about five minutes on Google, and you can have Google advertising on your site. If you don't want to go to Google, then you can go to DoubleClick, which I guess Google just bought. Or, you can go to Advertising.com, which AOL owns, or you can go to aQuantive, which Microsoft now owns.

The point is, there are places that any individual can go to get ads on their site and to make some amount of money on their site. The thing is, to make significant money in advertising, you need either a very large size or a very directed web site. Both of those ways will do it; either high volume, low CPM, or low volume, high CPM.

> *"To make significant money in advertising, you need either a very large size or a very directed web site."*

The placing of ads or ad words on a site is easy. This makes it a low CPM and thus generally not enough of a revenue generator by itself. Additional information or characteristics are needed.

Oh, yeah. When people use the term "advertising"—that is a very broad statement. It is like, advertising—how targeted is it? How integrated into the product is it? Is it video? Is it text? Is it banners? The concept of advertising is so broad in the Web. I think there are a lot of people saying there has to be this advertising fatigue thing, but I don't think that's the case at all. Maybe there is a lot of advertising fatigue around a standard banner ad, but there's not going to be advertising fatigue around from banner to video to product placement to integration with product. It is much deeper than that.

I think there are other ways to monetize. One is clearly premium services. If you give something to your users that is above and beyond what they expect, then that is fantastic and users will love that and they may be willing to pay you for that.

Another clear way to monetize is to forget the whole consumer space; there are enterprises out there that will pay you for enterprise web sites. There is a big movement right now toward bringing Web 2.0 technologies to the enterprise. I think that is another way to monetize a web site that monetizes the whole Web 2.0 application thing.

Is this something Meebo is doing? It seems that Meebo is a great service that enterprises would like, especially if you could lock it into an enterprise and secure it.

> "There is a big movement right now toward bringing Web 2.0 technologies to the enterprise."

We are really focused on consumers. Something we learned early on is that you are going to build a very different kind of organization if you are going after the enterprise. Service and support are a much bigger part of it. Enterprise sales is a bigger piece of it. Even the features you do, like security, is a different kind of security for an enterprise than for consumers. It is just a different kind of company.

You made a comment about the open APIs. Open concept, open APIs versus Open Source. How important is Open Source in a Web 2.0 World?

Open Source has been really, really, really good for Meebo. A lot of our code base is open source. Everything from the way we access the IM network, which is based on GAIM, to our web servers, which are lighttpd—an Open Source web server. We probably spent next to nothing on software and some money on hardware. We either coded it ourselves, or it was available in Open Source. The other great thing about Open Source is that you can then go in there and fiddle with the code to make it better. That's huge. And, it is also supported by the Open Source community. Also huge. Then when we find bugs in GAIM, we contribute back. For example, when we found bugs in lighttpd, we let Jan, who is kind of the administrator of lighttpd, know. He fixes them and everybody else benefits. Huge.

Do you have any worries that somebody will take the Open Source and create "Meebo 2"?

One of the big defendability points of Meebo is that it is insanely hard to scale. One of the things we've done is put out on our blog what we use, the different technology we use, yada, yada. The reality is that how you get all the different things to talk to each other and to interact together is the real secret sauce behind Meebo in particular.

Coming back to Web 2.0, what would you consider the most misunderstood thing?

You know, I'm not sure that I've seen much that has been a big misunderstanding. I think that everybody says, "I don't think I know what Web 2.0

> "*Nobody really knows what Web 2.0 is.*"

is" because nobody really knows what Web 2.0 is. It just refers to this resurgence of innovation around the Web, which is a great thing. It would be really hard for me to say that was wrong, because I don't think there is anything right or wrong about Web 2.0.

What issues do you see with Web 2.0? Do you see areas of Web 2.0 where people are having trouble inside or outside of Meebo?

The biggest challenge here is really finding really, really great people to join the team. Hiring is incredibly tough because Web 2.0 is hot. Lots of people are starting stuff, which means anyone who is really, really great already has a job. So finding folks to work on your projects is very, very challenging. Other than that, there are other parts of functionality you'd love to get in web browsers. You'd wish that they could handle more code base, but it is all minor.

At the end of the day, it is a really great environment to be doing stuff in right now.

That leads to my next question, what is the coolest thing that you've done or you've seen with Web 2.0?

Hmmm...

You paused. I expected you to say Meebo!

I'm trying not to say Meebo, even though it is the Web 2.0 product I use the most. By Far.

Going beyond Meebo, I think personally that YouTube is really, really cool for two reasons. One, just as Meebo's goal is to make IM super available, they made web video super available. There wasn't web video before YouTube; it was download and install.

And the thing I think is so cool is that it lets stories that would be hidden, come out. You see these videos of police taking part in actions that you wonder if they should be taking part in. You see quotes of people on the news that are kind of interesting quotes. There are stories that come out and things that are made public that would otherwise not have been.

> *"It really has to be interesting content."*

It is very, very, very hard to get any given video to really become viral and spread around the Web. It really has to be interesting content. So, if you've somehow done something either because you're really creative and you want that to happen or because you've done something that you're not supposed to be doing and it rises to that level, you have to realize that this is a very open-data kind of a world.

What I think is very cool about Meebo from a Web 2.0 concept, and one of the reasons I like it so much, it is similar to the YouTube thing about getting videos out. We get all of these emails all the time from users that say thank you, thank you, thank you. Because of you, I can now talk to my friends, or now I can talk to my family. So many soldiers in Iraq email us and say, "Because of you can I can now IM with my family back home." And people in offices are able to talk to their friends. That's awesome. We've made those people's lives materially happier and that is really cool.

You've cost businesses how much in productivity?

Fortunately we don't see it that way.

Moving into the financial side. With Web 2.0, there is an argument that things such as AJAX cost money and that the payoff is not there. Do you see Web 2.0 as a whole being financially justified?

I don't know that I fully understand the question. Who is trying to financially justify the cost of Web 2.0, the companies building stuff in it, existing companies starting to add it, or others?

Both or all of them. Companies looking to add it, or those building an average web application today.

That's easy. If you don't do it, then you'll lose market share, and you'll wish you did. At the end of the day, the great thing about the Web is that if you have really smart people, they can do really awesome stuff. And the user experience without doubt with this Web 2.0 stuff is a lot better. I don't have to sit and wait for a web page to completely reload. I can get on IM with a very snappy, very fast, software-like experience that I understand.

And people who don't do that, people who say, "Oh, no, no, forget about that stuff. It's not cost effective. I'm just going to keep my old program," they are just going to lose users. And if it is in the enterprise and they are forcing reloads of a page all the time, someone else will come along and say that they can make your employees more efficient because they can allow your users to get in and out without forcing reloads. They can save your users five minutes per use. They are going to migrate your users over to this new stuff.

Another issue brought up regarding Web 2.0 is that if your business model is based on advertising or ad/page views, then Web 2.0 has the ability to decrease those due to the fact that you aren't forcing page loads.

It is kind of funny. I was actually in a meeting where someone said they weren't doing AJAX, because they were paid on page-view thing. Here

> *"The market forces efficiency."*

is the thing: if they don't move to AJAX then they will definitely lose their users because someone is going to do it in a way more snappy, efficient way. And the users will end up moving.

I think that the market forces efficiency. The thing is, throughout time, there are folks who used to have the latest technology, which has become less efficient. They tend to make money based on this less efficient approach. Then at some point, someone realizes the there is inefficiency and they make it efficient. Then those people that were making the exploit are really unhappy because they can no longer make money from the inefficiency.

This happens all the time. That is innovation. I don't think that it is a horrible thing that folks will have to figure out other ways to make money other than by just serving up a bunch of page loads because it is just making things more efficient at the end of the day. And by the way, since so many things are going to go over to not page-loads, and since there is a fundamentally fair price that an advertiser should pay for x amount of exposure to a user, maybe the system will just change. Nielsen just moved from kind of fundamentally calculating page views to fundamentally calculating time. I'd say that is a *way* better method anyway. If there are a thousand page views over the course of 10 minutes, then each of those page views is kind of worthless, but the advertisers are being billed for a thousand page views. But really they had the user for ten minutes. Whether you had the user for 10 minutes on one page or on a thousand pages, I'm not sure that, in reality, the advertiser got any greater advantage [from] being on the thousand page views than being on that one page view. In fact, it might have been better on the one page view because then you really stuck like you were there the whole time for 10 minutes; it is probably worth a lot more.

So the quality instead of the quantity of the impression. Shifting back again to Web 2.0, what do you see as being next: Web 3.0 or the Semantic Web?

That's a great question. I don't think that Web 3.0 is really defined yet. Some people have said Semantic Web. I'm not sure I fully understand that yet because I've not looked into it enough yet.

I think that each wave of innovation happens because a couple of fundamental technologies come out that enable new things. In this wave it was Flash video, it was the concept of social networking, and it was AJAX. It was also the blogging platforms and the associated chronological search as opposed to relevancy search.

> "If other people follow Apple's lead...then you'll see this huge uptick in applications for mobile."

Those are the kind of things that spurred all of this innovation. That is what everyone is kind of using to create all these new things. Then people bite off big chunks to make things happen. So the AJAX thing happens. Someone bites off word processing. Someone bites of instant messaging. But then two years after AJAX happens, someone bites off the intersection of instant messaging with RSS reading with news feeds with...it kind of gets pretty niche.

But then, something happens where there is again this big technology thing that may not be initially obvious when it happens, but it is there and it spurs a whole new level of innovation. These days, I actually am feeling like it is going to be mobile. People have been excited about mobile for a long time. But it is really, really, really hard to be an entrepreneur and start a business on mobile because it is so locked down by the carriers. They control the mobile world. There are three or four of them and that is it. But with the iPhone and the advent of a very, very rich browser environment on a mobile device, all of a sudden the sky is the limit. You can develop anything for that mobile platform.

Like yesterday, late at night we put out Meebo for the iPhone. We always told people that once there was a rich browser platform on the mobile, then we will build a mobile application. And so Apple put one out and we did it.

Wouldn't Meebo work on Windows Mobile?

The Windows Mobile browsers are not nearly as powerful. Safari on the iPhone can do JavaScript. And because it can do JavaScript, you can do a very snappy, rich, fast interface that users will actually use. But that is neat! If other people follow Apple's lead, like from Ericsson, Samsung, and Nokia, which I bet they will, then you'll see this huge uptick in applications for mobile.

Are you fighting against mobile providers' text-messaging services?

Oh, yes. I am the first one to say that. On the mobile it is not clear that instant messaging beats SMS right now. Not at all. I think that SMS integrates better with the phone, even with the browser. I think that SMS uses less battery. The benefit of IM is that you have the whole buddy list there, but in the phone you already have your phone book.

So, I think that you have to have value-add beyond traditional just send and receive text on the mobile to make IM truly compelling. So we did things like having the whole chat history load into the iPhone. And your buddy icon that you selected at Meebo.com—that is instantly in your iPhone version too. And it is really great that SMS puts the most recent message at the top, so we worked the buddy list on the mobile and we will have the most recent message at the top.

We tried to give advantages beyond traditional IM on the mobile when we did the iPhone implementation. And I think more will definitely come of that. I completely agree that IM is one thing, but I'm talking about mobile [being] much broader than that.

What are your thoughts on Software as a Service (SaaS) or Software plus Services (S+S)?

I think the whole AJAX thing has fundamentally enabled Software as a Service. What is Meebo? It is an IM client that looks a heck of a lot like software, but it is delivered through the Web. What is Salesforce.com? It is the exemplar software service and it is a software package delivered through the Web.

I think that Software as a Service was the lead-in, if you will, to all of this stuff. And they did it a little bit before AJAX was available to make it snappy and such. Now I think people are going to take advantage of all the AJAX stuff to make it better.

Sound Bites

Meebo has seen phenomenal growth in a short period of time. While relatively new, by having over six million unique visitors monthly, it has taught its founders key lessons. These lessons include insights on Web 2.0. The following are some of the insights provided from the interview with Seth Sternberg:

- Advertising on the Web is now very, very efficient—an efficient, liquid market.
- There are a lot of are people saying there has to be this advertising fatigue thing, but I don't think that is the case at all.
- You are going to build a very different kind of organization if you are going after the enterprise.
- Because of Open Source you can go in and fiddle with the code to make it better.
- Everybody says, "I don't think I know what Web 2.0 is" because nobody really knows what Web 2.0 is.
- I don't think there is anything right or wrong about Web 2.0.

- If you don't do Web 2.0, then you'll lose market share and you'll wish you did.
- At the end of the day, the great thing about the Web is that if you have really smart people, they can do really awesome stuff.
- The market forces efficiency.
- Folks will have to figure out ways to make money other than by just serving up a bunch of page loads.
- Without a doubt, the user experience with this Web 2.0 stuff is a lot better.

Joshua Schachter: del.icio.us

13

> "We find ourselves in a world where we have unfathomable riches of which we've only scratched the surface. If computer technology stopped advancing for a few years right here, we probably wouldn't be in terrible shape."
>
> —Joshua Schachter

Chances are very good that if you are reading this book, you use the Web. Chances are also good that if you use the Web, you likely have a few sites that are your favorites. Additionally, there is likely a large number of sites you visit that you'd like to come back to. Most browsers will allow you to create a bookmark or mark a page as a favorite so that you can find it later. Unfortunately, if you have more than one computer, if you are currently not

del.icio.us
social bookmarking

del.icio.us search
login | register | help

» **all your bookmarks in one place**
» bookmark things for yourself and friends
» **check out what other people are bookmarking**

learn more...   » **get started** «

Tags
A tag is simply a word you use to describe a bookmark. Unlike folders, you make up tags when you need them and you can use as many as you like. The result is a better way to organize your bookmarks and a great way to discover interesting things on the Web.
learn more

hotlist what's hot right now on del.icio.us

tags to watch   more ...

HOT NOW   see also: popular | recent

investing
Monday view: Cheap solar power poised to undercut oil and gas by half | Monday View | Columnists | Business | Money | Te...
Google Finance
Virtual Stock Exchange - Home

On the fundamentals of programming : Codeulate. save this   **109** people
first posted by robotbrett   tags
programming learning education blog development

How to create custom ringtones in GarageBand 4.1.1   **105** people
save this
first posted by loerincz   tags
iphone garageband apple ringtones mac

web
Rails Envy: Acts_As_Ferret Tutorial
Wired News: The Web's Best Calendars
OpenID: an actually distributed identity system

thumbnail coming soon
P-99: Ninety-Nine Prolog Problems save this   **112** people
first posted by schopra2   tags
programming prolog problems tutorial puzzles

utilities

www.delicious.com

at your computer, or if you are using a different browser within your computer, then using a single browser's favorites simply doesn't help you get back to the sites you like.

The answer to this dilemma is to store your favorites on the Web. That is where del.icio.us comes into play. It allows you to store your favorites on the Web, so that you can then access them from anywhere, on any browser on any computer. More than that, you can also share your favorite links with friends, family, or the world.

In addition to storing and sharing your favorites, using del.icio.us also allows you to add tags to them. Using tags provides you the ability to easily categorize, sort, and search your favorites.

Del.icio.us, however, is also about social bookmarking. You can search other people's favorites using the tags they have added as well. This makes it easy to find out what web sites others thought were worth adding to their favorites.

The Limiting Factor Is Imagination and Implementation Skill

Joshua Schachter is the founder and creator of del.icio.us. Even after Yahoo! acquired del.icio.us in 2005, Joshua has continued as the director of engineering for del.icio.us. His experience with del.icio.us provides great insight into Web 2.0.

Can you tell a little bit about yourself and about what del.icio.us is?

> *"There is a lower transaction cost for trying those things out."*

I founded del.icio.us in 2003 or so, and it is a system for saving bookmarks and finding things that you have found previously, organizing those things, and basically providing a sort of memory for the Web.

How would you or del.icio.us define Web 2.0?

Honestly, when I started working on del.icio.us, it was just a thing I was building. I never really thought of Web 2.0 and it wasn't a key concept in my vocabulary or necessary for the building of this.

I think it is an artifact of the economic conditions of the ability for people to take passion in a topic and actually implement something. So, instead of millions of dollars of Sun gear and Java, they're able to build a low-end PHP/Linux sort of environment for building pretty much anything. These could be built and tried out at a very low scale. Any success ends up on the heels of failure of some sort. So, we as a developer community are able to try out lots of ideas, many more than previously, because there is a lower transaction cost for trying those things out; it's just sort of a low-water mark in terms of the difficulty and cost of building something.

When you ask people to name Web 2.0 sites, del.icio.us is a site name that often comes up. Do you think this is because of the low barrier to entry or are there other factors?

I built del.icio.us not because I had a business plan, not because I thought there would be money there, but because I wanted it; I had the ability to build something and the desire to see it happen.

Is Web 2.0 also the ability and desire with a low barrier to entry?

I sort of wonder if Web 2.0 is less the name of a specific phenomenon and more of a label we put on particular observation. But, boy—there sure are a lot of web sites out there lately. Do we confuse the state of the art, in terms of web applications, like AJAX and such, as artifacts of Web 2.0 or merely contemporaneous—they showed up at about the same time.

> *"The cost of implementation and the cost of failure are so low that we're able to prototype and try lots and lots of things, very, very quickly."*

So when people say, "Web 2.0, oh that is AJAX..."

It's not. Certainly, I remember when the AJAX article came out—it showed up bookmarked on del.icio.us. So, I was certainly doing that before it had a name. There's still very little AJAX, as it is, in del.icio.us itself.

One concept that comes up quite often in discussions on Web 2.0 is the idea of "community." How does community fit into Web 2.0?

I'm not sure that it does. There have certainly been large communities on the Web before this—there was Topica, Yahoo! Groups, instant-messaging protocols, Friendster; I'm not sure that this is necessarily a component.

What would you consider an important feature of Web 2.0?

Like I said, I don't think it's a thing, but more the name of an observation, so that doesn't hold. I think that economically, the cost of implementation and the cost of failure are so low that we're able to prototype and try lots and lots of things, very, very quickly. Things that work include sites that have community; they're very efficient in terms of cost to produce, that kind of stuff—so I think it all fits in sort of a line. Then when you connect the dots, you get an arrow point to Web 2.0; I don't think it's the other way around.

So if you look at Web 2.0 as just a term, then are there things you believe people are misunderstanding about it?

> *"Semantic Web is about data, not about the Web."*

I think because it's vaguely defined, it's also vaguely used. If vaguely defined and vaguely used are true, then how can you tell when you're using it correctly?

Looking at something different, Web 3.0, the Semantic Web—what are your thoughts on that?

I think it's similarly misunderstood. A great deal of people who talk about it look at the name and guess what it might be, rather than actually understanding it.

How would you define Semantic Web then?

I think it's a way to exchange databases with foreign schemas, and harmonize schemas across these databases. The semantics are around the definition of the schema rather than the definition of the data.

So then do you believe the Semantic Web is happening?

Semantic Web is about data, not about the Web. I don't think it's the same kind of thing. If the Semantic Web is version three of "something," then SQL was version two of it, not the Web.

Because it is not the Semantic Web, what would you say *is* the next big thing on the Web?

It's a variety of little things that will come together once again, change the costs and technologies. I don't think it will be one thing. It is continued decrease in costs of implementation; prototyping and shipping are going to be the same thing, or close in distance. I think that more and more computation will be pushed to the edge (onto the browser or the desktop). Data stores will get smarter, bigger, and faster and more appropriate for web-scale use. We don't have anything like that; the big boys do. All of these speak to decreasing costs.

I'm an amateur economist at times, and everything at the end of the day can be phrased in these terms.

Hitting one other tangent area, do you consider Software as a Service (SaaS) fact or fiction?

I think that it's going to continue to operate in a middle ground. I think that people tend to want to own their entire stack when their livelihood depends on it.

If the service they need is better supplied by someone other than themselves, that's a very interesting proposition. If S3 and EC2 had been available when I started building del.icio.us, I might have ended up someplace completely different. I learned quite clearly that my expertise was not getting hardware wrapped and routed, and that was actually quite difficult. If I could have punted on those problems, that would have made life a great deal easier—and cheaper—inexpensive to scale, and so on and so forth.

S3 AND EC2

S3 and EC2 are services provided by Amazon.com. S3 is a Simple Storage Service. EC2 is the Amazon Elastic Compute Cloud, which provides the service of processing power.

So then things like security...

Security, ownership of data, that kind of thing—those are important.

So where do you see us being with these things today?

I think it's technological, rather than political. Building software is still deeply voodoo and not science in the vaguest sense. People don't agree on terms, or methodology, or technology, parts, components...and there are radically different ways that people implement and even think about problems. So, there's a huge range. I don't know if it ever will be science—or similar to it—but right now it is deep, magical voodoo.

We are talking about Web 2.0 and online issues. What is your opinion on connectivity? Will it get better or is it good enough?

We find ourselves in a world where we have unfathomable riches of which we've only scratched the surface. If computer technology stopped advancing for a few years right here, we probably wouldn't be in terrible shape. Because our technology *is* mostly voodoo, we throw away most of our amazing performance. But we have these fat, wide, low-latency networks that allow incredible things. Like, you have almost instantaneous video to the desktop. That will get a little bit better, but right now the limiting factor is imagination and implementation skill.

> *"Now that [Web 2.0] is here, it is obvious that this was going to happen."*

Again, this goes back to the idea that it's not the technology—it's the cost of implementation and your passion for an idea that are the limiting factors. As the costs come down, it's just the matter of having the idea and the skill and the passion itself.

And you believe cost will continue to go down?

Likely, yes. That generally happens, right?

Yes. So is there anything you'd like to add about Web 2.0?

I honestly don't think in those terms, and I rarely even say "Web 2.0;" I don't even think about tagging for the most part, which I think is a major component or at least one of the things that people frequently attribute to Web 2.0.

There are people who considered Web 2.0 to be just a term being applied to just a period of time.

Ideas that just sort of happen seem like they were filled with inevitability from the start; they don't actually work out that way when you look at the true story. Now that it is here, it is obvious that this was going to happen, but at the time there were a lot of people doing a lot of different little things, moving the state of the art and the state of thought forward. When you look back five years ago, all the pieces were there and ready to come together; at the time, no one was that smart.

So all the pieces, the technology, were there five years ago, but they simply hadn't been put together yet—such as with del.icio.us...

When you talk to a sculptor, they say that they merely remove the excess material; that the thing was already there. In this case, the need was there, just not the implementation. So del.icio.us chipped away at all the stuff that you didn't need to have to get the stuff done, to just reveal what you actually want to do. I think that's why it is successful. It lets people do the things they need.

Sound Bites

Social bookmarking is the core of what del.icio.us is. Just as we can learn from other people's bookmarks, we can also learn from other people. Following are a few tidbits to be gleamed from Joshua Schachter:

- Instead of spending millions of dollars on technology, people are able to build a low-end PHP/Linux sort of environment for building pretty much anything. As such, you are able to try out a lot of ideas, many more than previously, because there are lower transaction costs for trying things out.
- Web 2.0 is less the name of a specific phenomenon, and more of a label we put on particular observations.
- Because Web .20 is vaguely defined, it's also similarly vaguely used.
- If the Semantic Web is version three of "something," then SQL was version two of it, not the Web.
- People don't agree on terms, methodology, technology, parts, or components, and there are radically different ways that people implement and even think about problems. Right now it is deep, magical voodoo.
- If computer technology stopped advancing for a few years right here, we probably wouldn't be in terrible shape.

Ranjith Kumaran: YouSendIt

14

"That's where Web 2.0 started; it was to help people more easily get into services like ours, which are brain-dead simple to use. So, it has allowed people to have conversations that they wouldn't necessarily have been able to have."

—*Ranjith Kumaran*

While social networking and video sites are often among the most talked-about sites on the Web, there are a lot of other sites that are also important and growing. One thing that links a lot of these sites is their ability to focus on doing something well.

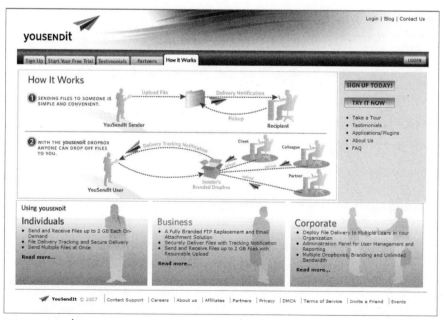

www.yousendit.com

YouSendIt is a site that has a primary focus and they do it well. That focus is the transferring of information and files to others. In the past, this has generally been done with FTP software; however, with the changes that have occurred on the Web, and with the larger averages size of files that are being sent, there are now easier options, one being YouSendIt.com. They make sending and receiving files a much easier, much more "on demand" endeavor.

While YouSendIt has a focus on what they do, you'll find that their task touches on many of the critical issues that people face with the Web. This includes securely sending information as well as tracking where information has been sent. For some perspective on current Web trends, including Web 2.0, one of the co-founders of YouSendIt, Ranjith Kumaran, has some experience to share.

At a High Level, Web 2.0 is About Enabling Interesting Conversations and Collaboration

Ranjith is a founder of YouSendIt, where he's currently responsible for product management and corporate marketing. His experiences prior to YouSendIt include Verisity Design (which was acquired by Cadence in 2005), as well as Red Hat, where he architected Open Source software.

Can you tell a little about yourself and YouSendIt?

> *"We try to allow data to move very freely from one place to another."*

I'm Ranjith Kumaran and I'm the founder of YouSendIt.com. What YouSendIt does, we're the leading company that allows users to send, receive, and track large files, actually files of any size, on the Web today. We primarily cater to businesses and professionals, but we have a vested reach into the consumer space as well.

Jumping right to the key question, how would you define Web 2.0 today?

It's a pretty nebulous topic, but there are maybe three things that I grok about 2.0. I'll start at the highest level, which I think is the ability for the Web to connect people and enable collaboration. A lot of this is enabled through allowing the re-syndication of data and services by anyone. We try to allow data to move very freely from one place to another. We try to provide information around the question, "Is there an interesting conversation going on around that file transfer?," so there's a lot of metadata that we provide around that transaction.

As far as services are concerned, we have opened up our API to allow other people to build more interesting services on top of ours. On our web site, there's a long list of plugins for enabling workflows, primarily in the creative professional

> *"The more people you can serve, the more value everyone gets out of it."*

space. If you're creating data and manipulating it, we want you to be able to move it to the people that care about the final product. So at a high level, it is about enabling interesting conversations and collaboration.

Some of the more subtle things that I've been tracking are the network effects that are built around these services and sites. Basically, the more people you can serve, the more value everyone gets out of it. For instance, in YouSendIt's relationship with our customers, it's actually how we enable our customers' relationships with their customers that is important.

We allow our customers to talk to their customers, and vice versa. We've built an ecosystem of businesses and services, all powered through the YouSendIt service.

I like all things long tail. What I really like about YouSendIt and Web 2.0 in general is the breadth of use cases that we see. Things that move through our system start anywhere from geo-seismic data that oil companies are sending around, to crochet patterns. This is something a traditional service constrained by shelf space couldn't address. Those are my favorites.

What would you consider the most important feature of Web 2.0?

It's the ability for people to easily adopt services and thus connect to more people and start more conversations. That's where it started; it was to help people more easily get into services like ours, which are brain-dead simple to use. So, it has allowed people to have conversations that they wouldn't necessarily have been able to have.

The term AJAX has been used a lot today, as have the topics of AIR, Silverlight, and more. Would you consider this Web 2.0?

> *"What we're finding is that 80 percent of collaborative efforts do happen asynchronously."*

I think the new and interesting types of UIs [User Interfaces] and interactions have enabled Web 2.0; I don't think we get a lot of that in what is now called Web 1.0. Really interesting desktop-like interactions couldn't have been possible previously. It's all sort of rolled into the Web 2.0 ball of wax, but I think it's more of an enabler than one of the fundamentals. One of the most important things of new services and applications is complex user interaction, and I think that AJAX does enable more robust user interactions.

As a tangent, Adobe AIR and Google Gears are about moving applications out of the browser and back to the desktop. Do you have any thoughts on that?

It's a good question, because we always talk about real-time collaboration and off-line collaboration, or asynchronous collaboration. A lot of the cases where people are using YouSendIt are asynchronous; people are moving data and someone will mash it up with something else and send it back, and it doesn't happen in real time. What we're finding is that 80 percent of collaborative efforts do happen asynchronously. So I think it is very important to be able to push some of these applications back out of the browser and onto the desktop, but to make it as accessible and as easy to use —and as connected as possible.

Does YouSendIt have a piece that works from the desktop?

We do. It's pretty basic. It just allows…that's not true. There's a very basic one that sits on your desktop, and you can drag files into it, and they get delivered faster and more securely, and things like that.

We also have plug-ins to other applications, so if you're inside Acrobat and you touched up a photo for a magazine, you don't need to leave Acrobat to move that file to someone who's waiting for it. We call that "getting embedded in the workflow," and we're very interested in that. We don't want people to leave their creative environment to use our service, so this is a good example of pushing it back to the desktop but keeping it as accessible as possible.

I see that you have plug-ins for Photoshop, Corel Draw, Outlook, and others.

The most popular ones are our own desktop clients and the Outlook plug-in.

Back to Web 2.0, what would you consider the most misunderstood thing about Web 2.0?

> *"I think people see Web 2.0 as something that happened all of a sudden."*

Sometimes I think people see Web 2.0 as something that happened all of a sudden, but things like AJAX, for example, have been around quite a while; it's just been refined over time. I think that's what surprises me most, the way folks think that it happened overnight. It's a 10-year-old overnight success, I guess.

You mentioned sharing information, which is what YouSendIt does. Do you see a change in feelings about security? Is there still a hesitance?

Yeah, some things like wikis and the YouSendIt service have more of a grassroots adoption. The way we've been successful at getting into places that otherwise would be hesitant to try our services and other third-party services is through grassroots initiatives, which means we make it so accessible that inevitably some critical mass of people will use it inside a corporation and they'll take it to the IT department and say, "Hey, we're already using this—let's figure out a way to build it into our workflow; we're going to be using it anyway." At that point, the IT group will step in and look at the hygiene behind the service.

It's actually been surprising; we haven't had the pushback that you'd traditionally expect from IT organizations. I think it's gotten to a point where they're just happy being able to enable their users.

So, people have given up worrying about security?

I don't think that they've given up; there's a balance between how you want to enable your team to be productive and at the same time, the onus is still on vendors like us to make sure that we live up to the promises that we make on security and availability.

Looking back at Web 2.0, are there any benefits that you have recognized?

> *"What I've found out, in Silicon Valley at least, is that people almost expect for us to make a big deal about Web 2.0."*

I think definitely technology-wise and distribution-wise, some of the network effects and viral effects have been tremendously important for us. I think a recent statistic for us is 70 percent of our users tell us that our service came recommended from other users. That's how they found out about us. The viral nature, the ease of usability that we've been able to solve, has been critical. It certainly couldn't have been done 10 years ago without the design paradigms or UI enhancements that have become prevalent on the Web.

Are there issues you see with Web 2.0?

There's kind of a stigma. What I've found out, in Silicon Valley at least, is that people almost expect for us to make a big deal about Web 2.0, and we're pretty low-key about it. We're happy being a very usable, viable service that our users get value out of. I get questions like, "Gee, when are you going to add "[insert flavor-of-the-week-service-here]?"—like tags, RSS feeds, things like that.

Our philosophy here is if our users aren't asking for it, we're going to leave it out. There's almost a stigma that if you're not following the latest and greatest thing—like Web 2.0, it's either not a viable company, or a cool company, but we're just happy listening to our customers and providing a valuable service.

Can you survive long-term as a single-service, or niche, company? Or is there a push to do more?

I think so, and we're naturally getting pulled in that direction. Historically we've done one thing really well, which is deliver files. Now we're getting into workflows and users are asking us, "Gee, I can open up the browser and use you guys, but can you automate that and make it happen behind the scenes? Can you embed it into my workflow? And also, what are the other services that you can layer on top of moving the file? Can you transform the file? Can you authenticate it? Can you get into asynchronous collaboration?"

Features like revision control, previewing; things like that. I'm glad that we started off doing one thing really well and learned a lot doing it. Now that we've cracked the code on that, our users are constantly asking us for more.

What do you see as being the next big thing after Web 2.0?

Tough question. I meet a lot of companies and entrepreneurs, and I kind of go by that feeling I get sometimes: that I'm looking into the future!

There's a lot of activity going on around the Semantic Web. Can we get machines to do some of the more mundane data gathering and distribution? Defining relationships between links and pages, data and content, and services—I think that's going to be one of the next big things.

> *"From a service perspective, I'm seeing a lot more services almost make web pages obsolete."*

Also, I've been seeing a lot of activity in the area of opening up social graphs. Facebook blazed the trail there, but once initiatives like OpenSocial gain critical mass, what services can you build on top of the social graph? So we're asking questions like, "How do you make rapid distribution more efficient?"—we're leveraging things like that.

From a service perspective, I'm seeing a lot more services that almost make web pages obsolete, so they treat the Web more like at thousand different applications that you can pull together and that customize an environment where you can get data without having to browse different web sites and web pages. Again, Facebook and some of the virtual worlds have shown some interesting models there: how can you share content, create content, without web pages as the delivery mechanism?

That's again pretty important to us. We're seeing this even inside the enterprise. Virtual meeting spaces, things like that being used. We're trying to connect those—meeting rooms and the data shared between them.

Lastly, we do have a free service, which is supported by advertising, but there are a lot of neat things around the next wave and more interesting types of advertising that can go out on the Web, really enabling brand advocates to inform other folks through the opening up of the social graph and some of the different types of distribution.

Do you see advertising becoming more targeted than it is now?

It has to be. It's in its infancy right now. It's a tough problem, but I think there's a lot of brainpower going into it to say, "Okay, how can we leverage all the data that we're collecting?"

We collect a lot of data about our users' transactions and interactions; how can we reflect that back to the user to better enable their workflows and make their businesses more efficient. Those are going to be the things that will be interesting as we go forward.

You mentioned Semantic Web. It sounds like you believe that is a good thing and that it will happen.

Definitely. I think it will be an automated thing combined with people augmenting it. I've already seen some things like that happening. Some of the facial- and image-recognition technologies are out there. People are already using them and augmenting that with Mechanical Turk. I think we're a long way from it being 100 percent automated, but, slow and steady.

Software as a Service (SaaS) and Software plus Services (S+S): fact or fiction?

> *"By outsourcing a lot of the services through companies like ours, people are becoming more productive."*

They have to be a fact. I think what we're seeing from our users is that by outsourcing a lot of the services through companies like ours, people are becoming more productive. That's the way it has to continue. It allows people to concentrate and focus on what their core competencies are, allowing us to scale services up or down as we need to make that more efficient. I think that's going to continue.

So do you see desktop applications going away?

I think the desktop is pretty engrained right now in the way people do things, but I think it's almost coming full circle to where the desktop is more of a terminal to more sophisticated applications on the Web. There will always be an offline component as well. Like I said, we're seeing workflows where only 20 percent is done online, 80 percent offline. I think there will be a steady shift, but we're probably a little ways away from 100 percent Web.

Do you believe there will ever be an "always connected" paradigm or world?

Yes.

In the foreseeable future? When do you believe "always connected" will happen?

I'd like to think in my lifetime. I don't think it's out of the realm of possibilities. Even if you look at where we were 10 years ago, folks are definitely more connected than 10 years ago, and the trends seem to show that continuing.

Whether that's a good thing or not, I don't know—I certainly don't want to be that guy at the park with my kids—answering email.

Is Web 2.0 something the average company needs to worry about?

I don't think they need to worry about it. I think that if the services are acceptable, and they are easy to get into and out of, then it shouldn't be something that occupies your mind. I think that's just the way services are going; it will just be very natural for people to adopt them.

Do you have anything you would like to add?

A lot of the things that I've been seeing and tracking have been Web 2.0 "in the office." I think they call it "Office 2.0." That's an interesting phenomenon. When I started the company it wasn't as accepted as it is now with a lot of the online applications and services like ours.

People have started adopting it at a faster rate in the last 12 months, and probably because a lot of the desktop services have moved that way—Microsoft and some of the Google apps and things like that make distribution of these things pretty broad. So, "Web 2.0 at the office" is something that's very near and dear to our hearts.

Hasn't AJAX helped in making this happen?

Yes, definitely. When I saw the mainstream web mail apps go AJAX—that was kind of the tipping point for me. It's here to stay, and people get it.

I mentioned Silverlight earlier; what are you seeing there, as far as adoption?

Right now, it is a 1.0 product that is nice for doing graphics. When Microsoft sets its mind on something, there is a good chance it will happen, or else it will disappear and we'll never hear about it again. It is interesting to see them trying to compete with Adobe, and it will be interesting to see what other products come into the space, products such as JavaFX and such.

Yeah, I've poked around with it a little over the last few months, and like you said, it seems like it's pretty early.

It is definitely early—it is definitely a 1.0 type of thing. While it is off topic, let me ask one final question. What are your thoughts on where Java is headed?

I remember when I was coming up, and one of the first things I did out of college was Java. At the time I was like, "Wow, this makes things so much easier and it makes so much sense." Now I have a bias towards very light-weight frameworks, applications, and environments, and I think that's kind of why I gravitated away from developing in Java to PHP, Ruby, and such.

That's my only gripe. I think it's still incredibly powerful and I think strategically, building an application in Java—the good thing is it's easier to hire and maintain and the libraries are more robust.

We definitely went through that decision early on in the company—the technology decision. At the end of the day, the kind of lightweight frameworks, the nature of our core applications are that we need to keep them as thin as possible. Kind of why we went with your standard LAMP stack.

LAMP

LAMP refers to using a software bundle that consists of Linux, Apache, MySQL, and programming languages such as Perl, PHP, or Python.

In the Web 2.0 space, there is still a lot of opportunity. Even the big sites have only a small percentage of the available market. I image your paradigm is the same—is it hard to own a market where there are so many people to target?

What we do is so horizontal. I think one of the early things I looked at was PayPal, and everybody uses money, everybody sends files. Very organized, trying to be kind of the best of the breed—building brand equity. Create a good user experience; then good things can happen.

Sound Bites

While YouSendIt might not be one of the first sites to come to mind when you think of Web 2.0, its founder, Ranjith Kumaran, has experience and insights that are relevant in a Web 2.0 world. Some of his notable perspectives follow.

- The ability of the Web to connect people and enable collaboration is enabled through allowing the re-syndication of data and services by anyone.
- At a high level, Web 2.0 is about enabling interesting conversations and collaboration. The more people you can service, the more value they get out of it.
- One of the most important things of new services applications is complex user interaction, and I think that AJAX does enable more robust user interactions.
- It is very important to be able to push some of these applications back out of the browser and onto the desktop, but make it as accessible and easy to use and connected as possible.
- Folks think that Web 2.0 happened overnight. It's a 10-year-old overnight success. Things like Ajax have been around for quite awhile.
- There's kind of a balance between how you want to enable your team to be productive and at the same time, the onus is still on vendors to make sure that we live up to the promises that we make on security and usability and availability. Additionally, by outsourcing a lot of the services through companies like ours, people are becoming more productive.
- If our users aren't asking for it, we're going to leave it out. There's almost a stigma if you're not following the latest and greatest thing.
- The desktop is pretty engrained right now in the way people do things, but I think it's almost coming full circle to where the desktop is more of a terminal to more sophisticated applications on the Web.

Garrett Camp:
StumbleUpon

15

"Web 2.0 is really about the user experience and not the underlying technologies"

—*Garrett Camp*

How often do you get that email from a friend or colleague pointing you to a web site they just happened to stumble upon? Simply using a search engine to find a site will get you results, but often there are some really good sites, or really appropriate sites, that automated search engines just don't bring to the top of the search. As such, search engines don't always give you the best results.

www.stumbleupon.com

StumbleUpon allows you to share those interesting sites that you stumble upon as well as helps you to discover sites others have found. By using the community, StumbleUpon gathers positive and negative ratings to help those sites that are really good float to the top while others sink out of sight. The overall result is that with a little bit of tagging and categorization, you can quickly find sites that others thought worthy of recommending on any given topic.

To make it easy to recommend sites, they've also created add-ins for Microsoft Internet Explorer and FireFox. With more than 4 million people contributing, it should be no surprise that you can get results.

It is About the User Experience, Not the Technologies

Garrett Camp is the founder and chief product officer for StumbleUpon. Since 2001 he has been helping others share the sites they stumble across. The result of this experience helps to provide some interesting insights into Web 2.0.

Can you tell a little bit about yourself and about StumbleUpon?

My name is Garrett Camp, and I am one of the founders and chief product officer of StumbleUpon. I started StumbleUpon about six years ago, in November of 2001.

> *"The Web becomes a lot more of an interactive platform rather than just a way to buy or read stuff."*

We were based in Canada, and I was doing both StumbleUpon and graduate school for four years until the end of 2005. After graduating I brought the company down from Calgary, Canada, to San Francisco in January 2006 and we raised some Angel funding. Once we had money, we started to hire people, and we've now grown from just 3 up to 20 people today.

StumbleUpon now has more than 4 million registered users and its central purpose is enabling personalized content discovery. What we are trying to do is show people interesting things on the Web; interesting recommendations that they normally wouldn't think to search for. We are not trying to replace search engines or become a search engine, but instead be a discovery tool for when you just want to be entertained or want to discover something interesting. We are primarily focused on discovery and are one of the leading companies focused on that right now.

How would you or StumbleUpon define Web 2.0?

I actually wasn't around during "Web 1.0," but I think 1.0 involved taking traditional business and publishing models, and moving them online. So you could buy clothes or dog food, or read the newspaper online; it was mostly an extension of offline business models, and there wasn't a lot of interaction with the users in a unique way.

To me, it feels like Web 2.0 is much more interactive. Sites have more participation from users, and there are community elements to it with things like profiles, reviews, ratings, and user-generated content.

Today it seems like every web site wants to add social or community features; ways for users to interact. I think that is the big difference…the Web becomes much more of an interactive platform rather than just a way to buy or read stuff.

I guess that is the way I define Web 2.0 and think about it. Many people look at it from the technical side with toolkits such as AJAX or Ruby on Rails, but I think those tools developed independently as a way to make pages more interactive and

> *"If it wasn't for Open Source, it would have been much harder to get started."*

responsive for the users. A difference I see from Web 1.0 is that by learning the basics of taking offline business models and putting them online, we are now developing new business models based on new forms of user interaction.

You mentioned AJAX and that some consider it a technology for doing Web 2.0, but that it is independent. What is your response to people who say AJAX is Web 2.0?

I would say they are technologies commonly used for Web 2.0. Even with that, I feel that "Web 2.0" is more of a marketing term than a technology thing. Tim O'Reilly first started using it to describe the second wave of the Web.

Technology-wise, AJAX is one of the central tools. But now it doesn't have to be only AJAX. There are other toolkits that enable pre-fetching data and not having to reload the entire page. These types of technologies have been associated with Web 2.0 interfaces, but you can still build a Web 2.0 app that is very social and unique compared to what we saw five years ago without them. It could be a straight PHP/file-based application. Web 2.0 is really about the user experience and not the underlying technologies.

Is there any feature that you would say stands out more than the rest?

I think that the LAMP platform has enabled a lot of it with the low-cost, robust, Open Source platforms. It seems like LAMP is the base on which most Web 2.0 systems are built. It is one of the core technologies that has allowed people to do so much with free tools. A lot of start-ups, including us, wouldn't have gotten this far if we had to pay for software or buy database licenses.

THE LAMP PLATFORM

LAMP stands for Linux, Apache, MySQL, and PHP. These products are Open Source and generally freely available. They can be used to create and run dynamic web sites at low to no cost.

So you believe that Open Source has enabled Web 2.0?

Definitely. I think the whole point is to be able to build apps in an interactive fashion based on user feedback and to start with something small instead of a big app with a grand launch. You can rent one box for $99 a month and start developing on it. If people start using your product and like it, they will give you feedback and you can improve the product from there.

At StumbleUpon, we developed incrementally and used Open Source software for everything. We wouldn't have been able to afford it otherwise. We had our hosting costs, our rent, and that was it. If it wasn't for Open Source, it would have been much harder to get started.

Is there anything about Web 2.0 that you believe people are misunderstanding or getting wrong?

I don't think so...it's just a loosely defined term. In some ways, I think of it as a second wave of popularity; I guess '99 was the first and now this is the second.

That's one way people think of it; I think of the participation and interactive aspects. There are many ways to define Web 2.0 and many different ways to interpret it.

You mentioned that Web 2.0 is the next wave. What do you believe will be the *next* wave?

I've actually thought a bit about what the third wave will be. We are starting to see the third wave now—you've probably heard about the terms "personalization" and "social graph," and they are definitely part of it.

The first wave of the Web, when it was small, used people to organize manually; Yahoo!, DMOZ, web-rings, etc. The second wave began when there [had] become too much content to keep track of or organize manually, and we shifted toward a search paradigm relying on crawlers and automated indexing. That is where AltaVista came in and Google became popular.

Today, from an information-retrieval perspective, I think the third wave is going to combine both manual and automated approaches; we will have algorithmic organization and distribution of content, but the difference is that the users submit, rate, and review the content instead of using

> *"[The Semantic Web is] a great idea, but the problem is that it never got widespread adoption."*

crawlers, which try to predict what should be in the index. I think these types of hybrid systems which combine community participation with algorithmic processing have a lot of potential. This approach is pretty much what StumbleUpon is trying to do. We use both approaches to create a recommendation engine driven by four million users.

The third wave is trying to utilize human input to define what good content is, and it has the technology to help manage and organize that information. Discovery, recommendation, personalization, and generated content are all parts of the third wave.

The Semantic Web is a term that comes up a lot. Do you see it being a part of the next waves?

The Semantic Web is mostly an academic term for bringing structure to the Web. Instead of having unstructured HTML documents where you didn't know what meant what, you would use extensible tags and better formatting to indicate what is an address, who is a person, and meaningful things like that. It's a great idea, but the problem is that it never got widespread adoption.

StumbleUpon and Facebook were developed in the spirit of the Semantic Web but were created and used by a wider audience. They are applications that everyone can use instead of a set of standards for web publishers to adopt. Much of what Facebook is doing is creating a social graph of your friends and acquaintances so that graph can be used to bring meaningful things to your attention. It has a lot of the same design principles as the intended Semantic Web; it just happens to be done by a company, and is focusing on the user experience instead of getting adopted by all web publishers. The Semantic Web is coming, just not in the way we initially expected.

Is there anything out there that you would say is really cool that you've seen that would be considered Web 2.0?

I like Facebook and StumbleUpon for content discovery; I like Last.fm and Pandora for browsing music. Del.icio.us is pretty cool for bookmarking, and I like Digg for watching trends in tech. Those sites are all pretty well-known. A few smaller ones that are interesting are Farecast for prediction of airline ticket prices and many other small "crowd-sourcing" applications like Predictify for forecasting events.

> *"Personalized search hasn't really taken off yet."*

There is actually a lot going on and a lot of start-ups, but recently I haven't followed many of them closely because I am focused on StumbleUpon and not exploring other products as much as I used to. Now I am just trying to internally manage all of the features we are trying to get out.

Are there any Web 2.0 features that you are using within SumbleUpon that are interesting?

The fact that we're doing one-click discovery and personalized recommendations is pretty interesting. Personalization and customization are something that never took off in the first wave of the Web. The "one-size-fits-all" approach to search is reaching its limits, but personalized search hasn't really taken off yet.

The interesting thing that we are doing is personalizing all our recommendations based on every single site the users stumble upon, rate, or review. Every single person's stumble tour is completely unique and every interaction with the toolbar—be it rating, tagging, or sharing—will improve the relevance of future stumbles.

We're doing this by blending both social and algorithmic approaches. When you first start using [StumbleUpon], you will get lots of popular and relevant sites, a Digg-like approach, but you'll soon start getting sites recommended by people with similar interests. So, if a new user rates three or four art sites, we will compare those to ratings from other users and start to show you other art sites along the same lines. I don't think anyone else is doing this kind of community recommendation approach quite like us.

> *"Today, if you have an idea you want to experiment with, it doesn't cost very much to try."*

Looking at Web 2.0 more broadly, are there any things you are seeing as issues?

Nothing comes to mind. There are always minor issues, but overall things are pretty good. Today, if you have an idea you want to experiment with, it doesn't cost very much to try.

In venture financing, we are already seeing more firms wanting to give entrepreneurs just $50,000 to $100,000 to get started rather than a million, because they realize that web start-ups aren't very capital-intensive. All you really need is enough funding to rent some servers, get a few people coding for a few months, and the server time to see if people like it. So there aren't many issues on the funding front.

There are some privacy issues, however. When people put something on a Facebook or online, they don't really think about it being public. I think about this, and most technical people think about this. Many of the people who just get into uploading tons of photos of themselves and their friends, tagging them, etc. do not really think that it's not a good idea; maybe their family or colleagues will see their photos.

You might have heard about the bank intern on Facebook. He told his boss he was sick, ended up going to some party, and a friend tagged him in a photo. So he was caught because his boss saw a picture of him at the party on their newsfeed when he was supposed to be sick. Facebook's initial release of the Beacon feature also drew some concern. In fact, I bought a pair of shoes on Zappos before I knew about the feature and the event ended up on a friend's newsfeed. He immediately wrote on my wall saying, "Tell Facebook to stop invading your privacy—I just found out what kind of shoes you bought." There are many people who bought Christmas gifts that were spoiled because the purchases were publicized. I know [they] didn't mean to violate anyone's privacy, but companies like Facebook need to have people willingly opt in to features that track their behavior.

> *"Software as a Service is a marketing term."*

It's an example of how companies need to think about how they collect data, display it publicly, and better understand what people's expectation of privacy is.

Who do you consider responsible for privacy? Is it the user, or is it the online sites and companies?

It depends. I think it is each company's responsibility to enable the people to realize what they are submitting to and what information will be made public.

StumbleUpon makes it really simple. Everything you rate goes to your public blog. It's all public knowledge; everything you rate or blog is out in the open unless you specify otherwise. But that is really the only action we display on your profile. We only publish recommendations that you willingly and explicitly give us, and there is no tracking of your browsing whatsoever. We don't really have many privacy issues because people understand that unless they click "I like it," it won't be public.

Let me ask about something somewhat related. What are your thoughts on Software as a Service (SaaS) or Software plus Services (S+S)? Are they fact or fiction?

I think Software as a Service is a marketing term. It is an okay term, and I guess that is generally what we are. Most people don't think of MySpace,

Facebook, or StumbleUpon as software; they just think about the service [each one] provides. In general, people think of the web tools more as services than software, and associate "software" more with something you install to your desktop.

Where do you see the Web going next? What do you see as the next big revolution?

It's hard to predict, and anything I predict will be wrong! I think in general, the whole idea of convergence is definitely happening. Already people are spending a lot more time online than they are interacting with traditional media. They are browsing on the Web instead of watching TV; listening to podcasts or MP3s from iTunes instead of the radio. Consumer attention is rapidly shifting and within a few years the majority of media consumed will be online.

Beyond that, it is hard to predict. Unlike Google, where you have to tell it exactly what you want, the general trends are leaning toward community interaction, social systems, personalization recommendations, and proactive information filtration.

Systems in the future will look at your past preferences and try to recommend what you personally will find interesting or useful. That is what StumbleUpon is doing in the context of web sites, photos, and videos online.

People want this to happen. There are now so many pages out there that you get hundreds of thousands of results for most queries, but people only look at the first couple pages of results. In the traditional approach to search we are relying on page rank to deliver something relevant within the top 20 to 30 results, even though it knows nothing about who we are. When I type something into a search engine, I should be getting very specific recommendations that are different from someone else's results, based on my past searches, including my personal preferences, who my friends are, and variables like that. Right now the majority of the searches are not being personalized in this fashion. I think this is something that becomes more important as the number of domains online continues to grow exponentially. As more and more content [becomes available] out there, it is going to be more important to look not only at the query, but who is performing the query to ensure the top results are personally relevant.

Sound Bites

StumbleUpon is about sharing what you find on the Web. It is about letting others know what cool things you might have found and learned. In much the same way, there are tidbits of information to stumble across and learn from Garrett Camp. Some notable items follow:

- Today, if you have an idea that you want experiment with, it doesn't cost very much to try.
- LAMP is one of the bases upon which many Web 2.0 systems are built. LAMP is one of the core technologies that has allowed people to do so much for free. A lot of start-ups, including StumbleUpon, would have had a difficult time if they had to pay for software or database licenses.
- The whole point of Open Source is to be able to build apps in an interactive fashion based on people's feedback, to start with something small and improve based on people's feedback.
- Companies need to think about how they collect data, use data, and what people's expectation of privacy is. It's each company's responsibility to make the people realize what they are submitting to, what information will be made public, and so forth.
- The general trends are toward community interaction, social systems, personalization, recommendations, and more proactive information filtering that will help us go beyond Google, where you must specify exactly what you want.

Rodrigo Madanes: Skype

16

> *"The most important thing is that even though we felt in the '90s that the Internet was having a big impact in people's lives, we're seeing in this decade that it's reconstructing a lot of industries and shifting a lot of value around while improving people's lives."*
>
> —Rodrigo Madanes

Skype is considered a Web 2.0 site and company; however, its web site is a minor part of what it is. Skype is used to make phone calls to other people through the use of peer-to-peer technology.

You can use Skype to call other Skype members free, or you can pay small fees to call other people on regular or mobile phones. In fact, Skype has made it easy to call other people no matter where they are in the world. Several

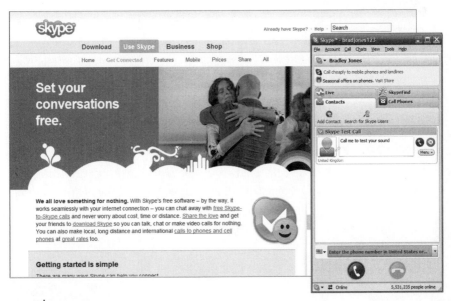

www.skype.com

interviews from this book were done with people who were using Skype. That allowed calls from London, New Zealand, and other far-off locations. In fact, Skype meant that the location did not matter.

Skype goes beyond a desktop browser. It requires that you download a program to your desktop in order to make calls. The downloaded program is similar to some of the common instant message programs, so it is easy to use.

While most phone calls are all about voice communication, Skype also allows for chatting and video. The power of the Internet is pulled into what you can do.

Web 2.0 Is Changing People's Lives and Changing Industries

Niklas Zennström and Janus Friis founded Skype in 2003. Since that time, a number of others have joined the team. Among them is Rodrigo Madanes, who leads the product strategy at Skype. While he could talk to you about user-centered design, virility, disruption, and a variety of other topics, he is also the person at Skype to talk to about Web 2.0.

Can you tell us a little bit about yourself and Skype?

Skype is a piece of software that people can use to talk for free, all over the world. As of version 2.0, they can even video-call with each other. Most people are familiar with Skype at this point, I believe.

> *"Broadly speaking, [Web 2.0] is the resurgence in web innovation."*

I am a technologist; I've been in the industry for about 15 years. I did my PhD in a flavor of human interaction, so, I've been studying how people use computers and how to make them friendlier.

What do you do at Skype?

I used to do product design. That would be working with everything that had to do with making Skype friendlier; that was one of the big innovations at Skype: Internet calling that worked and was easy to use. Now I'm the chief product strategist, which basically means that I look at where we're taking the products.

Jumping right in, how would you and Skype define Web 2.0?

For me, Web 2.0 is such a complex set of technologies and enablers. The best definition is that it is the resurgence of web innovation after the dot-com bust in 2002. It was in great part triggered by some technology and the critical mass of broadband users around the world. That led to the ability to have increased communication between people, watching videos, being able to have very interactive web pages, and more. Broadly speaking, it is the resurgence in web innovation.

Would those innovations be the things you just listed?

Yes, for me, the innovations focus on rich interactions between people. Voice and video calls, social networking, the ability to share TV and video clips, music, and all those kinds of rich interactions with people.

You mentioned technology. Often AJAX comes up when technology is mentioned around Web 2.0. Also mentioned are Adobe AIR and Microsoft Silverlight. Are these technologies Web 2.0?

No.

One of the facets is the enabling technologies that led to where we are now, so I would say that yes, the AJAX, the AIR, Flash, and those kinds of technologies have contributed and are components of Web 2.0. But, I would say that Web 2.0 is

> *"Telecommunications is at the beginning of what will be a longer transformation."*

the result of a critical mass of people with broadband, enabling technologies, large investments and start-ups, and a combination of low-cost, Open Source packages that enable these start-ups to accelerate very quickly—all of those things led to a transformation in the industries of telecommunications, advertising, and television.

That's the actual interesting phenomenon—that it is changing people's lives and changing industries. There are particular technologies that are being thrown around as having been instrumental, but the interesting part goes beyond the technologies.

What would you say is the most important thing about Web 2.0 today?

I would say that the most important thing is that even though we felt in the '90s that the Internet was having a big impact in people's lives, we're seeing in *this* decade that it's reconstructing a lot of industries and shifting a lot of value around while improving people's lives. And these are very large industries that are being reconstructed.

> *"One of the reasons I like my work is that the benefits are all very real."*

For instance, here at Skype we are seeing an impact on telecommunications. It is interesting. We could be simplistic and say that what's being reconstructed is voice calls becoming free, because you're using the Internet to talk across the world. But there's a lot more to it. There is the rich functionality, like presence, messaging, as well as the ability to migrate in a conversation between a chat, a voice call, and media sharing, all of which creates a lot of value and improves peoples' lives.

It's not just a change; it's also an improvement for consumers, and it's extremely liberating. I think telecommunications is at the beginning of what will be a longer transformation.

Are there any other industries you'd like to call out?

The one that most people know—because it's in the middle of a tornado—is advertising, which is mixed in with publishing, of course. That industry is actually seeing a transformation as all of the investments for advertising are shifting to the Internet.

The one that is beginning now, that I think is probably at the same age of maturity as telecommunications, is television and media. We've seen *some* impact, but I think there's a lot more to come.

Is there anything about Web 2.0 that you think people are misunderstanding or getting wrong?

To me the biggest misunderstanding, or perhaps the narrowest view, is the technical view that Web 2.0 is about AJAX or about a particular set of technologies. I see that as only one of the many components. What is interesting about the Internet for me is the resurging phenomena of improving people's lives and transforming industries.

For me the biggest misunderstanding is the thought that Web 2.0 equals AJAX or that it equals widgets.

What benefits are you or Skype seeing in regard to Web 2.0?

One of the reasons I like my work is that the benefits are all very *real*. I'll go to a party and be talking to someone, [and] they'll say, "Oh, you work at Skype? I talk to my dad every week on video, because he lives in Mexico and I live in London, and we get to see each other."

It is very simple and very much from the gut, but it is actually changing how relationships are maintained across the world.

I bet you are calling into this interview using Skype, and I know that several other interviews also had Skype to make the international calls easier.

It's making the world a lot smaller (Skype *and* Web 2.0).

Shifting back to the primary discussion, what issues do you see with Web 2.0?

I don't really see issues in terms of problems.

In most periods of substantial innovation, which tend to last five to ten years, you will encounter a number of obstacles and problems along the way. This is typical with technology and innovation. What you do is you figure out your way around it, either as a company or as an industry. It might take six months or it might

> *"People don't tend to see…how the Web is getting more homogenized and more easily 'cut and paste'-able."*

take two years to sort out a particular problem. I don't see them as issues, but more as things that happen when there are such big shifts in industries.

Do you see the Semantic Web, often called Web 3.0, as the next big shift in the industry?

I'm not sure. For a long time, we've been talking about the Semantic Web, and it's a particular "vision"—sort of very academic, if you will. It's a wonderful view—like what happened with the Internet, which grew so fast that there was no time to figure out the structure of data, and everything was dumped on the Web in many different ways—and none of it can be mixed and matched together to understand it. Every web site is different, and you have no way to have an integrated, structured view of the entire Web.

The Semantic Web, to me, is a way to figure out how to structure this whole set so that you can navigate it much better.

Will it happen overnight? No.

Will it happen over a longer period of time? Yes, and probably in somewhat unpredictable ways.

Interestingly, I think what we're seeing with widgets is a flavor of structuring that data. It's sort of a very small step towards Semantic Web. You can grab a widget, copy and paste it, and put it somewhere else. Years ago, that would have been unthinkable. But people don't tend to see that connection about how the Web is getting more homogenized and more easily "cut and paste"-able.

The Semantic Web is also about giving context and meaning to things. Do you think that widgets will gain more meaning?

Honestly, for it to be workable, it needs to be well-standardized. People need to add all the metadata in order to have semantics cutting across all kinds of web sites. I don't really want to get into the issues of ontologies and the technologies because it becomes a nightmare.

> *"We've seen a lot more benefit to consumers in this phase, and a lot more lagging response behind passing these benefits on to enterprises."*

I think it will happen, because if you look in a 10- to 20-year horizon, it doesn't make sense to have unstructured data being published. But, it needs to start in some niches, and from there, it will flourish.

I'm not so sure, however, that the next phase of innovation that we'll see in the next two to five years will necessarily be Semantic Web as the underpinning; I just don't know.

If not the Semantic Web, then what would you expect the next wave of innovation to be?

I think about that a lot and try to figure out where to be in that respect.

I think there are obvious evolutions, like the two that we discussed earlier. Telecommunications will continue to develop in terms of the migration of standard telecommunications to Internet technologies; a different form factor. This is because there are benefits such as presence, broadcasting, and being able to log in and out of everything in one place.

Of course the other is media.

It is sort of obvious that those are going to evolve in the near to medium term. Others, I don't know, really.

Switching topics a little bit, do you believe Software as a Service (SaaS) or Software plus Services (S+S) are fact or fiction?

I think those are fact—those things are real.

One of the interesting things that has happened with Web 2.0, although I don't have a great grasp of the history, is that it is one of the great technology phases that was mostly consumer-led. We've seen a lot more benefit to consumers in this phase, and a lot more lagging response behind passing these benefits on to enterprises.

Software as a Service has been used mostly in the context of enterprises. We're working with companies that do that: Skype enables Salesforce, which is one of those great company sites that offers SaaS.

> *"People were shocked that this could be easy and it could just work."*

A lot of software that people use on their desktop is going to be much more comfortably used on the Internet. Some of it will remain desktop apps, just because you can use leverage the CPUs and the audio/video qualities of your desktop much better than on the Web. But, yes, I think SaaS is fact.

We've talked about mobile a little bit, and Skype is based on mobile and broadband. There are places where connectivity is not available, especially broadband connectivity. Do you see the ability to be connected becoming pervasive everywhere?

I think it's one of those basic things like the telephone. You will end up having it; it's a question of local market conditions and how it evolves, but I don't see it as something that is going to be a stumbling block.

So then do you see us being "always connected" at some point?

Yes, I sort of see it like mobiles. People will have a mobile, but it will just be broadband.

Switching back to Web 2.0, what would you say is the coolest thing you've seen done in the Web 2.0 space?

Of course I have to talk about Skype!

I think it's really hard today to see the impact you had when it was a few years back. People had a hard time believing that they could make global calls for free. There was a general question of, "What's the catch?" along with statements such as, "It can't be free," and, "It can't sound better than my phone." People were shocked that this could be easy and it could just work.

I remember the impact that video had; then so many people started having video calls as a matter of fact. I'm always shocked at meeting people at a party, or dinner, or friends of friends, and seeing the pervasiveness of the use.

Sound Bites

While Skype is done with desktop software and mobile devices, it still happens on the Internet. As indicated in the above interview, the telecommunications industry is evolving, and Skype is at the center of it. Being in the heart of this, Rodrigo Madanes has some interesting insights into the changing industry and into Web 2.0. Many of those insights follow:

- By definition, Web 2.0 is the resurgence of web innovation after the dotcom bust in 2002. It was triggered in great part by technology and the critical mass of broadband users around the world, and led to people being able to communicate more.

- AJAX, AIR, Flash, and those kinds of technologies have contributed to and are components of Web 2.0, but Web 2.0 is the result of a critical mass of people with broadband, enabling technologies, large investments and start-ups, and a combination of low-cost, Open Source packages that enable these start-ups to accelerate very quickly—all of those things led to a transformation in the industries of telecommunications, advertising, and television.

- Even though we felt in the '90s that the Internet was having a big impact in people's lives, we're seeing in *this* decade that it's reconstructing a lot of industries and shifting a lot of value around while improving people's lives.

- In most periods of substantial innovation, which tend to last five to ten years, you will encounter a number of obstacles and problems along the way. This is typical with technology and innovation.

- The Semantic Web is a way to figure out how to structure this whole set of data on the Web so that you can navigate through it much better.

- You can grab a widget, copy and paste it, and put it somewhere else. Years ago, that would have been unthinkable. The Web is getting more homogenized and more easily "cut and paste"-able.

- Web 2.0 is one of the great technology phases that was mostly consumer-led. We've seen a lot more benefit to consumers in this phase and a lot more lagging response of passing these benefits on to enterprises.

Rod Smith:
IBM Corporation

17

> "Web 2.0 is about how businesses are changing, how
> people are collaborating, and how people are unlocking
> content to be used in new and innovative ways through
> customization, at orders of magnitude of less cost than
> they've ever had before."

—Rod Smith

IBM stands for International Business Machines and is a name that has
been around the computer industry for a long time. In fact, IBM incorporated nearly a century ago, in 1911. Its roots, however, go back even farther
than that.

www.ibm.com

IBM focuses on many areas, including products and services. The company is well-known in the mainframe arena and has also been a big proponent of Open Source, Linux, and more. It would take an entire book to describe what IBM has done and what they do now.

With such a vast history, IBM is a company worthy of being asked for an opinion on current and new technologies.

Web 2.0 Is That Intersection of Social Changes, Economic Changes, and Technology Changes

If you want to know what is happening with emerging technologies at IBM, then the person to talk to is Rod Smith, vice president, Emerging Internet Technologies. Rod has stated in interviews[1] that blogs, wikis, and innovative sites like Wikipedia and Google Maps are going to change the way that productivity applications are developed. Given that he's made such statements in the past, it is worth hearing what Rod has to say about Web 2.0 today.

Can you tell a little about yourself and what you do at IBM?

I lead our emerging Internet technology initiatives at IBM; I've done it since 1995.

Back then, I was also the Java CTO and was thinking about how we help grow Java from the language into an open middleware platform that would garner broad industry adoption.

My team has also been very involved in Open Source, particularly through the Apache Foundation, and open standards around application and data interoperability; we were very early innovators in XML, providing the early, W3C, standards-based parser to an Apache project. This then evolved into working on open distributed computing standards and technologies, such as SOAP, which evolved into Web Services. Today this is what we refer to as SOA—a loosely coupled programming model architecture enterprises are embracing.

All this set the stage for work that we're doing today in Web 2.0 and enterprise mash-up areas.

---

[1] IBM Executive Declares Web 2.0 Technology to Drive New Business Applications, http://www-03.ibm.com/press/us/en/pressrelease/19821.wss.

Internally, many folks refer to us as the "clue train;" we're responsible for collaborating broadly in the industry on shaping emerging standards and technologies, sizing up the potential business value by working closely with customers to get early feedback and guidance through proof-of-concepts and providing our product teams with insights as they help these technologies mature. Customers today are eager to hear what is on the horizon—it's a fast-changing world today. So, that's what I do, and we've had a really fun time doing it.

How would you define Web 2.0?

We stick close to the O'Reilly definition: it is the intersection of social changes, economic changes, and technology changes. That is what makes Web 2.0 elusive; it hasn't been about one technology. It's about how businesses are changing, how people are collaborating, and how people are unlocking content to be used in new and innovative ways—much faster and simpler than ever before.

Today's business folks are discovering emergent business opportunities and asking how they can harness these opportunities quickly to add new value. And they look at the potential Web 2.0 offers in terms of the mash-ups, for example, where domain experts collaborate and assemble new solutions in days or weeks—especially line-of-business and IT folks—and they've realized that, as businesses, they've put up barriers toward quick innovations. Businesses want to create the same kind of culture and capabilities Web 2.0 is enabling—inside their enterprises.

So, a good example in the Web 2.0 world is that I get challenged when I talk with line-of-business folks. They lay out a solution they'd like to see, and then they ask, "Can you come back to me in 30 days with something running?" Five years ago, that would have been impossible.

> *"Today, with Web 2.0, we can come back to [vendors] quickly and engage them at a business level."*

Usually if you tell a vendor that, they go away, they might build charts, they might do some proof of concepts, and they might come back in six to nine months with something running. It's all on spec—on trying to get a deeper understanding of the customer's needs.

Today, with Web 2.0 technologies, we can come back to them quickly and engage them at a business level with a solution and say, "Is this what you have in mind?" We might get it right; we might get it completely wrong. But, 30 days' worth of investment demonstrates the agility Web 2.0 brings to a relationship with customers. We can move quickly, and then I can evolve it with the customer at that point.

The term "remixability" has been used before. In what ways do you see people doing remixability?

Two years ago, we went to corporations and talked about leveraging syndication fees, RSS, and ATOM to unlock their content, so it could be remixed by their business partner; many folks in data centers scratched their heads, not really understanding the value of their data beyond the normal enterprise applications.

Today when I go back to those customers, 70 to 80 percent of them are enabling syndication feeds. And they're doing it because it's a very cost-effective way to pass information or get information to their business partners and others, and it doesn't have to be high-performance.

> *"Now you're seeing IT and the line of business [side] really collaborate."*

The part that I think drove people crazy on remixability in the past is that as soon as you get to a data center, they think about the high-performance transactional nature of content and how to ensure enterprise-grade scalability. They don't think about this whole "long tail" aspect of business opportunities. Remixability is using content to go after niche markets, and XML, syndication feeds, widgets, enable them to tap opportunities as a cost point orders of magnitude cheaper that with prior technologies.

You mentioned barriers. Often there are barriers to information and information access. Do you see changes in how people are working with information as a result of Web 2.0?

There are two or three things that are happening, and this comes back to empowering people, as much as anything else. When folks have information that they want to share with their business ecosystem, prior to Web 2.0 you asked your IT department, "Go open up an interface, or build a certain application so that my business partners can get to that information." Today, they look at syndication feeds as one way, a very inexpensive way, to keep their partners up to speed on what they think is relevant information.

But there's another dimension to that. What we've learned in talking to the line-of-business people is that they need to stay involved in the decisions of publishing and making information available. It's not an IT-only respon- sibility. So the line-of-business folks tell us, "I want to be in the loop [con- cerning] when content should be refreshed; I can tell you when that content has new business value." That's very different from, "IT, please take care of it; I never want to see it again."

So now you're seeing IT and the line of business really collaborate—under- standing the business value of their assets, the content.

Do you see the sharing of information impacting the consumer? Do you see consumers being more open with information?

We're often seeing the aspects of that, from a user-generated standpoint. IBM holds an annual virtual event called The Innovation Jam. The first couple years, we did strictly internal IBMers; then we opened it up to IBMers and Partners. Last year, we opened it up to IBMers, Partners, and families and friends. We said, "Tell us what your ideas are; tell us what you think are areas we should be working in." We had a huge turnout and IBM invested $100 million to develop the top ideas.

Other companies are looking for and are experiencing that very same thing. They're finding that users want to share information and want a cost-effective channel to do that.

> *"It doesn't take 18 months to respond to a new opportunity."*

Web 2.0 offers them that and it seems to resonate quite well.

Do you see consumers driving businesses more than they have in the past?

Yes, I do. It comes in two ways. One is that we show businesses that it doesn't take 18 months to respond to a new opportunity. Now you're seeing businesses turn to their customers, and say, "What things would *you* like?" We can respond faster now. They feel like they can be engaged. They don't feel like they have to be apologizing for the fact that things take some time, as they did before.

So we're now seeing a lot of folks that are doing more of what we call "un-conferences"—getting their lead customers and their people together and really cross-pollinating ideas that a business can try to turn around and harvest and harness and go to market with quickly.

IBM has been around "forever." There used to be the two- to six-year project cycle, and that was for phase one. Do you see the days of these large-scale project time frames being gone?

Oh, no! I don't see it gone—I see this new idea of Web 2.0–style applications that can address the IT backlog, so we'll have a class of applications that can be addressed in days or weeks rather than be relegated to longer project cycles.

IBM has an Information On Demand (IOD) conference and one of the applications we saw (I hope you're sitting down) is IMS that added a REST interface that returned an ATOM feed, and it was one of the most popular pedestals at IOD. Now, IMS has been around for 30-plus years but here were customers envisioning how enhancing IMS with Web 2.0 capabilities could provide them the IMS content they needed at a fraction of the normal development costs. Now those specialized application requests by a line-of-business or business partner could be satisfied—and that's a big deal.

> *"Some innovations will be successful business-wise and some will fail. And that's a good thing."*

The mantra we've heard from customers is, "I want my content to be mashable." Initially, I thought I understood this—pretty simple. But I learned after lots of discussions that businesses use this simple statement to mean, "I want to see my content and services reused in ways they were not originally intended."

Web 2.0 really does bring customization costs down to a level that I think makes it feasible to really innovate fast. Some innovations will be successful business-wise, and some will fail. And that's a good thing; you want to have some successes and some failures, at the right cost point.

Do you see people trying to remix a lot of the old technologies?

Absolutely—which is fun. Existing applications all have content locked away that lines-of-businesses would like to use for new business opportunities—but, again, the development costs outweighed the benefits.

The interesting part to me is that there are all of these hardened applications with little flexibility, and Web 2.0 is giving them flexibility. The Rich Internet experience that goes along with it is, I think, very important from a business perspective. The web browser is great for reach, but for years now businesses have complained to me that they lose business because of the somewhat clumsy browsing experience, and that can be directly tied to revenue. So the whole rich experience that AJAX is bringing to the table is not from a marketing standpoint; businesses are looking at how they can improve their revenue.

You mentioned AJAX. Is AJAX Web 2.0?

I think so. I think when customers look at it, they like the fact that Web 2.0 is browser-based. They like the fact that AJAX vendors are using standards, which means openness and choice for businesses. With AJAX, now you've got a different level of interaction granularity where widgets and feeds are communicating back to data sources on the backend. From an enterprise perspective, I would say RIAs (Rich Internet Applications) build on the SOA loosely coupled programming model.

What would you say is the single most important thing about Web 2.0?

Oooooh—very hard to do.

I think it's the way that we're really moving and empowering content-oriented developers. It's back to the data piece, and that to me is exciting. So, Web 2.0 is about how we're

> *"Applications don't have to live forever. They're 'disposable.'"*

seeing content services really expand business opportunities, and doing this in a simple manner that can be utilized by a very, very broad base of, I'll say developers, but experienced to technically astute line-of-business folks, if you will.

What would you consider the most misunderstood thing—the thing that people are getting wrong—about Web 2.0?

We've used the term "situational applications," which we've found resonated with customers extremely well. There are all these pent-up applications that they've not been able to afford to write before. The long tail applies to applications as well as content. I think the misunderstood part, for many businesses, is that some of these applications don't have to live forever. They're "disposable," and they really are situational: they're good for a certain partnership, and then they can go away.

If you say that to some IT organizations, they nearly have a heart attack. This is the worst nightmare in the world to them! Because they worry, through past experiences, they'll get saddled down the road with, "Please make this into such and such" and therefore they'll be measured by why it wasn't right in the first place in terms of enterprise scalability, security, and quality of service.

> *"Web 2.0 really is empowering and can help transform IT and line-of-business relationships."*

The second misunderstood thing is the value of simple access methods to data centers; their responsibility is to control and optimize access to (business) information. I think syndication feeds were viewed, until recently, as almost too simple—but exactly what many line-of-business folks were looking for.

In both cases, Web 2.0 will help transform IT and line-of-business relationships. But, some IT organizations are like, "Oh my, I've got another variable on how to control business," as opposed to, "How do I empower the business?"

What are some of the cool things IBM has done with Web 2.0?

Just look at what IBM Lotus has done around Lotus Connections and our Dogear offerings; those were all started from our CIO department. They are Web 2.0 applications that we've been using internally for the past couple years.

We're our own proving ground for Web 2.0. IBM is a large community, and if a piece of software is good, then our folks will use it and product groups will digest it.

Our CIO office has created a Web 2.0 situational application platform—it is a place where people deploy the situational apps. Our experience has been these Web 2.0 applications give significant cost savings to our different lines of business.

The fun part is that we get to go right to the customers. A lot of what Web 2.0 does is let businesses visualize their middleware investments.

That's rewarding to us and our developers to be able to short-circuit the development cycle and know we're constantly on the right path both with IT and business unit needs, as opposed to wringing our hands and hoping that we hit the right spot two years down the road.

What do you see as the next big thing after Web 2.0?

It's a funny question. I started Web Services in 1999, and in maybe 2003, somebody asked, "All the technology is laid out; what's the next big thing?" I said, "Well, culturally, businesses are still going to be absorbing SOA and this whole area for another five or six years. I think Web 2.0 is sparking a lot of imagination on what will be the value proposition of Web 2.0, three, four, or five years down the road."

Whether it's in the financial sector, or the media sector, it's really interesting how folks are really thinking about the dynamicity of information and wanting that expressed in ways beyond tag clouds and where we are today, so they can see semantic relationships and make really fast business decisions. I think we've just scratched the surface of what Web 2.0 [is capable of].

Sound Bites

IBM has been around for many decades. Rod Smith has been at IBM for over a decade himself, and during that time has been working with emerging technology. It is no surprise that he is experienced in the Web 2.0 space and thus has several interesting comments to make. Many of his thoughts follow:

- Web 2.0 is that intersection of social changes, economic changes, and technology changes. It's about how businesses are changing, how people are collaborating, and how people are unlocking content to be used in new and innovative ways through customization, at orders of magnitude of less cost than they've ever had before.
- Users want to share information, and in the past did not have a cost-effective channel with which to do that. Web 2.0 offers them that and they seem to resonate quite well with it. Line-of-business people need to be involved in the decisions of publishing and making that information available.
- A lot of folks that are getting their lead customers and their people together really do cross-pollinate on ideas that a business can try to turn around and harvest and harness and go to market quickly.

- Some innovations will be, business-wise, successful, and some will fail. And that's a good thing. You want to have some successes and some failures, at the right cost point.
- Now you've got a different level of granularity where you've got widgets and things talking back to data sources on the backend, but architecturally, it's just a nice extension.
- Applications don't have to live forever. They're "disposable," and they really are situational: they're good for a certain partnership, and then they can go away.
- Web 2.0 really is empowering and can help transform IT and line-of-business relationships. A lot of what Web 2.0 does is let you visualize your middleware investments.

Tim Harris:
Microsoft
Corporation

18

"Enterprises want to take advantage of the social and collaborative aspects of Web 2.0 but don't necessarily want the business models of Web 2.0 shoved down their throat."

—*Tim Harris*

Microsoft is a company that nearly everyone in the modernized world has heard mentioned. Being the creator of the leading web browser, Microsoft Internet Explorer, means that anyone working with Web 2.0 or the Web in general is also likely to be fully aware of Microsoft. While there are some that might say that a pre-Web company can't fully understand Web 2.0, there are more that are likely to say that a company like Microsoft will be involved in any major, current technology.

www.live.com & www.popfly.com

Microsoft is showing itself as a big player in the Web 2.0 market. As a tool maker, they have developed some of the key tools people are using to develop Web 2.0 web sites. This includes their ASP.NET AJAX Control Toolkit and ASP.NET AJAX Extensions. A newer tool provided by Microsoft also can be considered a Web 2.0 site. This is Popfly (www.popfly.com). On Popfly, you can use an interactive web site to develop your own site or to create a mashup using building blocks created from other sites. More important, you can inter-act with others and share your creations.

Microsoft's best-known Web 2.0 site, however, is Live Search (www.live.com). This portal is a starting point for a number of features that are generally con-sidered Web 2.0. On Live Search, you can find mail, messaging, blogging, and many other social features.

So what is Microsoft's view on Web 2.0? The best way to find out is to ask!

There Is No Consensus in the Industry of What Web 2.0 Is

While there are numerous big names at Microsoft, including well-known fig-ures such as Bill Gates, Steve Ballmer, and Ray Ozzie, if you want to get the details on specific areas, it is better to talk to the people more directly influ-encing the technology. Tim Harris works as a product manager in the Developer & Platform Evangelism (DPE) group in the Server & Tools Division. Such a position gives him the insights into what Microsoft is truly doing and where it is headed at a working level.

Jumping right in, let me ask the "easy" question: how would Microsoft define Web 2.0?

It is funny that you call that the easy question! You know that when we go out and talk to customers, ISPs, and all throughout the industry, and every person gives a different answer.

When people talk about Web 2.0, it really falls down onto the three pillars. There's the technology pillar where people are talking about things like RSS, ASP.NET AJAX, and technologies for building web sites and web applications. And then there's the business model pillar—the fact that busi-ness models have become inextricably linked to the software and so most of the focus there is on advertising models of all sorts of subscription mod-els and other business models around the delivery of software to the user.

The last pillar people have a tendency to talk about are these social constructs; the bidirectional communication that Web 2.0 enables—blogs, wikis, social mapping software, and things like that—things that create or give the end user the ability to communicate back to the people who are running the software.

Having said that, the way that Microsoft views Web 2.0 is that we take an expansive view where we look at the capabilities—the technologies, the business models, and the social constructs—and we wrap them into what we're calling Software plus Services (S+S). And by expansive view, I mean that we look at it from the perspective that to enable all these capabilities requires software running on the Internet and on the desktop. We need software to be able to interoperate when bits and pieces of it are running in different locations, and across all the different devices that people use in their lives today. People aren't just tethered to a desktop workstation or laptop these days. They expect to be able to have the same rich experience on mobile phones, on game consoles, on any of the different devices that they are using to access the information they want to get at.

Just to pick at a point, you mention game consoles. Would you say that Web 2.0 is applicable to the Xbox 360?

And I would submit that aspects of what people call Web 2.0 are already on the Xbox 360. With the Xbox Live service, we hit the technology side of it. We deliver the technology that enables things like information feeds to come down to the box to provide matching and collaboration between the people as in the matchmaking scenarios. From the business-model side, there is advertising, digital distribution of games, and the ability for game publishers to sell additional content on top of the games they sell in a box model, so new business models are definitely there. And then from a social model, people have their friends list, they can voice-chat with one another, they can text-chat with one another, they can meet up with their friends in these virtual spaces and play games. So I would submit that that is Web 2.0 in the sense

> *"People have a tendency to put Web 2.0 in the 'browser bucket,' and say that if it is not running in a browser it is not Web 2.0."*

of looking at it from the three pillars in so far as we've taken Xbox Live and integrated it with things like our web front end. So Xbox.com is another head that you can use to get into the Xbox Live experience. So even from within Xbox.com you can go through and send messages to your friends and you can look at all the stats for different games and stuff like that. And then there is also the instant messenger integration with MSN Messenger.

So yeah, I'd say that people have a tendency to put Web 2.0 in the "browser bucket," and say that if it is not running in a browser, it is not Web 2.0. And I think that is really the big difference between how Microsoft views Software plus Services and how most people view the Web. We don't necessarily say that if it is not running in a browser, it is not Web 2.0. Does it deliver on the social experience? Does it deliver on the ability to provide for different business models? Does it provide different capabilities through the technologies?

Microsoft has developed a lot of tools such as Popfly, the ASP.NET AJAX Control Toolkit, Silverlight, Live platform, and even XNA Game Studio for game development. Are you seeing people using these tools for Web 2.0 or are you seeing primarily an extension of previous development of standard applications? What kinds of Web 2.0 things do you see people building?

Oh man. It runs the gamut. There is everything from simple mashups with the Live platform, especially with mapping and stuff like that, all the way up to people building full-blown desktop applications that take advantage of technologies like RSS, synchronization, etc.

From a tools perspective, we are creating the tools that let developers build whatever they want to build—Visual Studio, Silverlight, our libraries for ASP.NET AJAX. Wherever we see the developer community needing tools to be able to do the things they want to do, those are the needs we try to fill. I think that is one of the main things, one of the unique advantages that Microsoft brings to bear, is the simple fact that we have this huge breadth. We are the only company that can provide developer tools that span all of the consumer scenarios, all of the enterprise scenarios, the consoles, mobile phones, desktop, and browse-based—you name it. To ask, "Is Microsoft seeing people use tools to build Web 2.0 applications?" The answer is, "Absolutely."

MySpace is using Microsoft tools. Developers like Facebook are using Microsoft tools on the back end. Anywhere from the back end to the front-end to the actual IDE that the developers are using, we have a presence.

You mention mashups. One of the concepts that comes up often is the idea of open APIs. Where do you see that going?

As far as APIs are concerned, we have a tendency to think of things in terms of APIs. We look at offerings that we are going to bring to market and we look at the perspective of, "Okay, cool. What are the APIs we are going to enable for developers to build on top of the platform we are going to bring to market?" That is an evolutionary process.

You can look at what we are doing with Live. We have our first iteration of APIs that are out there that we are letting people play with. But we are also internally looking at what we can do better, at what we can do to let developers build more consistent applications against this service platform.

That is in our blood. I don't see that changing. I see that expanding.

There are some companies that say that in order to be a Web 2.0 entity, you need to go beyond open APIs to Open Source and you can't play effectively in the Web 2.0 world unless you open your source. Any thoughts or comments on Web 2.0 and Open Source?

I think that there is definitely an agenda out there. One of the interesting things is that a lot of those Open Source companies are struggling from the business-model perspective. Well, cool; if all of my intellectual property is out there for everyone to see, then how do I turn around and monetize that rather than having everyone simply take it and copy it?

I think that the real key is making sure that the standards are there, the protocols are there, the interoperability is there. I don't think that includes taking what makes your company unique and giving it away.

We are seeing the evolution of things going to the Web and software going free, or near free, or claiming to be free from an up-front purchase price. Do you see Web 2.0 changing how money is made from applications?

It is obvious that business models are changing. It used to be that the business model for software and the software itself were completely separate entities. The packaging and distribution were completely separate from the development. That is not the case today. As applications are being delivered more and more over the Web and as people have an expectation or a desire for applications to have a low or zero up-front cost, the need for developers to be cognizant of the business model under which their application is going to be distributed is higher than ever. In fact, that is one of the main things that we are focusing on is the fact that developers have to be businessmen now. They need to be able to sit there and know that packaging and distribution are not separate from the actual delivery or coding of the software. I'd not say it is going to change—it is and has changed. The challenge right now is more educational rather than technological. Our challenge is getting people to understand how to get their arms around these new business models, especially the developer community.

So is it a good time to buy an advertising company?

Well, we just bought one, so I'd say yes. Advertising is just one of the business models that people look at as the embodiment of Web 2.0. When you talk about consumer software, that is where people jump to—you get the software for free, but you have advertising plastered all over it. That is kind of the new consumer web viewpoint, or consumer software viewpoint.

From the enterprise side of software, that doesn't necessarily hold true. What company wants their employees surfing ads when they are supposed to be doing the job? It is an interesting take because enterprises want to take advantage of the social and collaborative aspects of Web 2.0, but don't necessarily want the business models of Web 2.0 shoved down their throat.

> *"There is no consensus in the industry of what Web 2.0 is."*

From the Microsoft perspective, we are looking to provide to any number of business models, whether it is advertising-based, subscription-based, whether it is renting, leasing, purchasing. We are building our tools to allow developers to build applications with any number of business models.

What would you consider the more important features of Web 2.0? What is important within Web 2.0? Would that be one of the three pillars you mentioned?

If you kind of look at the three pillars I mentioned, then the business models and the technologies are sort of enablers for the social constructs. So I'd say the meaning of Web 2.0 is that there is this new social construct–type software that enables collaboration—that democratizes the publishing of information out to the Internet. So if I had to say that there was one that stands on top or stands above the rest, the big one is the social side of it, but then the technology and business pillars are absolutely enablers of that.

What do you think is the most misunderstood area of Web 2.0?

Wow. That is an interesting question. A lot of people think that if you build an AJAX application with an RSS feed that you've done Web 2.0. It comes back to the definition—how you define Web 2.0. That would be what I'd probably say is the most misunderstood piece. There is no consensus in the industry of what Web 2.0 is. Every company, every vendor defines Web 2.0 in a way that best suits what they bring to market. From that perspective, the most misunderstood thing about Web 2.0 is the definition itself. It is this nebulous thing that is out there.

Separate from misunderstandings, do you see issues with Web 2.0 or with where Web 2.0 is headed?

Looking at it through the lens of developers. They are trying to get their arms and heads around Web 2.0. There is the architectural side of it. Now suddenly developers have to worry about things like, "Am I connected or disconnected? Am I going to be able to scale to potentially millions of users? Am I going to be able to take advantage of the local processing power of the device that the application is running on or am I going to rely on some back end service in the cloud and what happens if that service is not available for whatever reason?"

It is an interesting time to be a developer because you don't own your application from end to end. You are relying on others—and developers hate taking dependencies on others—for your application. The challenge from a business perspective is that now you have to figure out things like service-level agreements between all of these different services that you are using as part of your application. Who is responsible for monetization? How do I monetize a service if I open up a bunch of APIs and just let people start using it? How do I monetize that if people are able to just go through and mash that up in other applications?

So there are a lot of challenges. Most of the challenges aren't technical. Most of the challenges are from a business perspective, from an intellectual-property perspective, and from a model perspective.

What is the coolest thing you or Microsoft has done with Web 2.0?

Wow. It is going to sound like a little bit of a cop out, but Microsoft Exchange Server is the conical example of a Web 2.0 app. If you look back in 1998 when we did DHTML and XMLHTTP and shipped those as a part of Internet Explorer 5, and essentially drove, or pioneered, the development of AJAX—we simply didn't give it a cool four-letter acronym.

> "It is hard to not say that Web 3.0 has already jumped the shark."

I'd say that back then we were doing essentially what would become a Web 2.0 app. It was an application that could be hosted, that could be run on premise; it could be run from a client side, on a desktop machine—you could access it through mobile phones. You could get information fed to you or you could go and grab it yourself. Obviously, it is a collaborative application. It is really a kind of conical example from a development standpoint of what Web 2.0 is all about. I can hit it through a browser, from a mobile phone; I can hit it from a desktop.

What are your thoughts or opinion on Web 3.0, the Semantic Web? Is it what is next after Web 2.0 or is there something else that will be after Web 2.0?

It is hard to not say that Web 3.0 has already jumped the shark.

Being able to go through and point to a particular thing and say that this is the next evolution—I don't think I'll be able to do that. I look at the next five years and I say that it will take that long for people to get their arms around where we are already. I think that the next big thing will be companies figuring out how to make use of the technologies that have been brought to market. It has taken almost 10 years for Web 2.0 to come about after the technological underpinnings were put into place.

Ten years seems to be the standard for technology adoption, although it is getting quicker.

Correct. So to ask me to look 10 years into the future to determine whether semantics are the next big thing? I think more and more that all the data that you see on the Web is going to get tagged. Metadata is becoming more and more prevalent in the information that is available on the Web. Now, whether that gets translated into semantics or into new, cool ways of sorting and filtering remains to be seen.

If we ignore semantics, what do you think Microsoft is going to be working on in five years that is going to be treated like Web 2.0 is treated today? What is the next big thing? Adapting technology is a given, but is there something coming?

I think that the next big thing is simply driving the seamlessness that we've talked about. We are at the beginnings of really enabling the seamlessness of use. Up-leveling the user experience; making it so that more and more of the devices that I use on a day-to-day basis get connected to the Net; that developers have a consistent way of enabling those devices to provide a rich experience for end users to be able to get what they want done.

Sound Bites

Microsoft is the best-known computer company in the world. Although the company predates the Internet, it has shown that it can keep up or catch up if necessary. In regard to Web 2.0, the following are a few interesting opinions provided by Microsoft in this interview:

- People have a tendency to put Web 2.0 in the "browser bucket," and say that if it is not running in a browser it is not Web 2.0.
- Microsoft is the only company that can provide developer tools that span all of the consumer scenarios, all of the enterprise scenarios, the consoles, mobile phones, desktop, and browser based—you name it.
- The real key is making sure that standards, protocols, and interoperability are there.
- It is obvious that business models are changing.
- The need for developers to be cognizant of the business model under which their application is going to be distributed is greater than ever.
- Enterprises want to take advantage of the social and collaborative aspects of Web 2.0, but don't necessarily want the business models of Web 2.0 shoved down their throat.
- A lot of people think that if you build an AJAX application with an RSS feed, you've done Web 2.0.
- There is no consensus in the industry of what Web 2.0 is.
- It is hard to not say that Web 3.0 has already "jumped the shark."
- It has taken almost 10 years for Web 2.0 to come about after the technological underpinnings were put into place.

Bob Brewin & Tim Bray: Sun Microsystems

19

> *"Anyone with reasonable smarts can have a good idea for a web property on Monday and can have something on the air two weeks from Thursday."*
>
> —Tim Bray

Most people have heard of the Java programming language and likely the company behind the programming language, Sun Microsystems, Inc. Using the slogan "The Network is the Computer," Sun is actually involved in hardware, operating systems, programming languages and more.

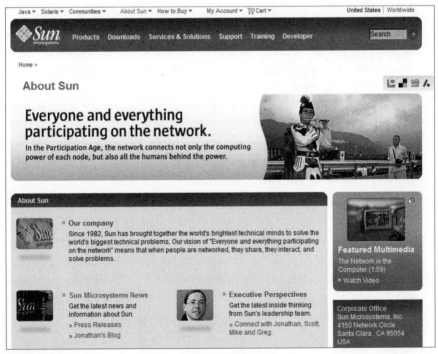

When it comes to web technologies, at Sun, the Java language and other initiatives that have occurred have been deeply involved with what is happening on the Web. Their work in hardware and operating systems has also given them perspectives that are worth noting in regard to the Web as well.

It Is All about the Information Flow

Not many people have the title of distinguished engineer at major software companies. At Sun, two distinguished engineers took time to answer a few questions about their perspectives, and that of Sun Microsystems, in regards to Web 2.0. Although there was general agreement in most of the comments; at times the two definitely had different perspectives—perspectives, however, that are both interesting.

Robert Brewin is a distinguished engineer and the chief technology officer for software at Sun Microsystems. He has been responsible for developer products and application platforms including the Java platform, mobility, enterprise software, and business-integration products. He has been chief architect for Sun's developer tools portfolio, where he led in such initiatives as strategic enhancements to the NetBeans IDE, the creation of Java Studio Creator, and more. He is responsible for Sun's role in Web 2.0 technologies.

Also at Sun is Tim Bray. Tim launched one of the first public web search engines in 1995, he co-invented XML 1.0, and he managed the Oxford English Dictionary project at the University of Waterloo from 1987 to 1989. He served as a Tim Berners-Lee appointee on the W3C Technical Architecture Group from 2002 to 2004. For Sun Microsystems, he is the director of web technologies.

Can you tell me a little bit about your roles at Sun?

Bob: I'm a CTO and VP for Sun Software. Like Tim, I'm a distinguished engineer. Most of what I look at and touch upon at Sun are those things that will layer on top of operating systems: much of the Java space, much of the developer space, much of the Web space. We have another CTO at Sun that focuses on the operating level, Tim Marsland. There is sort of a separation of roles, although there is obviously a lot of crossover.

In terms of areas that peak my interest around the whole Web 2.0 space, it is basically what I consider the "inversion of control and influence" that Web 2.0 has driven. Basically, it is a certain way to look at how things have changed and continue to change for the client and for what we expect out of our client, as well as for the enterprises and networks that provide that foundation.

Inversion of control, the way I've typically described it, is that in the good ol' days, whatever we provided—being the enterprise or the network—was what the client got. Essentially, they had this static portal with information that we decided to deploy.

I think it has completely flipped around now to where the enterprise is scrambling mightily to not only serve all the needs, but to basically handle the flow of information, which is tied into what Tim was interested in here. But it is about how all this information gets into the network and then gets disseminated back to all of the people who are participating.

> *"All the participants on the Web have an equal say in how the Web and the information on the Web resolves."*

Tim: My title is director of web technologies. I'm a distinguished engineer like Bob. I'm sort of a designated "wild-eyed crazy," sharing ideas about dangerous new things. I was deeply mixed up in the original introduction of blogging at Sun back in 2004, which kind of plunged us neck-deep in what we would now call the Web 2.0 waters. It has really been a tremendous success [in regard to Sun] as an enabler in a business and cultural view.

Web 2.0 is all about information flow; whether you call it inversion of control or inversion of information flow, it all shakes down to the same thing. The things that make the Web interesting these days are the things coming in from the edges, not the things coming out from the center. If you look at any two or three canonical Web 2.0 companies—Flickr, del.icio.us, YouTube, whatever—it is all about empowering the people at the edge to contribute to the richness of the Net. It is all about a culture of contribution. These contributions impinge on Sun's business at many levels. To start with, the enterprise's traditional IT departments are our largest customers and they are in the business of building web properties. They need to think a lot about how they are going to succeed in a world where they no longer control the flow of information. They need to surf and ride on the flow of information rather than trying to fight it.

Another thing that I think is really interesting is that the culture of contribution is not just at the end-user and content-contributor level, but it is also at the developer level. One of the things that's changed in the last few years is that it has become much easier to become a web developer. These new technologies have come along so that anyone with reasonable smarts can have a good idea for a web property on Monday and can have something on the air two weeks from Thursday. There is a culture of contribution that is extending the developer population, which is obviously a really important population for Sun.

> *"There are some hot Web 2.0 sites that are really very Web 1.0 in their technology."*

The combination of the Web becoming more interesting because of things coming in from the edges, and the technology becoming more interesting because of more contributors, is on balance and a real good thing for us because we are in the business of selling the infrastructure that all of this is going to run on.

You've hit on this, but let's ask the expected question: What is Web 2.0 to you?

Tim: Web 2.0 is the Internet based on the culture of contribution—the culture of contribution from the edges by individuals and by technology developers.

Bob: I'd take a different stab at that. Web 2.0 is a leveling of the playing field where the players are all equal. We all agree that there is this notion that the information flow is not one-way, it is not unidirectional, so all the people and all the participants on the Web have an equal say in how the Web and the information on the Web resolves.

What would your reaction be to people that say that Web 2.0 is Ajax, JavaFX, or Adobe AIR?

Bob: Frankly, I think it is an implementation detail. Again, Web 2.0 is not a technology. How technology manifests fundamentally is an aspect of what the Web is.

Tim: Those are all good, new technologies that I believe are going to improve user experiences. There are some hot Web 2.0 sites that are very

Web 1.0 in their technology. The technology is the facilitator, and it reduces friction, but it is not a dispenser of things. The dispenser of things is the new information flows and the culture of contribution.

You've already indicated this to some extent, but let me ask what you consider the most important aspect or feature of what you are calling Web 2.0?

Tim: The fact that you can be part of it. The fact that if you want to contribute, you don't have to be a journalist, an analyst, or a university professor. The fact that if you want to build a web site, you don't have to have studied Java EE for years. That is a big deal.

Bob: To quote a commercial, "Not only can you be a founder, but you can be a member." I think that is where it gets very interesting. There isn't a single-entity control or anything anymore. That is the beauty of it.

Looking at the other side of the question, what do you believe people are getting wrong or misunderstanding about Web 2.0 and all the hype?

Tim: The hype is the problem. If you go around the Bay and not just Silicon Valley, it is definitely getting a little bit "bubblicious" these days. That's okay. At the end of the day bubbles tend to have good aftermath. One thing that is good about this bubble is that it is less expensive than the Web 1.0 bubble was. So, the hangover will be less painful once we wake up. There is no doubt that people are painting the Web 2.0 label on anything they are trying to sell these days.

Do you think there is a bubble, and do you think it is going to burst?

Bob: Is there a bubble in the sense of Web 2.0? No. I think there is a bubble in the sense of the hype. I think that it is becoming pragmatic, and people are realizing that there is something real here, and they are understanding how they can build to this thing. Not only that, but they can then leverage it and use it. In terms of the ultimate endgame that it is going to solve world hunger, I think that people have made that bubble go away.

The other thing I'd like to address is the misconception that Web 2.0 is just about a specific technology—that it is just Ajax, or Java, or Ruby, or one of the many technologies being used by developers.

It is all those things and more in terms of implementation. But it is actually how we use it, and how it contributes to the overall social fabric that we have—that is what Web 2.0 is all about.

Tim: It is really dangerous to identify Web 2.0 with a particular technology. Obviously, one company at the center of all of this is Google, and yet a huge proportion of the Google core applications are built in Java. You just really can't tag and tabulate alongside something and make a direct conclusion that way.

From Sun's perspective, what are some of the benefits you have seen from Web 2.0?

Tim: The easiest one to understand is that we are in the business of providing infrastructure for networked applications. We've been saying that "The Network is The Computer" for more than 20 years now. Anything that makes the Internet bigger and better and gets more people involved is good for Sun. That is not rocket science. We are totally, unambiguously in favor of anything that makes the Net a better place. Clearly some of these new applications and new developer technologies that have come along qualify for that, so we are cheerleaders alright!

Keeping the focus on Sun, let me ask what you think are the "coolest" things going on at Sun in regards to Web 2.0.

Bob: I can think of two. Actually, I can think of a ton. I'll cover a couple of them.

> *"One of the important defining characteristics of the new-style web applications is 'time to market.'"*

First is when I take a look at the advances in client technology in the sense of enabling rich clients, especially mobile devices that connect to the Web and the Web 2.0 experience. That would be Java and JavaFX Mobile. I look at the efforts that are going on in terms of support and the bringing together and implementation of Ruby on Rails and JRuby. And again, it is both, not just one or the other.

When looking at systems and services, I see things like Niagara and Niagara 2. In terms of shipped hardware, it's better support for the massively scaled sort of web infrastructure. And then things like Thumper—the sort of disk storage coupled with CPU processing built on Solaris on the back-end. All of those things are hugely exciting.

WHAT ARE NIAGARA, NIAGARA 2, AND THUMPER?

Bob mentioned Niagara, Niagara 2, and Thumper. Niagara and Niagara 2 are processors from Sun. These are multicore processors that can work with multiple threads. In layman's terms, these are powerhouse processors when compared to a standard PC's processor. A multicore, multithreaded processor is capable of doing multiple things at a time. With eight cores, up to eight simultaneous processes can happen concurrently.

Thumper is a storage technology that was hinted at in 2004 and released in 2006. The result was Sun's Fire X4500 Server that combined an x64 server with loads of storage at what they considered a reasonable price.

Tim: We've talked about the technical side; let me talk about the nontechnical side. We at Sun are living the Web 2.0 story. We have become a highly transparent company. We are doing major public initiatives entirely via our blogging platform without doing traditional press releases. We have a very, very high proportion of people doing blogging, starting with our CEO at the top. The increased transparency and intimacy with our developer community and other constituencies has been a huge shot in the arm for the business. The ROI has been immense; especially considering the "I" part in the ROI is vanishing. Web 2.0: you don't have to sell us hard on it because we've seen it work, and it works for us.

One of the important defining characteristics of the new-style web applications is "time to market." Everything is happening very fast. If you have a new idea, you need to get it on the air in weeks rather than months. The work we are doing in developer support with NetBeans and the products is very much focused on applying the new set of tools that are available for developers. You should be able to get a good idea on Monday and have a prototype on the air on Thursday.

You mentioned return on investment. There are those that say Web 2.0 Features don't necessarily return on their costs. Do you see most Web 2.0 features being financially feasible?

Tim: I see them as being extremely cheap to deploy. It just does not cost very much to put up a blogging platform or social-network site. You can get all of the pieces you need from us or from other people and have something up in almost no time at all. I am a bit baffled by people saying there are high costs there.

The amount it cost us to put up our blogging platform to have thousands of employees talk to the world every day was almost embarrassingly small. On the other side of it, from the point of view of Sun, the benefits of increasing the bandwidth and transparency of our communication with our corporate contingencies have been overwhelming. The "I" is small and the "R" is huge.

Bob: The only thing I would add to that is that Sun as a company has this phrase that we use both internally and externally. One of the ways Sun derives value is by increasing the volume. Yes, there may be cases where directly implementing Web 2.0 technology may not directly drive revenue ideas and ROI, but looking at the larger picture, it is phenomenally huge. The more people are participating and using technology, products, sites, communities—all of those things, in the end, drive huge amounts of volume, which provides huge amounts of opportunity for driving ROI.

One of the benefits that Sun has over many Web 2.0 companies is that your revenue isn't driven by ad revenue or other "page view"–style revenue models. Web 2.0 can make a page more usable and decrease such views in the short term.

Tim: That seems like really backward thinking to me. Making your sites less usable to increase page views strikes me as bad.

Bob: The other side of this is, while it's an interesting way to view the world, fundamentally it strikes me that people who are building sites like that are very likely applying a sort of Web 1.0 methodology in building Web 2.0 sites. One of the advantages of many of the technologies that we implement on those things allows you to be more dynamic on your content and how you are engaging the customer. You may have fewer page counts, but you know what? You are tailoring those sites to the people visiting them. It is a huge advantage.

Changing focus, what do you see after Web 2.0? What do you see next?

Bob: Web 3…

Tim: *<laughing>*

Bob: My tongue in cheek!

If you look at Web 3.0 as the Semantic Web, then even though you say that tongue in cheek, there is a serious question there: What do you think of the Semantic Web as being the next thing? That was going to be my follow-up question, so now you have two questions to answer!

Bob: I'll start with the first one. I'll let "Mr. Semantic" answer the second one.

I think we are going to see huge volume and an explosion in growth in the face of clients who traditionally have not connected to the Web very well. This notion that all devices are isolated and not well-connected to the network will suddenly start to include things to leverage a more universally available and global IP network and all the assets on there. I'm thinking of technologies such as mobile phones, set-top boxes, your car's stereo, in-car navigation system. That is why when I mention things like client technologies and JavaFX Mobile; I am very excited. That plus the explosion and evolution of technology that forms the underpinnings that will allow everyone to participate on the Web in ways that they haven't been able to in the past.

Tim: Specifically in regard to what people call the Semantic Web. It is an interesting idea that is simply unproven. I have yet to see a killer Semantic Web app. And I think that it is an interesting research area, but it is still a research area. I don't think that we've quite connected the dots to make something that is going to change the world. Obviously it is something worth working on.

There is also the digital divide. There are still a lot of people that just aren't connected yet. If you look at the actual number of people that are participating in blogs, posting videos, posting links, doing their photographs on Flickr and stuff like that, then your first impression is, "Gosh, that is a lot of people."

But I think that's backwards. If you look at it and consider the number of people that might potentially want to participate, then we are just beginning, and there is a lot more room— an order of magnitude of more room to bring more people into participating in the Web. The big upside to Sun and for its core community in the short term is to reduce the friction, whether by empowering all the mobile devices as Bob talked about, or by making the authoring environments, the photo-taking environment, and the video-editing environment better, then we have the potential to ride the bus we are currently riding a long way. Not only will this be good for business; it will be good for the world. It will make the world and the Net a better world.

So do you think the Semantic Web will happen?

Tim: Personally, I'm unconvinced. The Semantic Web was first talked about in 1998, so we are seven or eight years into it now. I still haven't seen a killer app. Show me a killer app, and I'll start taking it seriously.

The terms Software as a Service (SaaS), Software plus Services (S+S) seems to be mixed in with Web 2.0. What are your thoughts on these?

Bob: Fundamentally, I think it is extremely real. SaaS is one of the ways that people are really leveraging the network in ways they haven't been able to before. This leveraging is around the notion of delivering the functionality, quality, and services that software provides, but not in its standard form. There are a number of ways to look at that, which go from being able to leverage certain full application services via the Web that are connecting to some other services or computers that are on the Net somewhere doing some useful work, to being able to reuse assets. Again, this is one of the ways I try to describe it—and poorly, by the way; this sort of evolution of computing from sort of functional-based programming to an object-oriented one is what gave birth to support services, which is where we are today.

This topic also brings up some issues that I don't think we've quite solved yet. So, while SaaS is being used as something such as accounting, or something as simple as using Google Maps, it does not provide a real, well-established and proven technology, framework, best practice, or blueprint for doing things like ensuring reliability, availability, scalability, and trust for all those services. I think this is the fundamental problem we still have to deal with.

It is emerging. I think, in fact, that we are building things on top of services. But, for me as a developer or a business, to be able to compose or derive an application or service that is built out of ones, tens, or hundreds of services provided to me from who-knows-where across the Net, I think is still a ways off.

Tim: Bob is right here. There is a huge amount of undiscovered territory here, and we are really in the first generation of addressing this. I think you'll find broad agreement from most leaders in the industry that we have to do this. The wins are just too big. From the point of view of an IT professional, being able to provide services without having to deploy software to an infinite number of desktops and then maintain them is such a huge cost win.

Then there is the deeper business issue, which is something Jonathan Schwartz, our CEO, talks about quite a bit. You really want to monetize things at the point of value. The traditional approach where you write big software-licensing checks now and then derive the business value for it 18 months later is getting increasingly hard to sell. With SaaS, if you use it this month, you get value this month, you pay this month. It is just a more rational and standard approach to business. We certainly haven't solved all the problems. I'm certain that is where a high proportion of the industry is going to be.

Tim, When you were working on XML many years ago, were things like Ajax and Web 2.0 something you would have imagined?

Tim: My predictions of what XML was primarily going to be used for were by and large completely wrong.

Having said that, Ajax isn't exactly a new thing. At the same time we were doing XML in 1996 and 1997, Microsoft was doing this whacky thing called Dynamic HTML, which if you looked at it closely was more or less exactly Ajax. So, the technology is not that new of a thing. What is new is that people are using it in clever and portable ways to enhance the user experience. It apparently seems to have taken the industry a decade or so to get good value out of this particular technology. No, I could not claim to have foreseen all the weird stuff that XML is being used for.

Do you see any particular technologies standing out in the next rendition of Web evolution?

Bob: There are a number that stand out, but I don't think you can single out any one in particular. We are seeing sets of things that are emerging that reinforce this notion, such as things like domain-specific languages (DSLs) for implementation—i.e., Ruby and others. I think we will see more of these technologies as opposed to universal solutions such as XML.

We are going to start building things or use things that are specifically designed to solve a specific problem rather than trying to slam a bunch of square pegs into all the round holes we can find.

Tim: There is interesting technology at every level of the stack. Go right onto the hardware, and here at Sun we are shipping these massively parallel processors with more cores and lower wattages and so on. That turns out to be a superb match to the kinds of things people are doing in Web 2.0. That's an interesting technology.

> *"If you have something to offer, it will get noticed."*

But then at the very top level, there is a whole swarm of issues around identity—the notion of how you establish who you are in a web of many interlocking social networks. There is as much policy as there is technology in that one. Wherever you look it is interesting.

What makes Web 2.0 what it is? What makes it stand out? Tim is working on the Atom protocol and some of the things that help with web publishing, but what makes it different?

Tim: I think it is if you can imagine it, you can build it; you can play. Anybody can be a first-class citizen. You don't have to work for a big company. You don't have to have a professorship at a university. You can pitch in and start playing. If you have something to offer, it will get noticed.

Bob: Yeah, I agree with that. The interesting twist on what we are doing is not so much that there is this whole participatory thing that is limited to people using it, but to people creating it. That is where it gets truly interesting.

The number of small companies that have been born and then sold for like half a billion dollars continues. I think I'm in the wrong business....

Tim: Sun is a very enthusiastic cheerleader for Web 2.0.

Bob: Although we are cheerleaders, there is still so much more to be done. Watch this space. Especially as we continue to round out things around the technical side and implementation of languages and tools for building things on the Web and Web 2.0, plus solutions for building reliability, scalability, and trust. Those are some things that we are investing a great deal of time and energy to figure out how we can help evolve the Web to start to use those things for services.

Sound Bites

When you talk to two distinguished engineers from Sun Microsystems, you can expect a lot of interesting comments. Tim Bray and Bob Brewin did not disappoint. Here are a few of their interesting comments:

- People have a tendency to put Web 2.0 in the "browser bucket" and say that if it is not running in a browser it is not Web 2.0. Web 2.0 is a leveling of the playing field where the players are all equal.
- It is all about empowering the people at the edge to contribute to the richness of the Net. The things that make the Web interesting these days are the things coming in from the edges, not the things coming out from the center.
- Enterprises need to think a lot about how they are going to succeed in a world where they no longer control the flow of information. They need to surf and ride on the flow of information rather than trying to fight it.
- Anyone with reasonable smarts can have a good idea for a web property on Monday and can have something on the air two weeks from Thursday.
- It is really dangerous to identify Web 2.0 with a particular technology. There are some hot Web 2.0 sites that are really Web 1.0 in their technology.
- There may be cases where directly implementing Web 2.0 technology may not directly drive revenue ideas and ROI, but looking at the larger picture, it is phenomenally huge.
- If you look at Web 2.0 features and consider the number of people that might potentially want to participate, then we are just beginning.
- The traditional approach where you write big software-licensing checks now and then derive the business value for it 18 months later is getting increasingly hard to sell. One of these really defining characteristics of the new-style web applications is that "time to market" is very important.

Michele Turner:
Adobe Systems Incorporated

20

> *"[Web 2.0] is all about giving a lot of control back to the user and leveraging that infrastructure that we built with "Web 1.0" to enable extremely rich experiences now, that we couldn't do back in the day."*
>
> —Michele Turner

I f you use the Web, chances are you are familiar with Adobe Flash. If you are familiar with Flash, then you are familiar with at least one of Adobe's products. In addition to Flash there is a good chance you've also heard of PDF files and it is statistically likely that you've seen or installed the Adobe Reader that reads documents in the PDF format.

www.adobe.com

Adobe, however, is more than just Flash and Reader. Their products include Adobe ColdFusion, Dreamweaver, Flex, InDesign, Photoshop, Premiere, Director, RoboHelp, and many, many more. The products cover a number of different categories including design, publishing, developer tools, digital imaging, eLearning, web design, web publishing, video, and audio.

Few companies can boast a 98 percent penetration within a market. Adobe, however, can with their Flash Player. Additionally, few companies are currently able to target both designers and developers effectively, but yet again Adobe is succeeding. In the Web 2.0 space, this seems to have given them an advantage.

Adobe is a major player in the web space. When you look at some of what they have done as well as where they are headed, it is easy to believe that Adobe will continue to be a major player.

We Are on the Edge of This Very Exciting Time

Michele Turner is an executive from Adobe; however, she brings a vast amount of experience as well. Michele has worked at Netflix, where she was a vice president fro product marketing and design. She worked at AOL as a senior vice president of marketing. At Excite@Home she was a senior vice president as well as the general manager for development. Her credentials go on to include companies such as Silicon Graphics, Sun Microsystems, and Stanford Telecommunications. With experiences from such prominent companies, it is no surprise she has interesting insights into Web 2.0.

Can you tell us a bit about yourself and what you do?

I'm Michele Turner and I'm vice president of platform product management and developer relations for Adobe. My background: I spent some time at AOL. At AOL I ran personalization and part of their communications products. I had responsibility for myAOL and other products there.

> *"User-generated content; content is king."*

I also did a couple of Web 2.0 startups before I came to Adobe. So I've done the big Internet companies, the little Internet companies, and kind of followed the whole thing from Web 1.0 to Web 2.0.

You mention Web 2.0 a couple of times. Let me ask the big question. From your and Adobe's perspectives, what is Web 2.0?

I don't have a canned answer for you. It is a lot of things. A lot of it is an evolution out of Web 1.0 from the technologies. We built the infrastructure in Web 1.0 to do a lot of the stuff we're seeing today; We're taking advantage a lot of that infrastructure in the trends that have defined Web 2.0, which is user-generated content; content is king, giving the users a lot of control, opening up APIs, opening up feeds and being able to bring lots of different content types together to create new experiences.

Those are the major things that start to define Web 2.0. That and changes to the user interfaces.

Two years ago you could look at a site and say, "That's Web 2.0" just by the look of it. That is changing a bit as we start to mature along this line. There is definitely a really increased focus on user interfaces and user experiences as well.

In summary, it is all about giving a lot of control back to the user and leveraging that infrastructure that we built with "Web 1.0" to enable extremely rich experiences now; we couldn't do that back in the day.

I have a little story from when I was at Excite@Home. This was in 1999 and the guy who was director for engineering for myExcite came up to me and said, "Hey, you know this new technology, which is not too new, Netscape built it and it is called RSS. It stands for Rich Site Summary." It wasn't even Really Simple Syndication then. It would let us take any RSS-enabled web pages and make a summary of those web pages. Users could just pick and we could pull it straight onto their myExcite. They could really personalize their site.

I thought, gosh, that is so cool. Let's do it. And, we did it.

The problem was—and this was probably around 2000—the content wasn't there. The bulk of the sites that were there were either recipe finders or Bible quotes. It just

> *"Until we made the content compelling, it really didn't take off."*

wasn't very compelling. The feeds we were buying had a lot better content. That has completely evolved over the last seven years to what we have now, which is a system of very robust RSS where you can pull in any kind of feed that you want. You can get very high relevancy to what you are interested in. It can be extremely specific, from your Little League schedule to something that is broader, to watching someone's blog post on a regular basis.

I see that as a really interesting trend. All of this technology was there since Web 1.0, but the content wasn't. Until we made the content compelling, it really didn't take off.

You can look at this with Flash content as well. Flash has been out there—it's 10 years old. Flash started out primarily for animation and cartoons on the Web and has evolved into the dominant video standard for video on the Web. Seventy percent of all video on the Web is Flash.

So as technology has evolved, sites like YouTube—talk about your quintessential Web 2.0 site—have evolved user-generated content. Users are able to create their own videos and post them up on YouTube. They really don't need to have knowledge of Flash offerings, but it is all Flash up there.

What that has evolved into for us is a really interesting model with Flash player where we don't rely on any distribution model to get Flash out there—at all. Flash Player is on 98 percent of all internet-connected desktops worldwide. We can update a new version, a new rev, of the software to 85 percent of all desktops within nine months. It does this by content pull, which is remarkable.

> *"There are different levels of how you use AJAX."*

We don't think that there has been any other technology that has been able to update itself so pervasively in the history of technology.

Talk about Web 2.0, and you have to talk about how important user-generated content is to driving technology as well. It is all tied together.

Following up on that, the term AJAX is thrown around probably as much as Web 2.0. How do you see AJAX, Adobe AIR, Microsoft Silverlight, and other technologies fit into Web 2.0?

AJAX is one of the technologies that fits into the whole user-experience part of Web 2.0. A couple of years ago you could look at a site and tell it was Web 2.0.

The core of that has evolved into "more effective user experiences." I think that Rich Internet Application development environments—RIA development environments—such as AJAX, such as what we are doing with Flex,

ActionScript, and Adobe AIR as a runtime, and Microsoft Silverlight as well, they are all RIA technologies, and they are all very important to driving, to creating, Rich Internet experiences.

It is interesting. I think there are different levels of how you use AJAX. At Netflix we had an interesting issue. You would look at a movie box shot, but in order to find out what was on that box, you would have to click through. Every time you clicked through, you were pushing the users deeper and deeper into the site. They kept getting lost. Netflix is an incredibly personalized site—if you use it, you know.

We kept getting complaints from users because they would lose context. They couldn't necessarily get back to their original state. They would be on one page looking at a movie, but there might another movie on that page they wanted to look at. But as soon as they clicked, they changed their state and couldn't find that other movie again.

So, we created this concept called the "back-of-the-box." Using AJAX, you mouse over the box shot and it brings up the back-of-the-box description. That is how a RIA really provides a much more effective user experience and just makes the whole process of getting through a massive amount of data so much easier for a user.

That is what is important about these technologies, whether it is AJAX, Flash, or Silverlight—designers or developers are making the perusal of massive amounts of data so much simpler.

> *"Flex is probably one of the best programming environments for creating RIAs."*

AJAX is one of the development environments for AIR. There are effectively two programming models for AIR. One is Flash/Flex, which is our programming model. The other is AJAX.

We are doing a lot more work around AJAX inside of Adobe. We have a very strong story with AJAX on the Dreamweaver side. There is a recent SitePoint survey that shows that something like 35 percent of all AJAX developers are using Dreamweaver. A lot of them are not doing application development. They are just doing web page development. It is not a technology that we are not familiar with. We have a good user base there, but there is a lot more in terms of what we will be doing with that, as it is a very strong model for Web 2.0.

You've mentioned Adobe Flex a couple of times. How does Flex fit into Web 2.0?

Flex is a programming language with an IDE (Integrated Development Environment). It compiles code to run in the Flash Player or Adobe AIR.

> *"Everyone is integrating Web 2.0 patterns into their web sites today."*

If you are a programmer and you are familiar with Java or any of the OO [object-oriented] languages, then Flex is supereasy to get started with. ActionScript, the scripting language, is JavaScript, ECMAScript. Its libraries are set around the mindset of creating video. When I first looked at ActionScript, it was like, "Wow, how do you build applications out of this?" It is a different model; it was built for a different use case than Flex.

Flex is for a software developer. It is relatively easy to get up and running with. We have an extremely rich component set and charting tools for building wonderful, interactive applications. Flex is probably one of the best programming environments for creating RIAs.

Shifting back to Web 2.0 specifically, what would you consider one of the most misunderstood areas of Web 2.0?

For me, one of the most misunderstood things is that it is just a fad that we are going through, and that it is just for 25-year olds who are creating their ad hoc web sites that they are going to throw up on to the Web.

I think what we have seen as I've watched Web 2.0 evolve over the last four or five years now is that it is like many other trends. It starts out relatively nascent with a lot of really good ideas and it needs to grow and evolve. But the whole notion that it started with, that we need to give users control, that user-generated content is important, and we need to be out there figuring out how to use it, has really taken over major web sites. From Google to AOL, everyone is integrating Web 2.0 patterns into their web sites today. All those key elements of community and sharing and shared content, these are now integrated into mainstream web sites.

So, I don't think it is a fad at all.

One of the things created from Web 2.0 is Ruby on Rails. It made it easy for anyone to get a Web 2.0 application up and running quickly. So we have this proliferation of applications that have no business model. There is a whole story on that.

But what we've seen is that the trends that have the highest benefit to the end user have the pieces of Web 2.0, such as user-generated content, better community support, better personalization, the ability for me as a user to go in and select what I want and to cull out all the stuff that I don't want. This is all being incorporated into the major sites today.

> *"The trends in the consumer space are toward much cleaner, effective patterns and user designs that are coming out of Web 2.0."*

Based on how you've described Web 2.0, with it being about community and having community being involved, can the concepts you've described behind Web 2.0 be applied to an "offline" enterprise?

There are a couple of ways that I see Web 2.0 impacting the enterprise. One reason I'm getting ready to go on a trip is to talk to our European Executive council about how Web 2.0 trends can impact the enterprise.

I see two major ways. One is user interface. The trends in the consumer space are toward much cleaner, effective patterns and user designs that are coming out of Web 2.0; it is going to have an impact on the enterprise because whether I'm using Google at home or whether I'm using Microsoft Windows XP at work, I'm getting used to better user interfaces, and that's what I'm starting to expect.

I have a whole bunch of AIR applications on my desktop and they are beautiful. They are gorgeous. They are easy to figure out. Then I pull up a not-to-be-named but fairly standard enterprise product and its UI is horrific. It is tough. It's hard. It's not intuitive at all. I think that those user interface trends, the design trends, are going to start impacting the enterprise as we see that poor UI impacts productivity.

This is another place where Adobe has had an enormous impact on Web 2.0. A majority of the designers out there have Creative Suite, particularly Photoshop, Fireworks, InDesign, or some element of the Flash offering on their desktop in the workspace today, designing these new UIs. We are behind that change in UI, that sort of UI revolution that is happening.

> *"We definitely don't see [SaaS] as a fad, but as where software is going to a large degree."*

The other area that I think is important for the enterprise is that all of these companies have invested in Web Services infrastructures over the last six to ten years. Now they can do something much more significant with them. They can take their internal content and turn them into feeds that provide information for the finance group, the marketing group, whatever. They can allow employees or customers to start pulling together data much more effectively than they could before.

I think the service-oriented architecture investment can definitely be seen driving Web 2.0 into the enterprise. We are starting to see that a lot. We have a number of enterprises using Flex today. They are using Flex charting and components, pulling it together with our Data Services. They are doing it because they have all this data on the back end and they need an easy way to get it represented internally into corporate intranets, to their sales team, or to whomever. It is a much easier way to create a better UI experience.

Enterprises, as much as anyone else, have massive amounts of data. How do you make it easy for a human being to get through that massive amount of data to create an effective experience for them?

You've mentioned Service Oriented Architectures (SOA). Software as a Service (SaaS) or Software plus Services (S+S)—do you see these as fact or fiction?

> *"We are going to be redefining the Rich in RIA."*

I think there is a huge amount of substance behind SaaS. It is definitely something Adobe is looking at very hard. We are looking internally at how we can add services to some of our applications, or how we create new, services-based end-user applications.

We have a VoIP service in pre-alpha right now, so it is very early. Adjunct to that is a product called Share. Share is a collaborative sharing service that is in beta right now. These are just two examples. We are very invested in this at Adobe. We definitely don't see it as a fad, but as where software is going to a large degree.

From a developer angle, we are making the APIs behind these services available to developers. I am super excited about this. We are going to be redefining the Rich in RIA as we enable developers to just seamlessly pull voice services or video conferencing or shared desktops into their applications. Now, not only do you have the data and these UI components, but we are also making it very easy to pull in multimedia as well. I see that as a trend that is going to be very, very strong and it is going to change the face of applications that we see today.

Web 2.0 is here and happening. What do you see as the next big revolution on the Web?

I'm at Adobe, so I'm going to tell you that it is web-enabled desktop applications. If you are not familiar with Adobe AIR, it is really relevant to this.

I came to Adobe because I learned about what was then code-named Apollo, I thought, "Oh my gosh, here is my opportunity to be involved in this thing that is the *"Having access to your local data is really, really key."* next generation of the Web." What we are seeing is that so many companies, whether they are corporate enterprises or they're commercial Internet companies, have invested in this whole massive Web Services architecture. We are enabling them to take that investment and expand it to the desktop and marry the best of the desktop with the best of the Web.

We are seeing some really phenomenal applications coming from our partners and we are really excited about that. There are certain things that applications built with Adobe AIR give you, such as online/offline access. There are a couple of ways to do that today, but having it integrated into your desktop application rather than going out to a browser application is very normal to people because you have it with Microsoft Outlook and in Apple iTunes. Having access to your local data is really, really key.

There are a lot of times that you have information on your desktop that you might want to pull into your application from the Web, and AIR makes that seamless. What is so exciting about this is that when we made AIR available to developers, we knew we'd see things we hadn't even imagined. We are seeing that today. We are seeing a generation of hybrid applications where they have a mode that is on the browser and a mode that is on the desktop.

> *"We are on the edge of this very exciting time with these web-enabled desktop applications."*

Because of the open nature of Twitter, there is now an application called Tweeter that is a sweet little AIR application that runs on your desktop. I use Tweeter on the desktop because it works better for me than a browser does. Twitter gets lost in the browser tabs.

I think we are on the edge of this very exciting time with these web-enabled desktop applications. You've seen the trend with widgets. We are all watching the Facebook widgets that are taking off right now. But what I'm talking about are full-blown applications that are significant and that are rivaling big experiences on the Web that people aren't expecting. Not simple media players. If you have not seen eBay Desktop, then you should play with it because it really lets you see what is possible with a web-enabled application on the desktop.

That is where I see it going and what I see as the next big trend.

Does the online/offline connectivity then become a non-issue?

No, I see it as an issue. I see it being tackled in a couple of ways. Google is looking at it with Google Gears. Mozilla is looking at it now with Mozilla Prism. We've enabled it through Adobe AIR.

Now, with something like the Buzzword word processor, I can write a document on the plane and queue it to upload when I step off the plane. When I hit that wireless network, then boom, the document is out there in the shared cloud so others can share the document with me.

There are just a lot of instances where I'd like to be working and not be dependent on a connection. As much as we'd like to say Wi-Fi is everywhere, it just isn't. Just look at how often your cell phone fails. That is very mature technology and it is not consistent.

I think online/offline support is going to be very important, especially for the foreseeable future.

Web 3.0, the Semantic Web. Is it a valid concept that will happen in the future?

I do think that it is a really interesting concept, and that if it does happen it is going to take a while.

I did some consulting for a company that was doing semantic search, and it's really hard technology to get right. Again, Web 2.0 came from the evolution of taking some of the fundamental things we got right with Web 1.0 and improving on them. Web 3.0, I think, is going to be the same kind of thing. Ultimately the content is what drives these things, and the explosion of content driven by Web 2.0 trends may help enable the Semantic Web to be realized.

I'm also watching what is going on with the social platforms. There is Facebook and other major ones coming out. I'm watching that from a developer-relations standpoint to say, "What can we do with you guys?" I'm also watching it form a trends standpoint. A lot of the people using the platforms are going to be the folks building Web 3.0, so what does that mean to us?

> *"Online/offline support is going to be very important, especially for the foreseeable future."*

Is there anything about Web 2.0 that you'd like to add?

At Adobe, we see ourselves as the enabler of Web 2.0. From Creative Suite being used to create so much of the content and the user interfaces on the Web, to our programming languages Flex and ActionScript that are delivering RIAs, in the browser with Flash Player and on the desktop with AIR, and by being the premier format for video on the Web with Flash, Adobe is a part of nearly every Web 2.0 experience today.

Sound Bites

Adobe is enabling people to create interesting applications on the Web with Adobe Flash Player, Adobe AIR, Adobe Flex, and other products. Michele Turner speaks for Adobe and provides a number of great insights into where

Adobe is helping in the Web 2.0 space and about Web 2.0 in general. Some of her notable observations follow:

- All of this technology was there since Web 1.0, but the content wasn't. Until we made the content compelling, it really didn't take off. Now with Web 2.0, it is about giving a lot of control back to the user and leveraging that infrastructure that was built with "Web 1.0" to enable extremely rich experiences now, that couldn't be done back in the day.

- Flash Player is on 98 percent of all desktops worldwide. Adobe can update a new version, a new rev, of the software to 85 percent of all desktops within nine months. It does this by content pull. What other software product can do this?

- An RIA really provides a much more effective user experience and just makes the whole process of getting through a massive amount of data so much easier for a user.

- That is what is important about these technologies, whether it is AJAX, Flash, or Silverlight—designers or developers are making the perusal of massive amounts of data so much simpler.

- Pieces of Web 2.0 such as user-generated content, better community support, better personalization, the ability to go in and select what is wanted and to cull out all the stuff not wanted—this is all being incorporated into the major sites today.

- The trends in the consumer space are towards much cleaner, more effective patterns and user designs that are coming out of Web 2.0.

- The whole service-oriented architecture that has been invested in can definitely be seen driving Web 2.0 into the enterprise. We definitely don't see SaaS as a fad, but as where software is going to a large degree.

- As much as we'd like to say Wi-Fi is everywhere, it just isn't. Just look at how often your cell phone fails. That is very mature technology and it is not consistent.

- Online/offline support is going to be very important for the foreseeable future. We are on the edge of this really, really exciting time with web-enabled desktop applications.

Index

professionals, LinkedIn for professional
networking, 119
project management, Zoho Project, 80
"promiscuous linking", LinkedIn preventing,
121–122
public information, availability on Web, 39
publishing. *See* self-publishing

R

Reader, Adobe, 243–244
Read/Write Web
MacManus on, 92–93
overview of, 91–92
Web 2.0 concepts (Vegesna), 85
recommendations
Amazon, 38
StumbleUpon, 190, 195
rel attribute, HREF tags, 64
relationships
impact of Skype on, 203
LinkedIn and relationship management,
122
reliability, Twitter business model focusing
on, 151
remixability
in blogs/blogging, 124–125
of content (Smith), 212
of old technologies (Smith), 214–215
return on investment (ROI), Web 2.0
development and, 235–236
RIAs (Rich Internet Applications)
building on SOA model, 215
Microsoft and Adobe for Web-enabling the
desktop, 95
user experience and, 246–247
rich media
business perspective on, 215
embeddable chat rooms, 157
enabled on Web 2.0, 245
innovations in, 201
rich clients in mobile devices, 234
technologies supporting rich interfaces,
137
video advertising and, 41
ROI (return on investment), Web 2.0
development and, 235–236
RSS feeds
availability of content and, 245–246
Bloglines consuming, 30, 32

monetization models and Bloglines and,
40–41
remixability of, 212
technologies supporting Web 2.0 (Harris),
222
Technorati and, 63, 73
Web 2.0 technologies built on, 224
Ruby on Rails
as domain-specific language, 240
ease of creating Web 2.0 applications with,
248–249
rich clients in mobile devices, 234

S

S+S (Software plus Services)
Bianchini on, 50
Bray and Brewin on, 238–239
Camp on, 196–197
Engleman on, 42
Kumaran on, 184
MacManus on, 97–98
Madanes on, 205
Mancini on, 10–11
Meckler on, 26
Microsoft program for integrating Web 2.0
capabilities, 223
Schachter on, 173–174
Sternberg on, 166
Stone on, 152–153
Turner on, 250–251
Vegesna on, 88
Walker on, 141–142
S3 (Simple Storage Service), Amazon, 173
SaaS (Software as a Service)
Bray and Brewin on potential of, 238–239
Camp on, 196–197
Engleman on, 42
Gartner report of predictions regarding, 114
Kang on, 106–107
Kumaran on, 184
MacManus on, 97–98
Madanes on, 205
Mancini on, 10–11
Meckler on, 26
Schachter on, 173–174
Sternberg on, 166
Stone on, 152–153
Turner on, 250–251
Vegesna on, 88, 89
Walker on, 141–142

Heroes are everywhere.

978-0-470-24204-9

978-0-470-19739-4

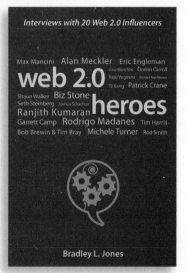

978-0-470-24199-8